"From the hands of two renowned and respected preacher-scholars, *Inspired Preaching* will enable pastors to think more biblically—and creatively—about their task as expositors of the Word of God. I commend the book highly for its up-to-date perspectives and usefulness!"

David Alan Black
Professor of New Testament and Greek
Southeastern Baptist Theological Seminary

"*Inspired Preaching* is a carefully researched and well-written volume on the preaching found in the New Testament. Moreover, it is a practical handbook for contemporary students and pastors on interpreting and preaching the New Testament. I know of no book that brings together these two approaches in one volume in such a helpful and interrelated fashion. Wells and Luter have done an excellent job of guiding readers to an understanding of the challenges in faithfully proclaiming the New Testament for our day. Students and preachers will find much help in these pages. I gladly recommend this book."

David S. Dockery
President, Union University

"In an age of pulpit gimmicks and evangelical hoopla, this book is a clarion call for the church to reclaim the God-ordained means of Spirit-filled preaching in its worship and witness. Written with passion and conviction, this book instructs and provokes and also, as the title suggests, inspires. May the Lord use it to encourage a new generation of faithful proclaimers."

Timothy George
Dean, Beeson Divinity School of Samford University
Executive Editor, *Christianity Today*

"Evangelicals are countercultural in insisting on the centrality of preaching. We believe that the preached word creates life, just as it did when Ezekiel proclaimed the word to the dry bones. It is salutary, then, to return to the first preachers of the Christian Church, whose preaching is captured in the New Testament. Luter and Wells fix our atter'   ~~ ~~ Jesus and the apostles as proclaimers of the word. Not all will agree   ' ~ ~uthors rightly stress the importance of oral p   New Testament documents have a homileti

D1292292

einer
.ment
The Soum..... ~~,   iinary
Louisville, ᴋentucky

inspired
preaching

inspired
preaching

A SURVEY OF PREACHING
FOUND IN THE NEW TESTAMENT

C. RICHARD WELLS
& A. BOYD LUTER

BROADMAN
& HOLMAN
PUBLISHERS

NASHVILLE, TENNESSEE

0–8054–2417–2

Published by Broadman & Holman Publishers
Nashville, Tennessee

Dewey Decimal Classification: 251
Subject Heading: PREACHING

Unless otherwise noted Scripture is quoted from the New American
Standard Bible, © Copyright The Lockman Foundation, 1960, 1962, 1963,
1968, 1971, 1972, 1973, 1975, 1977, 1995. Other versions are identified as
follows: KJV, King James Version. NIV, the Holy Bible, New International
Version, © copyright 1973, 1978, 1984. Phillips: reprinted with permission
of Macmillan Publishing Co., Inc. from J. B. Phillips: The New Testament in
Modern English, revised edition, © J. B. Phillips 1958, 1960, 1972.

1 2 3 4 5 6 7 8 9 10 10 09 08 07 06 05 04 03 02

Ad Memoriam
W. A. Criswell, 1909–2002

To Carol
The Wife of My Youth
"Many daughters have done nobly, but you excel them all"
(Proverbs 31:29).

C. Richard Wells

To Joanna, Natalie and Tim, with much love. You indeed are a gift from
the Lord! (Psalm 127:3).

A. Boyd Luter

Contents

Preface

We often call a small child that seemingly cannot sit still a "wiggle-worm." In a very real sense, the book you are about to read qualifies to be called a literary "wiggle-worm." By that, we mean that what *Inspired Preaching* started out to be, and what it ended up being, are at two different places, because our understanding of the subject matter related to preaching and the New Testament simply wouldn't stay still.

In a nutshell, here's what happened: Richard proposed to Boyd co-writing a book surveying the preaching in the Bible, to honor W. A. Criswell, the far-famed pastor emeritus of First Baptist Church, Dallas, and founder and chancellor of The Criswell College. Our intent was to blend the insights, experience, and writing style of Richard, as a veteran preacher and long-term professor of homiletics, with that of Boyd, a biblical studies professor who had been a pastor for nearly ten years.

The flexibility in time for research and reflection allowed by Broadman & Holman turned out to be a key factor in our completing the manuscript. For this, we express our deep appreciation to Leonard Goss, our skilled editor, and along with John Landers all those at Broadman & Holman who graciously flexed with our time realities (which included at one point the demise of the hard drive on Boyd's laptop computer). The primary villain in the passage of time, however, was the frustration of administration. Richard's role as president of The Criswell College and Boyd's as dean of faculty made unrelenting demands. Finding consistent time to write proved harder than when we were both full-time faculty members.

Even though the larger chunks of time needed for writing were not readily available, the opportunities to continue reading relevant materials, our classroom teaching and other writing responsibilities overlapped the subject matter. As a result, our knowledge base, our sense of the "big picture" and the significance of the subject for a twenty-first century audience continued to grow rapidly.

After some months, we realized that the stacking up of insights was not taking us where we had intended to go. So, we approached Broadman &

Holman and asked permission to move our book in a different direction: to limit our study to the New Testament and, at the same time, to broaden its scope to survey the preaching *in* the New Testament, but also to examine the New Testament books *as* preaching (i.e., as wholes and as straightforwardly "sermonic" in their current form).

The understanding and support we received from Len Goss in allowing this shift of focus relatively "late in the game," so to speak, was invaluable. We believe *Inspired Preaching* will prove to be a much stronger contribution to the understanding of the pastors, teachers, students, and others who read it, as a result of our "mid-course correction."

By now you have every right to ask: "What changed and developed in your thinking that makes *Inspired Preaching* distinctive and better?" In keeping with the rapidly growing body of research that has emerged in recent years, *Inspired Preaching* proceeds from the assumption that the cultures of the New Testament era were largely oral in character. In saying that, we are not repeating the standard scholarly mantras about "oral tradition" and the related theories of oral transmission of the events and stories recorded in the New Testament. Rather, we hold that, although writing was quite common in the first century, as witnessed by all the books of the New Testament, virtually all the other dynamics for producing the books were oral and rhetorical in nature.

For example, it is now practically without dispute that there was no such thing as silent reading during the New Testament era. The Ethiopian eunuch, overheard by Philip, serves as a prime example of that reality (Acts 8:30). In addition, though, it is very likely that most, if not all, of the New Testament books were dictated by the author to a secretary (e.g., Rom. 16:22). And, even if an author did do the actual writing of the document, every word would have been spoken out loud, likely with passion, the author visualizing his hearers with great pastoral concern, as it was recorded. Thus, not only did the New Testament books *faithfully record* selected examples of the preaching (usually as summaries of sermons) of the apostles and the other New Testament authors, they, at least as much, *forcefully embodied* that preaching in their (whole) written form.

We will consider both aspects in-depth in this book. In the portions that focus on the Gospels and Acts (chapters 1, 3, 4, 6, 7, and 8), there will be an extensive, fresh, and careful analysis of the examples of the "inspired preaching" of Jesus, the apostles, and others included in those books. In the material related to the Epistles and Revelation (chapters 2, 5, 9, 10, and 11), considerable attention will be given to the rhetorical structure of the books, as a clear indication of the oral preaching styles of the various writers.

This bottom-line oral quality of the New Testament books explains why they sound (and feel) much more like spoken, rather than written, communication. Even when we read them silently, they seem much more lively than typical written communication, which is meant to be read silently. They fairly plead to be read aloud (especially in the pulpit)! And, in our early twenty-first-century culture, which is becoming more and more oral and aural (e.g., When was the last time you saw a teenager on an airplane, or waiting for a ride somewhere, without headphones on?), we have much to learn from the oral communication style of the first century.

Amazingly, without ever having the opportunity to study the emerging understanding of the orality of the New Testament era, W. A. Criswell seemed to understand that historical reality instinctively, and he embodied it in his own electrifying exposition of Scripture. Holding a Ph.D. in New Testament interpretation from Southern Baptist Theological Seminary, Louisville, Kentucky, where he studied under such renowned New Testament scholars as A. T. Robertson and Hersey Davis, the nuances of the many and varied scholarly views were never lost on Dr. Criswell. However, in spite of his scholarly training and ability, "orality" clearly dominated the writing ministry of W. A. Criswell. He published fifty-six books, but the vast majority were transcribed sermon series, and all "shouted forth" the passion and power of his larger-than-life pulpit style, expressed in thousands and thousands of sermons. May the following treatment of the New Testament as *preaching, by preachers,* faithfully honor the memory and uphold the tradition of this preacher among preachers!

C. Richard Wells
A. Boyd Luter
Dallas, Texas
June 2002
Soli Deo Gloria!

PART I

Preaching and the
New Testament:

Surveying the Forest

CHAPTER

INSPIRED PREACHING IN THE NEW TESTAMENT: AN INTRODUCTORY LOOK

A. BOYD LUTER

> As good news addressed to the church, the written Gospels themselves are a form of preaching (kerygma). Moreover, the Gospels are rooted in the preaching of Jesus and the apostles.[1]

> "Jesus came . . . preaching" (Mark 1:14).[2]

> The tradition of preaching from the prophets, John the Baptist, and Jesus continued with the apostles (Acts 5:42). In addition, other persons shared in gospel proclamation (Acts 21:8; Eph. 4:11); in fact, the whole church at times became involved in forms of preaching (Acts 8:4). . . . From the beginning, preaching seems to have been varied in both mode and content.[3]

> One of the most characteristic features of Acts is the presence of many speeches interspersed throughout the narrative. Altogether these comprise nearly a third of the text of Acts, about 300 of its approximately 1,000 verses.[4]

THE WHOLE IS GREATER THAN THE SUMMARIZED SERMONS (THOUGH THE SUMMARIZED SERMONS ARE WHOLLY GREAT!)

The preaching recorded in the Gospels and Acts is (to be guilty of vast understatement) powerful stuff! It is, quite honestly, difficult to imagine more skillful and spellbinding communication than Jesus' masterpiece, the

Sermon on the Mount (Matt. 5–7). And consider the astoundingly far-reaching, heart-piercing impact (Acts 2:37) of Peter's sermon on the day of Pentecost (2:14–36): three thousand conversions (2:41)!

We live in a rapid-fire culture, which is very different from the New Testament era in many respects. However, we may be more alike in regard to one overlooked area than we ever notice: the tendency to summarize. For example, a running summary of the key points of the President's State of the Union address seems, to many among us, long and drawn out in comparison to the sound bites that are the staple of the nightly news.

As we look at Scripture through this kind of cultural lens, it never occurs to us to ask why the messages recorded in the New Testament are so *short*. By contrast, the information provided in the Scripture itself very clearly points to the fact that the actual presentation of what we have of Peter's second message in Acts lasted some two and one-half to three hours (compare Acts 3:1 and 4:1–3).[5] Longer still was Paul's seemingly impromptu "talk" (Gk. *logos*) to the believers in Troas (Acts 20:6–7), which began after the evening meal and the congregational taking of the Lord's Supper ("gathered together to break bread") and continued until midnight.[6]

Similarly, we believe the vast majority, if not all, of the sermons included in the New Testament books are likely summarized.[7] That perspective does not, however, undermine the nature of those sermons in any way. They are, without question, the most extraordinary (not to mention divinely inspired and inerrant!) examples of preaching available, worthy of our most reverent and meticulous study.

In keeping with that perspective, the remainder of this chapter will deal with, in overview: (1) the importance of preaching, as revealed in key passages in the New Testament; (2) the nature of preaching in the New Testament, as understood from the major terms used; and (3) the major instances of preaching seen within the books of the New Testament. The final section, a brief introductory consideration of the major book-length genres (i.e., literary forms) in the New Testament, will set the stage for the next chapter. There we will begin to lay out our case for viewing the New Testament books in their entirety (i.e., whole) as preaching.

THE PRIORITY OF PREACHING IN THE NEW TESTAMENT

Out of respect, many classic treatments of how to preach begin with a discussion, usually brief, of the importance of preaching.[8] The following section is our attempt, however feeble, to lay out seven principles that reflect the high regard for preaching reflected in the New Testament.

A Natural Outworking of Servant Leadership, as Modeled by Jesus Christ

The Lord Jesus pointedly preached the nature of servant leadership to the apostles (Matt. 20:20–28). Apparently that humbling lesson was branded on Peter's heart at that time, and he never forgot it. When, in later ministry, it was necessary for him to speak to the issue of proper leadership, he unashamedly presented it as an integral part of the way local church leaders are to handle their roles (1 Pet. 5:3).

Such church leadership roles require articulating the Word of God (1 Tim. 3:2; Titus 1:9). Hence, even as Jesus preached as a natural outgrowth of being the classic servant-leader (Matt. 20:28), so must preachers today view themselves as servant-leaders at core and pulpiteers in the overflow of such servant-leadership. That biblically informed perspective, as simple as it may seem, transforms entirely the way one perceives "greatness" (Matt. 20:25–28) in ministry, including greatness in preaching.

The Breadth and Depth Aspects of the Great Commission

Christ's marching orders to his church at the end of the first Gospel (Matt. 28:19–20), better known as the Great Commission,[9] are structured as an imperative with three related participles. The command is to "make disciples." The disciple-making process is made up of three steps: (1) go(ing);[10] (2) baptizing; and (3) teaching.

Going means to make the gospel message available (i.e., by proclamation) to "all the nations" (28:19). The *baptizing* (28:19) is for those hearers who respond to the *going* with the gospel in saving faith. The *teaching* is for those new believers who have been baptized and need to be taught in order to begin to grow toward full obedience (28:20).

Therefore, the Great Commission, as the Lord Jesus Christ laid it out, basically turns out to be a double-dose of preaching with baptism sandwiched in between. The "in-breadth" preaching is the offering of "the Good News" to everyone, everywhere ("all the nations"). The "in-depth" preaching is the ongoing biblical instruction of baptized believers that makes for the maturing of the next generation of those who will seek to carry out the Lord's commission by preaching "wide and deep." Together, it can be rightly said that these complementary aspects of preaching are designed to function as nothing less than our Lord's designated "one-two punch" to reach the world and biblically transform the hearers of his message of Good News.

The Source of Strengthening and Encouraging Instruction from the Lord

Since it is tucked away at the very end of the body of Paul's Epistle to the Romans, many people have never noticed the following words: "For whatever was written in earlier times was written for our instruction that through perseverance and the encouragement of the Scriptures we might have hope. Now may the God who gives perseverance and encouragement grant you to be of the same mind with one another according to Christ Jesus" (Rom. 15:4–5).

Now, at first glance, this passage may not seem to have anything to do with preaching. Such a view would, however, be premature and very short-sighted. That can be seen quite readily by comparing the flow of thought in these two verses:

- Biblical instruction (Gk. *didaskalia*) is intended to enhance the hearers' perseverance and encouragement and, ultimately, give them hope (Rom. 15:4).
- God is the giver of such perseverance and encouragement that leads to being of one mind in Christ (Rom. 15:5).

Obviously, Paul is here saying that God is the source (Rom. 15:5) of the "perseverance" and "encouragement" that come through instruction in the Scriptures (Rom. 15:4). Thus, there is great encouragement to preach and to persevere in doing so, that others might be encouraged and persevere as a result of hearing the proclamation.

The Expected Applicational Overflow of the God-Breathed Nature of Scripture

Inspired Scripture is to transform the life of the person being equipped for ministry (2 Tim. 3:16–17). But that change is not an end in itself. At least one very crucial part of the wider ministry role is faithful proclamation of the Bible (2 Tim. 4:2) and, relatedly, evangelism (2 Tim. 4:5). Hence, the Word of God is expected to first apply to the preacher and then, through him, to his hearers. There is no guarantee, though, that it will be received by those hearers (2 Tim. 4:2–4). With God's human "mouthpieces," the key issue is faithfulness (2 Tim. 4:5), not eloquence or success.

When we back off and consider this passage for a moment, it seems that Paul is basically saying to Timothy, "Just let Scripture 'do its thing.' Just allow it to do what the Lord designed it to do." Put another way, God breathed out (i.e., as inspired revelation) his Word to us, and, as a result, our belief structures and lifestyles are retooled. In turn, he expects us to faithfully "breathe out" (i.e., as inspiring preaching) his written Word that others might be doctrinally and behaviorally renovated.

The Ongoing Timely Application of Timeless Principles from God's Living, Active Word

Since one part or another of the psalm is quoted four times in the space of nineteen verses,[11] it is quite clear that Hebrews 3:7–4:13 is an extended practical exposition of Psalm 95:7–11. It is fascinating to track the thought of the writer of Hebrews in his use of the Psalm 95 citation.[12] He seems to have focused in particular on how David, in Psalm 95, had paralleled the sad events at what was named Massah and Meribah in Exodus 17, which had taken place well over four hundred years before David's time,[13] to the tendency toward hard-heartedness among his hearers in his day. From an interpretative standpoint, David viewed Exodus 17 as *timeless* in its application and, in Psalm 95, he did in fact apply that timeless truth in a very *timely* manner.

The author of Hebrews does much the same. He picks up on the word *today* in Psalm 95 and uses it repeatedly (Heb. 3:7, 15; 4:7) as his biblical base-point for timely application to his hearers. As a skilled preacher[14] but one who is very compassionate toward but realistic about the current stubborn and unbelieving mind-set of his audience, he hammers on the need to respond *now* (i.e., "today"). It could be said very accurately that he is "preaching for a verdict" in Hebrews 3–4. At the very least, the writer is seeking to let the "living and active" Word of God (in this case, Psalm 95) do its "piercing" (Heb. 4:12) and transforming work in his hearers' lives.

A Readily Available Blessing for All Engaged in the Process

It is sometimes noted that Revelation 1:3 is the only place in the Bible in which a blessing is pronounced for reading Scripture. Such a statement is totally well intended and is true . . . *as far as it goes.* It must be noted, however, that when the verse says, "Blessed is he who reads," it is not talking about sitting down and reading the Scripture silently, as is customary to us.

Rather, there is a very important reason "he who reads" is singular in Revelation 1:3, while "those who hear" is plural. The dynamics of this verse have to do with the oral setting of a church service. One person is standing and reading the Book of Revelation, while the congregation "hears" (there was no printed, or even hand-copied, document for the congregation to follow along during the reading).

Hence, the "reading" of Revelation 1:3 has basically the practical force of preaching and, again, it is preaching for a behavioral verdict. The process to receive the "blessing" in Revelation 1:3 is not complete until there has been application of what has been heard and resulting lifestyle transformation. That is what is meant by the last phrase: "And heed the things which are written."

Certainly, this verse should be dear to every believer. It is nothing less than a great "blessing" to internalize the Scriptures and let them have their way in our lives.

However, when the exegetical details above have been carefully sifted, it is clear that the original *direct* "blessing" was related to the oral reading and open-hearted hearing (i.e., "with ears to hear" [Rev. 2:7, 11, etc.]) of God's written Word, much like what we are calling "inspired preaching" in this book.[15] That "blessing" is also still available to God's people as they *hear* the Word read and let the complementary power of its oral quality sink in on them alongside the effects of standard silent reading.

The Primary Way the New Testament Was Produced and Propagated

As will be seen in the next chapter, the normal way in which most letters and many other documents of the New Testament era were produced was through an author dictating to a secretary.[16] The interesting thing about the Apocalypse is that, in this case, the primary (divine) author is the risen Christ (Rev. 1:5, 8). John serves as the human coauthor (1:4, 9) but, more than anything else, in the sense of serving as Christ's stenographer (1:11, 19).[17]

Thought of this way, Revelation begins to look like what could be called a "relay-team sermon." Christ does most of the initial (inspired) "talking," so to speak, then hands the baton to John for editorial comments and passing the baton on to the churches (Rev. 1:4, 11; chs. 2–3), where the Apocalypse is read by either the courier or some leader (1:3), though the Holy Spirit is also "speaking" ("hear what the Spirit says to the churches"; 2:7, 11, etc.) through the reading and hearing.

Since this is the focus of the discussion in the next chapter, it will be sufficient, at this point, to point out that such interaction between the author/preacher (sometimes the Lord, as here) and another person writing the proclaimed content is not a puzzling occurrence in the New Testament, not even a rarity. As will be seen consistently throughout this entire volume, such instances are actually "windows" into the prevailing oral culture that was the New Testament era. In order to properly understand what we are dealing with, we must face the mass of such evidence and its significant implications. Otherwise, it is like refusing to wear a pair of glasses that can correct our myopia (nearsightedness) when studying the New Testament.

THE TERMINOLOGY OF PREACHING IN THE NEW TESTAMENT

Before going further, it will be helpful to examine the primary words for preaching that are used in the New Testament. As will be seen, there are two primary terms for preaching in the New Testament, though there are also a number of other ways in which the function of preaching is described.[18]

Heralding the Word of the Lord: *Kerussō*

In the ancient world, the herald played the role of making public announcements or proclamations. In a society without print or telephones or television or e-mail (which we take for granted in our culture), the herald played a vitally important role.

There are two additional elements related to the role of "herald" (Gk. *kērux*) that need to be understood to explain why the term was applied so readily to preaching. In the first place, in almost all cases, the herald was not proclaiming the message (Gk. *kērugma*) on his own authority. He was speaking on behalf of someone else, often some high-ranking official. Secondly, the proclamation usually carried with it the force of an "appeal." In other words, it was anything but a monotone "announcement," such as the kind of thing that actor Ben Stein has perfected as his "signature" schtick.

The idea "to herald" (Gk. *kērusso*) is fairly common in the New Testament, being used about sixty times. Of these uses, one is found in 2 Timothy 4:2, a context spoken of above. When Paul commanded Timothy, "Preach the Word," it was precisely this kind of authoritative proclamation that the apostle had in mind. And that was particularly important for Timothy to hear at that point in time. He was naturally timid, anyway. But the wider context of 2 Timothy indicates that Timothy was thoroughly discouraged and beaten down, perhaps depressed. At the very least, in regard to his preaching responsibilities in the church at Ephesus, he was not oozing with personal confidence at the thought of going back into the congregational setting to preach.

By his use of *kērusso* here, Paul seems to be saying, "Tim, you have to take responsibility for what the Lord has called you to do and preach. But remember, you are not up there representing yourself, and you're not proclaiming your own message, expecting it to make all the difference in people's lives. You are 'heralding' the God-breathed message, which packs divine authority and has the power to transform your hearers, even as it has you."

That passage is disproportionately dear to me, because I am, naturally, a "timid Timothy" when it comes to preaching. Public speaking (of any sort) is the last thing in the world I would have done vocationally, if I had been allowed the final choice in the matter. But the Lord had other ideas. And, graciously, he continues to remind me that it is not my "word" that I proclaim. I represent him, and his Word packs a punch that mine never could. He wants me to be concerned with faithful "heralding" (2 Tim. 4:2–5) and he will take care of the rest.

So there's our first word for New Testament preaching in a nutshell: *Kērusso* means to herald as an authoritative appeal. And preaching is still to be viewed as just such an authoritative appeal (i.e., on behalf of the all-powerful Creator and sustainer of the universe, to those made in his image, for whom he cares very deeply) in our day as much as it was in societies in which they knew instantly the function and delegated authority of a "herald."

Delivering Good News: *Euangelizō*

The Greek verb *angellō* (from which we get "angel" [i.e., God's "messen-ger"]) means simply "to tell." It does not necessarily imply the tone of mes-sage being passed on, just that a message is being delivered. Theoretically, the message could be good, bad, or indifferent.

However, the addition of the little Greek prefix *eu*, with a range of mean-ing from good to splendid, changes things considerably. When the term *euan-gelizō* is used, the messenger is, unequivocally, delivering "Good News." There is nothing bad about it, other than in refusing to hear it or rejecting it.

So powerfully did the term *euangelizō* impact the ministry of preaching in the New Testament that we operate within a complex of its "kissing cousin" Greek terms to even carry on a decent discussion about preaching ministry. The Good News we deliver is, literally, "the Good News." That may sound like double-talk, but that is exactly what "gospel" (Gk. *euangelion*) means: "good news." And the person delivering that Good News can be called an "evangel-ist" (Gk. *euangelistes*). Some are evangelists specially gifted by the Lord (Eph. 4:11), though it appears that all are to "do the work of an evangelist" (2 Tim. 4:5[19]), in faithfully preaching the gospel message, whether they possess the gift of evangelism (another of our spin-off terms from *euangelizō*) or not.

Preachers sometimes need to be reminded that, literally *by definition*, we are in the business of preaching "Good News." In a world in which the morn-ing newspaper and the evening news are almost constantly focused on *bad news*, we can easily be sucked into that kind of mentality. In too many of our churches, we run into people whose countenances project the sense that "if there weren't *bad* news, as far as I'm concerned, there wouldn't be any news at all."

Nothing could be further from the truth! We preach "Good News." It is, in fact, "splendid news," *the best* news of all. As preachers, the Good News is that we can say to people, "I've got Good News" and the only sense in which "and I've got bad news" even comes up is in regard to those who turn away from the Good News. In that light, it is readily apparent why Paul could say, "I am not ashamed of the gospel *[Gk. euangelion]*, for it is the power of God for salvation to everyone who believes" (Rom. 1:16).

Preaching in Other Words

As important as these terms are, the full essence of New Testament preach-ing cannot be balled up in "heralding" and "preaching Good News." There are additional ways to express what is involved in preaching, as well as other nuances that need to be clarified.

For just a quick sampler: In Mark 2:2 Jesus "speaks" (Gk. *laleō*) the Word. In John 1:15 John the Baptist "testifies" (Gk. *martureō*). In Acts 2:40 Peter "exhorts" (Gk. *parakaleō*) on the day of Pentecost. In Acts 18:26 Apollos "spoke boldly" (Gk. *parrēsiazomai*) in the synagogue. In Acts 23:6 Paul "cried out" (Gk. *krazō*) in the Sanhedrin. In Ephesians 6:19 Paul "made known" (Gk. *gnorizō*) the mystery of the gospel.

We may be more comfortable with the term *preaching* (whether the "heralding" or "delivering Good News" angle is in view). But all these other terms deal with aspects or dimensions of preaching that are equally important. Thus, as with beautiful flowers, "a rose (in this case, preaching) by any other name smells just as sweet." It still delivers the authoritative Good News that turns lives right side up.

THE EXAMPLES OF PREACHING SEEN IN THE NEW TESTAMENT

Sometimes the impression is left that there were only a handful of great preachers in the New Testament era: Jesus, Paul, Peter, Apollos, and a few others. That is hardly the case—a point proven by the fact that the longest message recorded in the Book of Acts, one that was clearly characterized by wisdom and the power of the Holy Spirit (Acts 6:10; 7:55), was delivered by Stephen (7:2–53).

The following is an overview survey of some of the "preaching and preachers"[20] in the New Testament. Most of those we will see are "the usual suspects." Some may be surprising. Hopefully, all will be enlightening.

The Foundational Examples of Jesus and His Forerunners

In the Gospel of Matthew, before the beginning of Jesus' public ministry, John the Baptist comes on the scene "preaching" (Gk. *kērussō*) in the wilderness (3:1). Jesus' preaching ministry in Matthew is elegantly structured as five major messages,[21] the longest of which are the first (the Sermon the Mount), which is three chapters long, and the last (the Olivet Discourse), which is two chapters long. And, since Matthew records that Jesus fed crowds well in excess of 10,000 at least twice,[22] it is highly likely that Jesus regularly preached to massive crowds. Clearly, to Matthew, preaching was a major consideration, since in the neighborhood of one-third of the First Gospel is fairly directly related to preaching.

In the Gospel of Mark, by far the shortest (and often the tersest) Gospel, Jesus is the primary preacher. There are noteworthy examples of the Savior's preaching in Mark 3, 4, 7, 9, and 12. Mark's version of the Olivet Discourse, which is fairly similar to Matthew's, though lacking most of the parabolic material at the end of Matthew 24 and in chapter 25, is in Mark 13.

In the Third Gospel, there is a greater variety of those who could be said to "preach" in some sense. For example, even though their only hearers were each other, there is a sense in which Elizabeth and Mary "preached" to one another in regard to the messianic significance of the babies within their wombs (Luke 1:42–55).[23] Then, several months later, Zacharias, John the Baptist's father, who had been muted because of his unbelief (1:20), had his tongue loosened by the Holy Spirit and "prophesied" (1:68–79).

As in Matthew, the preaching of John the Baptist is recorded (Luke 3). The featured preacher, though, is definitely Jesus, with messages found in Luke 4, 6, 10, 11, 12, 13, 14, 15, 16, 17, 18, 19, 20, and 22. Luke's version of the Olivet Discourse is found in chapter 21. It is noteworthy that all the preaching in the middle section of Luke's Gospel (chs. 9–19), often called the "Travelogue," are distinctive to Luke.

In the Gospel of John, it is solely Jesus who does the preaching. Whether it is evangelistic preaching to Nicodemus (John 3) or the Samaritan woman (John 4), or didactic teaching to the apostles in the Upper Room Discourse (John 14–16), or a number of other extended didactic passages (e.g., John 5, 6, 8, 10, 12), John has recorded many magnificent sermons that enrich our feel for New Testament preaching.

As has been seen, in the Gospels the dominant preacher is Jesus. It is daunting for any sinful human preacher to seek to emulate the proclamation of the sinless God-Man, since it is impossible to duplicate his level of effectiveness. But, although none of us will ever be Jesus, because he was human and divine, much that is helpful can still be learned from his "inspired preaching," to make for "inspiring preaching" today, as will be seen at various points later in the book.[24]

The "Follower" Examples in the Book of Acts . . . and One More

The preaching in the Book of Acts changes dramatically from the Gospels, if for no greater reason than Jesus has ascended to heaven (Acts 1:9–10). It is the preaching of his primary followers, his closest disciples: apostolic preaching, dominated largely by Peter—with five major messages—and Paul—with seven major messages, but including several other notable (and surprising) examples.

The first great preacher of the infant church was unquestionably the apostle Peter. This does not seem strange to us, due to our immense respect for Peter as one of the "pillars" of the church (Gal. 2:9). However, from the standpoint of previous Scripture, it is nothing short of astounding! Consider his less-than-awe-inspiring record as the spokesman for the apostolic band following Jesus, in which he could plummet from a verbal spiritual "A+" to "Get behind me, Satan," in the space of seven verses (i.e., from Matt. 16:16 to 16:23).[25] Nor is the reader's confidence in the likelihood of Peter's becoming a great preacher enhanced much by his denial of Christ (Matt. 26:69).

However, it is a dramatically different Peter that we witness preaching on the day of Pentecost. In the power of the Holy Spirit, three thousand people were converted through Peter's message (Acts 2:41). By the conclusion of Peter's second recorded sermon, the number of *male* converts is recorded as "about five thousand" (4:4), which implies that there were many women and children not numbered, perhaps easily tripling or quadrupling the number.

But before we can get used to the extraordinary evangelistic harvest seen in Peter's first two messages in Acts, the nature of Peter's messages changes significantly. In Acts 4, he speaks to the "rulers and elders and scribes" (4:5). In chapters 10 and 11, it is Cornelius the Gentile and his household in Caesarea. Then, finally, at the Jerusalem council in Acts 15, Peter's message to the assembled "apostles and elders" (Acts 15:2) was to the effect that his ministry demonstrated that God was saving Gentiles "through the grace of the Lord Jesus, in the same way" as he was the Jews (Acts 15:11). That was a powerful testimony, coming from the apostle to the Jews.

Interestingly, the next "preacher" in Acts is a nonbeliever: Paul's former pharisaic mentor, the great Jewish teacher, Gamaliel. In his "sermon" to the Sanhedrin in Acts 5, Gamaliel counsels caution in acting against the rapidly growing church in Jerusalem by citing known events from relatively recent Jewish history. He then draws this conclusion: If the church is not of God, he says, it will fall apart. If it is of God, though, it cannot be overthrown and the Jews will "be found fighting against God." This, of course, turns out to be an ironic preview of the Jewish persecution of the spread of the gospel and the church throughout the rest of Acts.

Next is the courageous "unto death" sermon preached by Stephen in Acts 7. Its lengthy retelling of the history of Israel displays a remarkable grasp of how Jewish leaders had so often tended to be "stiff-necked and uncircumcised in heart and ears and always resisting the Holy Spirit" (Acts 7:51). The confrontational and convicting nature of Stephen's sermon was not exactly designed to "win friends and influence people." It, of course, got him stoned.

This tragic ending, of course, would seem to imply that Stephen's preaching was a failure. However, when all aspects are considered, virtually the opposite may well be the case. Certainly Stephen was faithful in his ministry of preaching, even "out of season"[26] (2 Tim. 4:2–5). And it may well be that a seed was planted in the mind and heart of Saul by the bold preaching of Stephen that later played a role in his conversion on the Damascus road (Acts 9).

The next preacher in Acts is Paul, and more of his messages are recorded than of any other preacher. Part of the reason is that four of his seven extended messages are in the context of defending himself within the Jewish and Roman legal systems (Acts 22, 23, 24, and 26). The other three are (1) in a Jewish synagogue in Pisidian Antioch (Acts 13); (2) to the philosophers on the Areopagus in Athens (Acts 17); and (3) to the elders of the church of Ephesus at Miletus (Acts 20). These sermons seem to have been chosen to reflect the diversity of Paul's preaching situations.

It is widely agreed that one of the ways in which Luke has structured the Book of Acts is to parallel the ministries of Peter (in Acts 1–12) and Paul (in Acts 13–28).[27] That being the case, it would be expected that there would be a parallel between the recorded observations of the explosive evangelistic response to Peter's preaching in Jerusalem in Acts 2–4 should be seen in the preaching ministry of Paul. That does, in fact, occur, as Luke describes the evangelistic overflow of Paul's preaching and teaching in Ephesus, particularly in the "school of Tyrannus," that, incredibly, reached "all who lived in [the Roman province of] Asia" (Acts 19:8–10).[28]

The final example of preaching in Acts is James, in Acts 15. It appears to have been included because it is the decisive persuasive message that led to the consensus reached by the Jerusalem council.

In summary, the Book of Acts records a wide array of examples of preaching. While there are a considerable number of parallels between the preaching of Peter and Paul, each ultimately demonstrates flexibility and effectiveness in preaching in varied Jewish and Gentile settings, as well as on multiple occasions before authorities with incarceration on the line. The varied preaching of Stephen and James, as well as the ironic inclusion of a message by the Pharisee, Gamaliel, adds spice to the mix. Suffice it to say that Acts is a rich resource for insight in regard to New Testament preaching, both its theological basis[29] and its outworking in ministry.

THE NEW TESTAMENT GENRES AS PREACHING

When I went to seminary in the early 1970s, many evangelicals were just beginning to realize that biblical hermeneutics might be somewhat more difficult than reading and understanding a newspaper.[30] What most didn't realize was that the analogy between a newspaper and the Bible was indeed a useful one, just not in the way that it had been used previously, in emphasizing the simplicity of biblical interpretation.

Think about it: In a newspaper, there are a number of different kinds of literature, ranging, for example, from front-page hard-news stories, to opinion/editorial pieces, to self-help features, to obituaries, to comic strips, to television or movie reviews. And (even though we tend to take this for granted, having grown up in a culture with newspapers), each of these types of writing must be interpreted on its own terms (i.e., by the established rules of interpretation of its field), *if* it is to be understood accurately. If, however, a person who had never seen a newspaper picked one up and tried to read and understand it, how successful would the attempt be, without obtaining at least some basic background knowledge of how various kinds of newspaper writing function? Not very, I'm afraid.

While there are several kinds of shorter literary forms in the New Testament,[31] it contains only three major types of literature: (1) historical-biographical books (the Gospels and Acts); (2) epistle/letter (from Romans through Jude); and (3) apocalyptic/prophecy (Revelation).[32] As with our newspapers, for accurate interpretation to take place, each of these genres must be understood in terms of the established literary conventions of its day for that type of literary communication.

Since we will be covering the entirety of the New Testament in the remainder of the book, it is not my purpose here to discuss these three major genres in any depth. It is rather to whet the appetite for the fact that, to a significant degree, it is the distinctiveness of each that provides its flair. If "variety is the spice of life," then, as will be seen, the New Testament is a spicy dish, indeed.[33]

As literature, the Gospels and Acts are unique in the ancient world, a truly artistic blend of history and theology in presenting the person, life, ministry, and saving work of our Lord Jesus Christ. As God's Word, they are completely historically trustworthy, while reflecting the theological perspectives and emphases the authors chose to communicate most effectively to their distinctive audiences. Since it is virtually certain that what each writer presents is reflective of previous oral teaching to some extent (at the least, their own preaching ministries about Jesus), and since the first words in the Second Gospel are "the beginning of the gospel of Jesus Christ" (Mark 1:1a), the feel of what we could call the "semi-sermonic" pervades these books.

What I mean to say here is that, although they record the preaching ministry of Christ in what are almost surely summarized sermons, the more sermonic aspect of the Gospels and Acts is actually that, in their canonical form, they "preach" just as they are. Yes, we break them down into "bite-size chunks" for the purpose of preaching an expositional series. That is a great help for more in-depth understanding of the biblical text. But from a "big-picture" standpoint, in answer to the foundational questions "Who is Jesus Christ?" and "How did the church of Jesus Christ get started?" reading a particular Gospel or Acts without comment, holistically, as an extended "sermon" is hard to beat.[34]

The New Testament Epistles bear a striking resemblance to the epistolary examples of that era that have survived (although, on average, they are several times longer than extra-biblical letters). Accordingly, they all have some form of introduction and conclusion, with a body sandwiched in between. In that respect, their format is basically identical with almost every sermon I have ever heard preached. This observation is, to some extent, a legitimate reflection of their oral/rhetorical quality, as will be seen clearly in the next chapter.

Beyond this basic form, though, the epistolary writings in the New Testament are anything but stereotypical. In length and feel, they run the gamut from the "brief note" feel of Philemon and 2 and 3 John to the sense of an extended logical treatise (e.g., Romans) or elegant rhetoric (e.g., Hebrews). Suffice it to say that the letters found in the New Testament are more like family members who have much in common but otherwise are very different. They are more than virtual clones of one another.[35]

From the standpoint of relating preaching to the epistolary genre, at the very least it should be observed that the New Testament letters have the shape and the various sizes and tones of most of the different kinds of messages you hear preached. Longer, shorter—more formal, less formal—usually delivered against the backdrop of some practical occasion or issues . . . as much of a "stand-in" for preaching as could be conceived in that day. No wonder Harvey can say, "Letter writing was as close to face-to-face communication as first-century correspondents could come."[36]

The Book of Revelation is more like Daniel or Ezekiel in the Old Testament than any other book in the New Testament. It is legitimate to refer to it as "apocalyptic," given that is as close to a title as we have for the book: "The Revelation (Gk. *apokalupsis*) of Jesus Christ" (Rev. 1:1). This explains all the mind-boggling "picture imagery" (i.e., vision symbolism) in the Apocalypse.

However, Revelation is not just apocalyptic. It is also more or less equally "prophecy" (1:3; which explains the specific predictions of a nonsymbolic nature) and, although this is not as high-profile, "epistle" (note the standard way New Testament letters begin [i.e., author, recipients, greetings] in 1:4), which is seen in the role the seven churches of Asia (1:4, 11; chs. 2–3) play in the book.[37]

In many respects, Revelation is an extended message by the glorified Christ to the churches (compare Rev. 2:1 and 2:7) through an angel recorded by John as a kind of human secretary (1:1–2, 11, 19). Thus, from the very beginning the Apocalypse has the feel of a sort of exotic sermon. Between the uniquely blended genres and the subject matter, much can be learned about powerful and provocative preaching.

In regard to the study of these genres, though, what is often not grasped by evangelicals is that the New Testament era was a time in which the transition from an oral to a written society was far from complete. As John Harvey aptly observes:

> The popular culture of the first century was, technically, a
> rhetorical culture. In a rhetorical culture, literacy is limited,
> and reading is vocal. Even the solitary reader reads aloud

(Acts 8:30). The normal mode of writing is by dictation, and that which is written down is intended to be read aloud to a group rather than silently by the individual. Such a culture is familiar with writing, but is, in essence, oral. The predominantly oral nature of a rhetorical culture requires speakers to arrange their material in ways that can be followed easily by a listener. Clues to the organization of thought are, of necessity, based on sound rather than on sight.[38]

In a culture of this type, communication was primarily conceived in the oral/aural dimension, even if it was written down and passed along in "literary" form. This means that, while we must, obviously, work with the written (literary) product of the New Testament books if we are to play fair with the realistic transitional nature of communication in the New Testament era, there is an equally important oral/rhetorical dimension that must be understood. Beginning to come to terms with that overlooked oral (dare I say "preaching") quality is the focus of the next chapter.

CHAPTER

THE NEW TESTAMENT AS INSPIRED PREACHING: APPRECIATING THE ORALITY FACTOR

A. BOYD LUTER

As he dictates, he sees in his mind's eye those whom he is addressing and speaks as he would if he were face to face with them. Even if he made use of amanuenses, the style is his own. . . . When the amanuensis was one of his close associates, like Timothy or Luke, some greater stylistic discretion may have been allowed to him. But when Paul warmed to his theme, it can have been no easy task for any one to write down his dictation. If the amanuenses followed the customary procedure, they could have taken down what Paul dictated with a stylus on wax tablets, possibly using some system of shorthand, and then transcribe the text in longhand on to a papyrus sheet or roll.

F. F. BRUCE[1]

Since the acts of both writing and reading were accompanied by vocalization, the structure of the text was marked by aural rather than visual indicators. Mnemonic clues were important because people usually made reference to written materials by using their memory rather than looking up a citation. These factors . . . must be considered when interpreting literature from this period.

C. W. DAVIS[2]

I, Tertius, who write this letter, greet you in the Lord (Rom. 16:22). Blessed is he who reads and those who hear the words of the prophecy, and heed the things which are written in it; for the time is near (Rev. 1:3).

WHAT'S WRONG WITH THIS PICTURE?

The scene is a recent chapel service at The Criswell College in Dallas. As the singing ends, a male student portraying the apostle Paul appears, sits down at a spotlighted table, picks up a quill pen, and begins to write. Though his lips do not move, the voice in his head is heard over the loudspeaker system, reading 2 Timothy 3:1–4:8.

While this chapel vignette was, indeed, moving and thought provoking, I must admit that it troubled me more than a little. Now, it certainly did not do such obvious violence to the actual dynamics of Paul's writing of what was almost surely his literary swan song[3] as portraying the apostle sitting at a computer (or even a typewriter). But it did assume the standard writing dynamics of the modern era and anachronistically overlayed them onto the apostle. In other words, what we naturally (if subconsciously) expect to see is what seems "normal" to us.

So, you might well ask, if the above description was historically inaccurate, what would the specific circumstances of the composition of a New Testament work, whether 2 Timothy or some other book, by a New Testament author such as Paul, have been like? Before answering that question, however, we need to back up and address the validity of the typical basic communication model almost invariably used in such discussions.

SIMPLICITY THAT IS SIMPLISTIC: BIBLICALLY CRITIQUING AN OVERSIMPLIFIED COMMUNICATION MODEL

Jeff Weima summarizes, "In any act of communication, one can distinguish between the sender, the message that person conveys, and the recipient of the message. When this model is applied to literary texts, these three components become (1) the author, (2) the text and (3) the reader."[4] This is not a bad model at all . . . as far as it goes. However, even though its one-two-three crispness has the great advantage of simplicity, which usually plays out in understandability, it also turns out to be a two-edged sword.

In this case, simplicity turns out to be *simplistic* (i.e., oversimplified), when it has to do with the communication process related to the New Testament documents. As will be seen, a communication model that accurately reflects what took place with the books of the New Testament is considerably more complicated. However, there is also a significant up side to this heightened complexity: The process is far, far richer than the simple three-factor model above.

Author

For an initial example, if, as Davis correctly asserts, "The acts of both writing and reading were accompanied by vocalization,"[5] then the *author* (component one of the three-part model above) is also both a *speaker* and a *hearer*. And, of course, since most people readily recognize that there is a very noticeable difference between "spoken communication style" and "written communication style," this is no small factor. Add on top of that the impact of having your own words fall on your ear (i.e., *aural* input) and you begin to see that, in the New Testament era, an "author," even in the simplest compositional situation, "wore three hats," so to speak.

Secretary

Actually, however, in regard to the New Testament books, it is very likely that, in the bulk of the cases, the author was *not* also the writer. Quite frequently, an amanuensis[6] (a secretarial figure,[7] similar to a stenographer of more recent times) would take down the dictated words of the author. Though there is very strong evidence supporting this point, as we shall see, there is only one New Testament "secretary" that we know by name: Tertius.

After nearly sixteen power-packed chapters (by the reckoning of verse and chapter divisions provided much later, of course) attributed to "Paul, a bondservant of Christ Jesus, called as an apostle" (Rom. 1:1), without warning, in Romans 16:22, we read, "I, Tertius, who write this letter, greet you in the Lord." I once heard someone in a Bible study ask if this could be Paul's "ghostwriter." Though that is laughable (it's better to laugh than to cry), that is how out of touch most of our culture has been, and still is, with the compositional realities of the New Testament books.

Even though Tertius is the only named amanuensis in the New Testament corpus, there is considerable additional evidence of their work. For example, in what may well have been Paul's earliest letter,[8] Galatians, suddenly, near the end of the epistle,[9] the reader encounters this wording: "See with what large letters I am writing to you with my own hand" (Gal. 6:11). The significance here seems to be that, only at the end of the body of the letter does the apostle take pen in hand (from the amanuensis) and, in doing so, he provides an oversized "signature" for his work.

Similarly, but apparently even more to the point of authoritatively "signing off" on a letter, are Paul's words at the end of 2 Thessalonians, usually also understood to be among the earliest of the Pauline Epistles:[10] "I, Paul, write this greeting with my own hand, and this is the distinguishing mark in every letter; this is the way I write" (2 Thess. 3:17). And, there may well be an intriguing viable explanation for the filled-out "signature" here: the intervening presence of a falsified epistle from Paul.

The errant eschatology that the apostle is obviously contending with in 2 Thessalonians appears to be due to "a letter as if from us, to the effect that the day of the Lord has come" (2 Thess. 2:2). And, if the natural question is asked (i.e., How could such a false letter get such ready acceptance?), the dynamics of the documents of the era combined with the Thessalonian correspondence provide a plausible explanation.

Paul did not "sign" 1 Thessalonians (as he had Galatians), perhaps not thinking that he needed to do so. So, with no "signature sample" to verify that the letter was Paul's, and given that different amanuenses and couriers[11] (i.e., letter-carriers, who were sometimes the same person as the amanuensis) were often used in that era, coupled with the reality that the Thessalonian believers were still basically little more than babes in Christ,[12] it may not have been that difficult to dupe them into believing a concocted letter was from Paul. Hence, having learned a painful, but valuable, lesson, the apostle added the extended signature portion in 2 Thessalonians, including the stated test for the legitimacy of his letters (apparently from this point in time forward): "This is a distinguishing mark in every letter; this is the way I write" (3:17).

Similar wording pointing to this Pauline signature pattern, and the presence of an amanuensis, is also seen in several of his later epistles: "The greeting is in my own hand—Paul" (1 Cor. 16:21)[13]; "I, Paul, write this greeting with my own hand" (Col. 4:18)[14]; and "I, Paul, am writing this with my own hand" (Philem. 19).[15]

Being a secretary in the New Testament era to someone like Paul would have been a tremendously challenging task. As Bruce describes, "If his amanuenses followed the customary procedure, they could have taken down what Paul dictated with a stylus on wax tablets, possibly using some system of shorthand, and then transcribe the text in longhand on to a papyrus sheet or roll."[16] In order to make sure that the dictation had been recorded correctly, and that the transcribing was accurate, the process envisioned here likely required a repeated "out-loud" rereading of the document. As crucial as this would have been for the accuracy of the text,[17] though, it would have been virtually as important for the person who was the carrier of the document.

Courier

A most important, though often overlooked, role was played by the person who carried the particular New Testament document. Now, it is not known for sure if the role of the courier always (or even often) extended to the role of the "reader" (i.e., the public reading of the document within the congregational context).[18] However, in most cases, it certainly would be the logical thing to do, given the difficult (at best) readability of documents in the New Testament era. If nothing else, the reader in the church setting would have depended greatly on the courier to help clear up the many questions due to the difficult layout of the text.

As Michael Holmes elaborates on the writing format of the period: "Books were written in *scriptio continua* (i.e., without breaks between words) with minimal punctuation or other aids for a reader, generally in either one wide column or several narrow ones per page."[19] That means that, if the courier was the reader on the receiving end—and had not been able to hear the author articulate the full document in question—probably several times, there would inevitably have been significant hesitation, and not a few errors, in trying to make sense in the verbal "delivery" of that document.

Though Randy Richards's recent probing study of 1 Peter 5:12 comes down on the side of understanding Silvanus (Silas) as the carrier of the letter, instead of the secretary, it is not impossible (or even particularly implausible) that Silas played *both* roles. In fact, as pointed out above, it would have been very advantageous for Silas (and Peter's hearers) for him to serve as an amanuensis-courier.

While it cannot be known for sure, it is plausible that we see the couriers more or less named in a number of Paul's letters. Ephesians 6:21–22 probably indicates that Tychicus was serving as Paul's letter carrier, and he apparently did the same for Colossians (see Col. 4:7–8). Similarly, Philippians 2:25–30 likely refers to this key role for Epaphroditus. Also, the commendation of Paul for Phoebe in Romans 16:1–2, as well as her home base in Cenchrea,[20] may well indicate that she carried that great letter.

Reader

As far as is known, there was no such thing as a silent reader in the New Testament era. Our best window on that reality is the Ethiopian eunuch in Acts 8. While verse 28 initially sounds like it could at least allow reading in silence ("reading the prophet Isaiah"), verse 30 leaves no doubt that it is *not* silent reading: "Philip had run up and *heard* him reading Isaiah the prophet" (emphasis added).

The "congregational reader" was a vitally important figure. In order for the church members to be able to "hear" (i.e., understand) and "heed" (i.e., apply) the Scriptures (Rev. 1:3), they had to be read *accurately and well*. Since they were undoubtedly read whole, they also had to have been read through any number of times, in order for the memory function to begin to grasp, for recall, the content of the document.

EARS TO HEAR: SUMMARIZING A NEW TESTAMENT COMMUNICATION MODEL WE CAN IDENTIFY WITH TODAY

So, we have seen that there was a lot more to the communication task during the era in which the New Testament was produced than just the initial one-two-three of the standard communication model (i.e., author, text, reader). At the simplest, it was usually speaker/author/hearer, amanuensis, courier, text (which had been rewritten—[perhaps repeatedly]—for accuracy) and reader/hearer(s).

All of these factors combine into the undeniable realization that the New Testament was birthed in an era of "high residual orality."[21] But as we will see from the following summarial discussion and analogy, as well as the conclusion of this study, what goes around, comes around. In certain key respects, the present and future of communication is the past, in this case, the orality dimension.

Given my substantial familiarity with Philippians,[22] the following represents a brief initial attempt to describe the New Testament era communication process as it was carried out between Paul and the church at Philippi. There is filling in of gaps here and there, to be sure, but none of what is said is speculatively implausible.

A Philippians "Orality Scenario"

From his point of incarceration (likely house arrest in Rome),[23] the closest thing to being able to pay a personal visit to Philippi that Paul could do was to send them a letter.[24] So Paul "paced and preached" (i.e., with his beloved Philippian believers in the front of his mind) in his abode, "teaming" with Timothy (Phil. 1:1), as his coauthor/amanuensis,[25] to produce the letter as we have it.[26] Epaphroditus (2:25–30) was present, listening carefully to the entire production, even as it was read repeatedly, so that Timothy could ensure that he was doing full (and precisely accurate) justice to all of the apostle's thought patterns.

Epaphroditus then carried the letter and delivered it to the troubled[27] church at Philippi, in care of their "overseers and deacons" (Phil. 1:1). On the first day of corporate worship, he also delivered the letter as the reader in the congregational setting (see Rev. 1:3). Paul almost surely chose him for that key role because: (1) He was the appointed authoritative "messenger" (Gk. *apostolos*) from the Philippian church to Paul (Phil. 2:25); (2) he had a deep personal relationship and emotional bond with the congregation (2:26–30); and (3) the joy of Epaphroditus's return, after nearly dying (2:26–27, 30), would make hearing Paul's (and Timothy's) eventual pointed references to problems in the church somewhat easier to hear and face. Among Epaphroditus's initially excited, then shocked, hearers that day would have been the two primary "trouble-makers" in the congregation: the women Euodia and Syntyche (4:2–3).

A Contemporary Semiparallel

A current preacher had, about a decade earlier, founded a church hundreds of miles away. Although he strongly desired to go and visit the distant church, both because of the personal bond and also to speak to the pride and disunity problems that had emerged in the congregation (and which were worsening quickly!), he was unable to do so at that time.

He did, however, have a trusted associate, himself an effective preacher, who also knew the other church well and who could, in fact, go and represent the preacher.

The man who had planted the distant church years earlier knew that, in order to accomplish the congregational healing needed, his associate/ messenger had to be the absolute next best thing to his own actual physical presence. He had thought about just sending an audio or a videotape of a lovingly pointed message crafted to their needs. But then he realized that there was no technology readily available that would allow all members of the distant congregation to hear and see . . . and, even if the "tech" had been available, it would lack the personal touch.

What was the preacher to do? He taped his message, which was then very carefully transcribed by the church secretary. He then gave both the tape and transcript to his associate, who had also watched him deliver the message, as it was being taped. His instructions to the associate were to listen to the tape and read the transcript out loud over and over (with the people and needs in the far-off congregation in the spotlight of his mind!) until, in doing so, he could virtually reproduce every vocal and literary flourish and emphasis point that the preacher had crafted and featured in his original message.

When the associate arrived at the faraway church and read/"re-preached" the message, the impact was little short of incredible! Not only did it not seem stale and secondhand; the convicted and comforted congregation marveled at the fact that it was as if the associate was almost an extension, or echo, of their beloved founding pastor, still so far away geographically. While he had not been able to visit, the next best alternative had indeed been delivered to them, in writing and reading. The associate had proven to be a virtual message incarnate, as he spoke passionately and glowed with everything he said, which was right there on the paper he held in his hands throughout the sermon.

PARALLELLING THE EXPANDED COMMUNICATION MODEL TO A SHIFTING COMMUNICATION REALITY TODAY

John Harvey concludes his highly significant volume on Pauline orality, *Listening to the Text*, with the following sage commentary on the present state of our culture:

> The end of the twentieth century [experienced] another "paradigm shift": the shift from print media to electronic media. . . . It might be characterized as a shift from a literate culture to an aural-visual culture. People read less and are

entertained more. Sight and sound dominate popular culture. This is the age of the satellite dish and the hand-held television. A household without a computer, a compact disc player, and a videocassette recorder is considered "behind the times." The average television commercial lasts fifteen to thirty seconds, with the images changing at least once per second. Sound and motion hardware for computers is becoming commonplace, and time spent "surfing the internet" is rapidly overtaking time spent in front of the television. Sales of home video games are skyrocketing. Experiments in virtual reality seek to integrate input for all five of the senses into a single entertainment package. Although literacy is still important, popular communication has moved off the written page and away from silent documents to interactive technology and "talking books." In a very real sense, oral communication is again moving to the forefront.[28]

Whether we like it or not, we cannot make the stark reality of Harvey's analysis go away. If anything, as much as has already changed, the pace of movement in the direction he described is only accelerating.

So, what are we to do in our classrooms and our churches? It is anything but a caring or compassionate decision to just walk away from this far-ranging paradigm shift and return to our silent reading/study comfort zone. To do so is to ignore the fact that a skyrocketing proportion of our culture, most pointedly our younger students and church members (and our children, for those in the child-raising years!) simply do not hear the Word of the Lord in the way we do and are probably not going to come around to doing so, no matter how hard we beat them over the head to do so.

But some might say, "I don't want to be some shallow, trendy preacher or teacher. I want to be biblical in carrying out the ministry the Lord has given me!"

Wonderful! If that is indeed your conviction, you are headed in the right direction: *Back to the future!* Taken seriously, the transitionally oral-literate culture of the first century A.D., in which the New Testament was produced, can provide invaluable aid (and a classic, but also highly contemporary, communication model) for ministering to the again transitionally literate-oral culture of the beginning of the twenty-first century. In that sense, after two millennia of church history, the more things change, the more they remain the same.

PART II

The Preaching in the New Testament, the New Testament as Preaching:

Inspecting the Trees

CHAPTER

THE GOSPEL AND THE GOSPELS: THE INSPIRED PREACHING OF THE EVANGELISTS

C. RICHARD WELLS

It is like watching a man tinkering expertly with a piece of machinery, oblivious to the fact that what he is handling is a bomb.

LAURENCE CANTWELL[1]

ON HANDLING A BOMB: A FRESH LOOK AT THE GOSPELS

At least until the present age of biblical illiteracy, almost anyone could name the four Gospels, and most would say, if asked, that the Gospels are biographies of the most important person who ever lived. That would seem obvious. Over the centuries, however, the Gospels have generated no end of controversy. Modern biblical critics have debated almost everything about them; but even the ancients wondered why the one story of Jesus should be rendered so differently, and how they should distinguish the inspired accounts of Christ from the spurious.[2] What would seem obvious—that Matthew, Mark, Luke, and John wrote biographies of Jesus Christ—is not obvious at all.

Questions about the Gospels arise in part because we have "no parallels to the Gospel form."[3] Are they *biographies*? Clearly not. Mark, for example, says nothing of Jesus before adulthood, and John denies outright that his Gospel is a biography.[4] Justin Martyr called the Gospels "apostolic *memoirs,*" which might suggest that a Gospel is merely a collection of sayings and stories. But the Greek *apomnēmoneumata* refers to the *source* of the tradition (i.e., with the apostles' remembrance), rather than a genre of literature.[5] Morton Smith likened the Gospels to the Greek *aretalogy* (hero story);[6] but Jesus is not

29

a "hero" in any typical sense. Every other attempt to classify the Gospels like-wise wrecks on shoals.[7] The Gospel is historical but not history, biographical but not biography, story but not fiction, in short, "a new creation,"[8] or as Laurence Cantwell puts it, "a prodigy in the history of world literature."[9]

The Problem with the "Synoptic Problem"

In this chapter, we want to take a fresh look at this "prodigy" of world lit-erature; and we begin with the familiar "Synoptic Problem." As every semi-narian knows, Matthew, Mark, and Luke exhibit striking similarities, but striking differences as well. The problem is how to account for both. Oversimplified, our seminarian learns to resolve the problem as follows. Mark wrote first. Matthew and Luke then adapted Mark, using a source (Q) common to both (but not to Mark), adding material peculiar to each (labeled M and L).[10] This "solution" assumes that the Evangelists made use primarily of *written* (as opposed to *oral*) sources in their work.[11]

Long before B. H. Streeter popularized the documentary solution to the Synoptic Problem, B. F. Westcott advanced a very different explanation of Gospel origins. We naturally think, said Westcott, that the Gospels were *liter-ary* from the beginning. "But this idea is an anachronism both in fact and in thought," for the leaders of the early church had no intention of "forming a permanent Christian literature."[12] Their Jewish culture—emphasizing oral training and the sufficiency of the Scriptures—disinclined them to write any-thing, still less to *add* anything to the Law, Prophets, and Writings. Furthermore, their Master had commissioned them to *preach*, not write;[13] and the surpassing greatness of their message served only to focus this homiletical vision, which persisted, according to Westcott, even in the sub-apostolic age. In short, the Gospels "were the results and not the foundation of *the Apostolic preaching*." The "primary Gospel was proved, so to speak, in life, before it was fixed in writing."[14]

Westcott had the early church on his side. In his *History of the Church*, Eusebius of Caesarea informs us that the followers of Jesus had "neither the ability nor the desire to present the teachings of the Master with rhetorical subtlety or literary skill." Rather, "they proclaimed the knowledge of the Kingdom of Heaven . . . giving very little thought to the business of writing books." Of the Twelve, "Matthew and John alone have left us memoirs of the Lord's doings, and there is firm tradition that they took to writing of neces-sity."[15] This testimony is extensive and consistent for each of the Gospels.

To be sure, most modern scholars acknowledge an early oral tradition behind the Gospels; and some, notably Rudolf Bultmann and the form crit-ics, presuppose an extensive oral prehistory for the Gospels.[16] As Martin Dibelius famously declared, "In the beginning was the sermon."[17] We might almost expect Bishop Westcott to say, "Amen." But form critics make both too much and too little of the sermon. In their attempts to analyze the oral tradition according to *forms*—narratives, discourses, pronouncement stories, miracle stories, sayings, legends, and the like—and to reconstruct the *Sitz im Leben* (setting in life) of the Gospel pericopes, they have proved most ingenious. Yet they make too little of the oral tradition as a whole, which they consider little more than folk stories passed along by early Christian communities, gathering accretions along the way that obscure the authentic Jesus. Those we call the Evangelists were in actuality only *collectors* (and possibly *editors*). They did not *compose*, still less *remember*, and certainly did not *preach* the Gospels.

Bultmann and the form critics got it partly right—"In the beginning was the sermon!"—but they also got it very wrong, because they failed to treat the "sermon" as a real sermon. True, a moderate form critic like C. H. Dodd can say that "the fourfold Gospel taken as a whole is an expression of the original apostolic preaching."[18] But this preaching (the kerygma as he called it) amounted to a theological outline, barely discernable, like a sunken galleon, under the murky interpretations of the early church. The form critics painstakingly analyze the pericopes in hope of recovering doubloons and manage to extract a few stray coins from the sand. But they miss troves abrim with treasure. To change the metaphor, the form critic resembles "a man tinkering expertly with a piece of machinery, oblivious to the fact that what he is handling is a bomb."[19]

Not to put too fine an edge on it, the problem with the Synoptic Problem is the solution. The Gospel is a "prodigy in the history of world literature" because it isn't exactly literature at all, but *apostolic preaching reduced to script*—resembling the recorded sermons of Chrysostom or Augustine more than, say, William Shirer's *Gandhi*.[20] Are the Gospels *historical* and factual? Most certainly. Are they *history?* Certainly not, for "no New Testament writer," James Denney observed, "ever *remembered* Christ."[21] The early church, says Ralph Martin, was not "continually harking back to some 'golden age' when Jesus was with them . . . or seeking to recapture a lost Camelot of spiritual life when Jesus lived on earth. On the contrary, they were conscious of his living presence in the present."[22] The apostles were not creating an archive but telling a story. And the Evangelists did not compose scrapbooks of memories; they made transcripts of the glad tidings! In the beginning was the sermon!

The Gospel Bomb

Reading Gospels scholarship, writes Lawrence Cantwell, is indeed "like watching a man tinkering expertly with a piece of machinery, oblivious to the fact that what he is handling is a bomb."[23] We can be sure that if he realizes it is a bomb, he will stop "tinkering"! Likewise, recognizing the original orality of the Gospels should change the way we look at them.

First, the original orality of the Gospels should strengthen our confidence in their authenticity and reliability. Birger Gerhardsson has shown that the apostles' reluctance to write testifies to "a commonplace which we recognize from elsewhere in Antiquity . . . that which can be learned from the written page cannot be compared with that which may be learned from the lips of a living person."[24] For the postapostolic writers, the very fact that the earliest *evangelium* was *not written* proved its authenticity. The Gospel witnesses were either personal disciples or interpreters of a disciple "guaranteed to be familiar with his proclamation and teaching,"[25] who wrote only as a kind of emergency measure.[26]

Second, the original orality of the Gospels encourages us to preach the whole Gospel. George Beasley-Murray argues against the form critics, that "the earliest preachers . . . [understood] that the *whole work of Jesus*—not just the cross—was a revelation of the kingdom of God for the salvation of the world."[27] The Gospels are not, after all, merely "passion narratives with extended introductions."[28] From the infancy narratives in Luke, to the discourses in Matthew, to the parables of the kingdom in Mark, to character sketches in John, each part of each Gospel proclaims the kingdom of God.

Third, original orality focuses our attention on the distinctiveness of each Gospel. In its preoccupation with literary antecedents, modern critical scholarship has not only ignored the most obvious explanation for the differences between the Gospels but has silenced the flesh-and-blood voices of the Evangelists. The Gospels are not mere redactions or collections but *"distinct views of a complex whole."* Bishop Westcott added,

> We never find even in the case of the Prophets that the personal character of the divine messenger is neutralized; and much more may we expect to find a distinct personality, so to speak, in the writing of the Evangelists, whose Inspiration was no ecstatic impulse, but the consecration of a whole life, the conversion of an entire being into a divine agency . . . the gospels, like the Gospel, are most divine because they are most human.[29]

Fourth, original orality reminds us that the Gospels have a missionary purpose. The early church made much of the fact there are *four* Gospels. They recognized that each Gospel portrays Jesus in a distinctive, paradigmatic way. They frequently linked these portraits to the four *zoë* of the Apocalypse (4:7) or the "living beings" of Ezekiel (1:10),[30] and most found significance in the number four, as such, the Gospels being the Word of God for (the four corners of) the world.[31] Be that as it may, both biblical and patristic evidences indicate that the Gospels took shape in connection with four great mission centers, associated with James (Matthew), Peter (Mark), Paul (Luke), and

John.[32] We can be sure that as the earliest preachers took the gospel from Jerusalem, like all good preachers, they would tailor the message of Christ to missional peculiarities of the cultures they sought to reach. We should expect each of the Gospels, therefore, "to meet the [needs] of a marked class" and, by extension, to satisfy "the requirements of those who embody . . . in changing shapes the feelings by which it was first inspired."[33]

We turn our attention then, to the Gospels themselves. In such limited space, we must content ourselves with brief and more or less illustrative answers to two questions. First, what evidences do we have that the Gospels were originally sermonic? Second, what difference might it make to interpret a particular Gospel homiletically?

"THE KINGDOM OF HEAVEN": THE INSPIRED PREACHING OF MATTHEW

Matthew: *Ho Telōnēs*

The Gospels are technically anonymous, but the authors are certainly not unknown. Not only is the witness of the early church strong and consistent; the writings themselves provide corroborating evidence,[34] including personal cues that not only help us identify the Evangelist but also enable us to hear his living voice.

The Church Fathers universally testify that our first Gospel is *kata Matthaion*, Matthew being one of the Twelve, the "publican."[35] The most celebrated testimony comes from Papias (cited by Eusebius): "Matthew composed the oracles [*ta logia*][36] in the Hebrew dialect;[37] but each interpreted them as he could."[38] Irenaeus bears a similar testimony,[39] as do Origen,[40] Cyril of Jerusalem,[41] Jerome,[42] and others. The Church Fathers also assert that Matthew wrote for Jewish believers, and with this, the style of the Gospel agrees. Matthew "feels" Jewish—replete with citations of the Old Testament and details of Jewish law, custom, and history.

Eusebius goes so far as to affirm the original orality of the Gospel. He writes: "Matthew had begun by preaching to Hebrews, and when he had made up his mind to go to others too, he committed his own gospel to writing in his native tongue, so that for those with whom he was no longer present the gap left by his departure was filled by what he wrote."[43] This amounts to saying that the Gospel of Matthew is a transcript of sermons Matthew had preached over a period of time. By this means, Matthew would continue to "preach" even in his absence, as the Gospel was read aloud.

Matthew has certainly left his impress on the Gospel. For example, only in Matthew's list of the Twelve does he bear the name *ho telōnēs*, "the taxgatherer" (Matt. 10:3). The reproach of the "publican" is legendary, of course;

and from the fact that all three Synoptics record Matthew's "call" at the tax desk in Capernaum,[44] we may guess how deeply the call of such a person affected the earliest preachers. But here again, Matthew has left his mark. All three Synoptics mention a reception following Matthew's call, hosted (Luke informs us) by Levi himself,[45] and prompting complaints from the Pharisees and scribes to Jesus' disciples that their Master eats and drinks with "tax-gatherers and sinners."

In all three Synoptics, Jesus cuts them off with a proverb ("It is not those who are healthy who need a physician, but those who are sick"),[46] to which he adds a mission statement: "I did not come to call the righteous, but sinners."[47] Between these two sayings, however, Matthew inserts another word from Jesus: "But go and learn what this means, 'I desire compassion, and not sacrifice.'"[48]

Matthew would have had good reason to remember those particular words from Jesus. With a name like Levi, Matthew might well have belonged to the priestly caste, or at least a pious Jewish family. But like the prodigal son, Matthew had left the father's house for the far country of unsavory companions and materialistic lifestyle. Whatever other motives he had, he was certainly disillusioned by the hypocrisy of Jewish traditionalism. It is striking that Matthew's Gospel records the bulk of the Lord's invective against those Pharisees and scribes who fancy themselves true sons of Abraham because they fast ceremoniously,[49] tithe herbs from the backyard,[50] and build the tombs of the prophets.[51]

Such people, like the prodigal's brother, had no place for their wayward sibling, and thus at the reception Matthew would have felt keenly the Lord's rebuke of the Pharisees. To "go and learn" was a standard charge of rabbis to young students. So Jesus deals them "a double rebuke," says Craig Blomberg. He treats them "as learners rather than teachers and . . . as beginners."[52] The scribes and Pharisees have yet to learn "lesson one" in the Law and the Prophets[53]—God loves sinners. Matthew himself is living proof.

As Matthew records (preaches!) it, Jesus' rebuke of the Pharisees constitutes a three-part sermon on God's care for sinners: (1) It is illustrated by ordinary human experience (9:12b—*everybody* knows that the "sick," not the "healthy," need a doctor); (2) It is based on the nature of God (9:13a—he loves compassion); and (3) It is actualized in the ministry of Jesus who "did not come to call the righteous, but sinners" (9:13b).

The Kingdom of Heaven

Nowhere is Matthew's distinctive homiletical thrust more apparent than in his use of the phrase, "kingdom of heaven," which occurs thirty-three times in his Gospel, and never again in the New Testament. The usual explanation for this anomaly is that Matthew employed a circumlocution, "reflecting pious Jewish avoidance of the divine name."[54] But this is manifestly not so.

On at least five occasions Matthew *does* have "kingdom of God,"[55] and he uses the divine name, "God," no less than fifty times! Besides, the rabbis themselves did not avoid altogether using "kingdom of God."[56] A better explanation is that "kingdom of heaven" is a double entendre. On one hand, the phrase expressed Jewish aspirations for the rule ("kingdom") of God. On the other hand, the phrase calls attention to the *character* of the kingdom. It is of *heaven,* not of earth.

The word *heaven* is, in fact, a thematic key to Matthew's Gospel, where it occurs twice as often as in Mark, Luke, and John combined.[57] It is not without significance that only in Matthew—the Jewish Gospel—does *John the Baptist* summarize the prophetic hope of Israel with the message that the "kingdom of heaven is at hand,"[58] the message Jesus repeats verbatim as he begins his own ministry (4:17), which gradually unfolds of the rule of the Father "in heaven."[59] In short, Matthew proclaims the Good News that Christ brings "heaven" to earth. As a "completed Jew," says Alfred Edersheim, Matthew preached that the "rule of heaven . . . the very substance of the Old Testament"[60] has come in Christ: "Wide as God's domain would be His Dominion; holy, as heaven in contrast to earth, and God to man, would be [its] character; and triumphantly lasting its continuance."[61]

MARK: A TRANSCRIPT FROM LIFE

The Interpreter of Peter

Papias (c. 60–c. 130) was bishop of Hieropolis in Phrygia. He was a "hearer" of the apostle John, and he knew Polycarp, the famous bishop of Smyrna and disciple of John. He knew (or knew of) many other followers of the apostles, some of whose writings he collected in a work called *Exposition of Dominical Oracles,* published about A.D. 110. The *Exposition* is lost to us, but numerous fragments survive in the works of Ireneaus and Eusebius, who recognized the extraordinary value of this testimony. In a celebrated passage, Papias tells how Mark's Gospel came into being. It is an extraordinary testimony, which we take leave to quote in full.

> This, too, the presbyter [doubtless John] used to say:
> "Mark, who had been Peter's interpreter, wrote down carefully, but not in order, all that he remembered of the Lord's sayings and doings. For he had not heard the Lord or been one of His followers. But later, as I said, one of Peter's. Peter used to adapt his teachings to the occasion, without making a systematic arrangement of the Lord's sayings, so that Mark was quite justified in writing down some things just as he remembered

them. For he had one purpose only—to leave out nothing that
he had heard, and to make no misstatement about it."[62]

The most striking feature of this testimony is that Papias traces Mark's
Gospel directly to Peter. Eusebius cites several other writers to the same effect;
to which we could add, among others,[63] the testimony of Jerome that Mark
was "the disciple and interpreter of Peter," and that he "wrote a short Gospel
at the request of the brethren at Rome embodying what he had heard Peter
tell."[64] The verdict of the early church is unanimous against modern critics
that the Gospel of Mark is genuine and apostolic, for he wrote under Peter's
authority—end of debate.[65]

There is another critical point in this testimony, however: Mark's Gospel
is a record of Peter's *preaching and teaching*. A century after Papias, Clement
of Alexandria (c. 155–c. 200) wrote in the *Hypotyposes*,[66] "So brightly shone
the light of true religion on the minds of Peter's hearers, that, not satisfied
with a single hearing . . . they resorted to appeals of every kind to induce
Mark, (whose gospel we have) as he was a follower of Peter, to leave them in
writing a summary of the instruction they had received by word of
mouth."[67]

Elsewhere in the *Hypotyposes*, Clement wrote, "When, at Rome, Peter had
opened the word, and by the Spirit had proclaimed the gospel, the large audience urged Mark, who had followed him for a long time and remembered
what had been said, to write it all down. This he did, making his gospel available to all who wanted it. When Peter heard about this, he made no objection and gave no special encouragement."[68] Irenaeus, a contemporary of
Clement, says plainly that Mark "transmitted to us in writing those things
preached by Peter."[69] In his *Demonstratio Evangelica*, Eusebius concluded that
"the whole of Mark is said to be a record of Peter's teaching."[70]

A TRANSCRIPT FROM LIFE

From the testimony of Papias, we note at least six affirmations about
Mark's Gospel. First, Mark was the "interpreter" of Peter. (The term
hermēneutēs signifies a "go-between" or "translator").[71] *Peter himself* (not a
document) was Mark's primary "source." Second, Mark wrote "carefully" (or
"accurately"), though "not in order." Third, although Mark had not himself
been an eyewitness follower of the Lord, as an associate of Peter, he had often
heard the apostle speak about Jesus. Fourth, for his part, Peter had no interest in a systematic written account of the life and ministry of Christ; rather, he
was a *preacher* who adapted "his teachings to the occasion." Fifth, Mark
recorded Peter's preaching as he remembered it. And sixth, in doing so, he
took pains to leave nothing out and to make no error.

According to Papias, Peter had no intention of producing a biography of Jesus but rather preached as the occasion demanded. Since we will deal at length with Peter and his preaching in chapters 5 and 7, we need only point out here that Mark's Gospel confirms the distinct impression we get from Papias—that Peter was a man of action, not reflection. He preferred to preach, not write, and even in his preaching, he preferred to focus on what Jesus did, rather than what he said. Mark is unquestionably the "Gospel of action."[72]

C. H. Dodd suggested that the second Gospel functions much like a "commentary" on Peter's preaching, following the basic thematic pattern we discern, for example, in Peter's sermon at the house of Cornelius.[73] A better analogy might be a "newspaper story." In the spirit of Peter, the Gospel of Mark is almost journalistic. What Jesus does is center stage, and how and when and where and why and to whom and with whom he does it. G. F. Maclear long ago observed that Mark (Peter) circumscribed the events of Christ's life with details that would "make them impressive to bystanders."[74] Mark calls special attention to the human experience of Jesus, his grief (7:34), his pity (6:34), anger (3:5), hunger (11:12), sleep (4:38), and more. Often Mark details the posture of Jesus, his gestures, or words,[75] and he takes pains to record particulars of person, number, time, and place that the other Gospels typically omit.[76]

Certain rhetorical features of Mark enhance this journalistic style. For example, more than twenty-five times Mark uses the word *immediately* (Gk. *euthus*) to make a lively transition. He habitually uses the present tense, even when a past (Gk. aorist) tense might seem more appropriate grammatically.[77]

"To sum up," said Maclear, "in substance and style and treatment, the Gospel of St. Mark is essentially a transcript from life."[78] Mark's "Good News" concerns Jesus "the Son of God"; but Jesus is *revealed as the Son of God* amidst the rough and tumble of the everyday. William Lane observed that Mark's "vivid style" puts "his listeners on the scene where they may visualize and experience what the evangelist has described;" and thus Mark intends "to involve men in the crisis of decision prompted by Jesus' presence."[79] Lane goes on to say that Mark uses questions, confusion, and misunderstandings[80] to create a "climate of tension" about the identity of the Son of God that "can be resolved only by the recognition of Jesus' dignity,"[81] which does come, when Peter confesses at Caesarea Philippi (8:29b) and when the centurion confesses at the foot of the cross (15:39).

Behind Mark's vivid style we hear the living voice of Peter himself, telling the story of Jesus' work in an everyday world and urging his hearers to confess, just as the centurion did: "Truly this man was the Son of God." Mark is a transcript from life. Mark's Christian faith is neither a topic for faculty lounges, political sloganeering, or pop psychology sprinkled with Bible verses. Christianity is Jesus Christ the Son of God, demonstrating his power in life and demanding our life in return.

This dynamic in Mark's (Peter's) "inspired preaching" may actually help explain the much controverted ending of the Gospel. Our seminary student is taught that Mark 16:9–20 does not appear in the best Greek manuscripts, and further, that the literary style of those verses differs so much from the rest of the Gospel as to make it certain "that from the beginning Mark circulated with the abrupt ending of chapter 16:8."[82] The "abrupt ending" has always been problematic, however, because it seems to end the ministry of Jesus on a note of failure. Many modern scholars would agree with Harvie Branscomb "that the Gospel did not or was not intended to end here."[83] It is conceivable that a longer original ending was indeed lost, and that early writers tried to fill in the gap.[84] It is also possible that Mark intended to write a companion volume similar to Acts and thus did not regard 16:8 "as the virtual end of the history."[85] There are other theories, more or less plausible, but in the end, they are quite unnecessary.

The "abrupt ending" makes perfect sense in a summary of Peter's preaching. It corresponds in fact to the "abrupt beginning" where "the evangelist [confronts] the reader with the fact of revelation in the person of John's Jesus."[86] Having proclaimed the message that Jesus *demonstrated* his deity in real life, we can easily imagine that Peter would end by urging his listeners to enter vicariously into the place of the women at the tomb, gripped by "trembling and astonishment" at hearing the resurrection news.[87] Mark intended his Gospel to end here precisely because the message of the gospel does *not* end here![88] The "fear" of the women (16:8) is not a sign of failure, only a sign that *we too* must decide how to respond to the news that "he has risen!"

FORGIVENESS TO THE NATIONS: THE INSPIRED PREACHING OF LUKE

Evangelist or Historian?

The beginning of Luke is unique among the Gospels. Matthew traces the lineage of the Son of David. Mark announces the Good News. John states a philosophical first principle. But Luke begins with what appears to be an introduction to a literary history. Just as, for example, Josephus introduced his history of the Jews to a certain Epaphroditus,[89] Luke introduced his history of Christ to a certain Theophilus, stating his purpose for writing and offering assurances of his credibility as a historian. So it might seem; but is it so?

Let's take a closer look at Luke's Prologue. First, the text itself:

> Inasmuch as many have undertaken to compile an account
> of the things accomplished among us, just as those who from
> the beginning were eyewitnesses and servants of the word have
> handed them down to us, it seemed fitting for me as well,
> having investigated everything carefully from the beginning, to
> write it out for you in consecutive order, most excellent
> Theophilus; so that you might know the exact truth about the
> things you have been taught (Luke 1:1–4).

From Luke's testimony, we can draw several conclusions. First, Luke indicates that others had attempted what he is about to undertake. Luke does not suggest that these efforts were faulty or misguided, but neither does Luke accord them any special value or influence. Further, while Luke does not specifically deny using these (or other) accounts, he does not say that he did so, only that he knew of efforts similar to his.

Second, Luke does not say these others had *written* narratives (as in the RSV), only that they had endeavored to draw up the mass of Gospel material and arrange it afresh [*anataxasthai*] "in a connected shape [*diēgēsin*]."[90] If these others fell short, it was only because they possessed fragmentary or ill-arranged materials.[91]

Third, the basis for Luke's (and the others') "accounts" was the apostolic preaching of the gospel handed down "to us" [*paredoson hēmin*].[92] This tradition came from "eyewitnesses," whom Luke also calls "servants of the word" (1:2).

Fourth, Luke did not intend primarily to write history but to record kerygma. This is evident from the fact that Luke *equates* the *pragmatōn* ("things," 1:4) handed down with *tou logou* ("the word" or "gospel;" 1:2). The "works" constitute the "word." Further, the word translated "accomplished" [*peplērophorōmenōn*] connotes "fulfilled," or perhaps even "fully believed" (1:1).[93] Either way, Luke would appear to mean that he intended to supply Theophilus with an orderly presentation of the orthodox kerygma.

Fifth, Luke's purpose was to augment and confirm what Theophilus had already learned, presumably through teaching and preaching (1:4). Here we are reminded of the patristic testimony concerning both Matthew and Mark.

Sixth, Luke says that he is qualified to write, *not* because he conducted dissertation-type research, but because he had personal familiarity with the gospel story. The NASB "investigated" is misleading, since the verb *parēkolouthēkoti* connotes personal observance or attendance, as of a teacher or teaching.[94] The RSV gives a better sense: "having followed all things closely."

Seventh, and finally, when Luke declares his intention to present the "things" of the gospel "in consecutive order," he by no means limits himself to *chronology*. The term *kathexēs* does not suggest sequential history, only an orderly arrangement.

Wescott believed that Luke's prologue set the stage for an "oral history."[95] The preaching of the eyewitnesses—no doubt the apostles—had passed more or less intact into various (written and oral) accounts. On the basis of his personal knowledge of the "things . . . handed down," Luke prepared an orderly arrangement of them to confirm for Theophilus what he had already been taught.[96]

The prologue of Acts confirms this interpretation; there Luke refers to the Gospel as the "first account . . . about all that Jesus began to do and teach."[97] The word for "account" is *logos* ("word"), which in Greek (as in English) has an extensive semantic range, from the pedestrian to the profound, but always conveys the idea that a mind *expresses* itself in a "word."[98] So, while Luke's phraseology in Acts may reflect the Greek literary convention whereby a "book" is dubbed a "word,"[99] we should remember that, just as a "word" in Greek is never merely a "book," the *Book* of Luke was not considered by its author a mere literary product but as an expression of truth.

Of course, Luke likely also had in mind the Hebrew "word" (*dābār*) which does not (as in Greek) merely *express*, but reveals, creates, transforms, judges—in short, *acts redemptively*. Significant in this connection is that in the New Testament the "word" is a virtual synonym for the preaching of the gospel. Thus Paul expresses gratitude that the Thessalonians received "the word of God's message . . . for what it really is, the word of God, which also performs its work in you who believe."[100] The proclamation of the truth-as-it-is-in-Jesus is the "word" that saves. Although it took the form of a literary work, therefore, Luke regarded his Gospel as just such a redemptive "word" for Theophilus.

THE "WORD" FOR THEOPHILUS

Despite several deliciously ingenious theories linking him to Seneca, Philo, or others, Theophilus remains a mystery to us, except as representative of a familiar kind of person. The evidence as a whole suggests that Theophilus was a Gentile of rank, and a believer, struggling with doubts over whether or not he really belonged in the church, which was "an originally Jewish movement."[101]

The early church consistently maintained that, as with Mark and Peter, Luke wrote under the influence of Paul.[102] Eusebius reports that some "actually suggested that Paul was in the habit of referring to Luke's gospel, whenever he said . . . 'According to my gospel.'"[103] It is not quite clear whether he agrees; but the companionship of Paul and Luke will not permit Eusebius to dismiss the suggestion out-of-hand.

Luke's "word" for Theophilus certainly bears the impress of the apostle to the Gentiles. It is the theme of Romans traced through "all that Jesus began to do and teach"—from the very human birth of one whose family tree begins s not at David, but at Adam (3:38), to the charge he left to his disciples that in his name they should proclaim "repentance for forgiveness of sins . . . to all the nations" (24:47). This is Luke's Gospel, which Paul proclaimed as "the power of God for salvation to everyone who believes, to the Jew first and also to the Greek" (Rom. 1:16).

THE INSPIRED PREACHING OF JOHN THE EVANGELIST

"The Theorem of the Logos"

"Last of all," wrote Clement of Alexandria in the *Hypotyposes*, "aware that the physical facts had been recorded in the gospels, encouraged by his pupils and irresistibly moved by the Spirit, John wrote a spiritual gospel."[104] Already when Clement wrote (c. A.D. 200), this "spiritual" gospel was being appropriated by various unorthodoxies. The earliest known commentary on John, for example, fell from the pen of one Heracleon, a mid-second century Gnostic. About the same time, an otherwise orthodox Roman elder named Gaius rejected the Gospel because it seemed to lend support to the Montanist heresy. It is striking, Leon Morris observes, that "with all these heretical associations, John still became universally accepted as canonical."[105]

On the other hand, it comes as no great surprise that the heretics would seize on the fourth Gospel. For among the Gospels, John is preeminently the Gospel of *ideas* rather than *events*.[106] Clement of Alexandria said as much himself. John did not intend to repeat the Synoptics; but to interpret what Frederic Godet called "the theorem of the Logos"[107] for a generation chronologically and culturally remote from Galilee and Golgotha: Ephesus in the late first century.[108] "The climate of opinion" there and then, says Bruce, "was not greatly concerned about historical fact and geographical location," an insistence on which, "it was thought, tended to obscure the universal relevance of eternal truth." So John "attached the utmost importance to eternal truth," but at the same time, "he insisted that eternal truth was manifested in time and place . . . when the Word appeared on earth in the human life of Jesus of Nazareth."[109] The "theorem of the Logos" has a name—Jesus.

Situated at the juncture of Asia and Europe, Ephesus was the queen city of hellenistic culture. She had grown phenomenally wealthy from the traders who plied her highways and harbor, and phenomenally diverse from the ideas that travelled with the merchants. The Ephesus where John lived and preached after his departure from Jerusalem[110] had become a "rendezvous" for orators, scholars, philosophers, and religious sectarians from both

Occident and Orient. "On such a theatre," wrote Frederic Godet, "the Palestinian apostle must have grown daily, not, doubtless, in the knowledge of the person and work of Jesus, but in the understanding of the manifold relationship, sympathetic or hostile, between the Gospel and the different tendencies of human theology."[111]

Paul had brought Christ into this intellectual and religious zoo with great effect,[112] but he also warned of "savage wolves" poised to attack the flock after his "departure."[113] It fell then to John—after years of reflecting on the immense significance of Jesus Christ, whose life, ministry, death, and resurrection he knew firsthand—to beat back the polymorphous zanies from the church doors in Ephesus. To keep the wolves at bay. To foil the philosophers with the "theorem of the Logos."

"That You May Believe . . . and Have Life"

John himself explicitly set forth as the purpose of his Gospel—"that you may believe that Jesus is the Christ, the Son of God; and that believing you may have life in His name."[114] From the wealth of material available to him,[115] John chose vignettes and sayings and discourses from the life and times of Jesus the Messiah, the Son of God, as texts for proclaiming his glory amidst the cacophony of alternative voices in Ephesus. Barnabas Lindars has stated that the "Gospel had its genesis in homilies preached by John,"[116] which confirms the testimony of Eusebius that John "had relied entirely on the spoken word until the Synoptics were in general circulation," and wrote only to fill in gaps, particularly on the early ministry of Jesus.[117]

Even as written, the Gospel itself can be read as a series of sermons by one who was an eyewitness of the Jesus-history, and who had lived long enough to leave no room for doubt about the transforming power of Jesus the Logos. So John preached a conviction and sought "in virtue of that conviction to bring life."[118]

The famous "born again" passage (3:1–21) provides a dramatic example. The scene is Jerusalem, where much of the Gospel is set.[119] In the person of Nicodemus, Jesus encounters a representative of what Friedrich Schleiermacher might call the "cultured despiser,"[120] for whom real religion has more or less given way to rational philosophy.[121] Even though he is "a man of the Pharisees . . . a ruler of the Jews" (3:1), Nicodemus finds himself simultaneously wary of Christ and drawn to him.[122] Nor was Nicodemus alone: "We know," he said, apparently speaking for some of his colleagues, "that You have come from God as a teacher" (3:2). Others might not be, but *they* at least were prepared to take the teaching of Jesus seriously. In truth, of course, they understood almost nothing about Jesus or his teaching; and Jesus dissolved their pretensions instantly—"Truly, truly [amēn, amēn], I say to you, unless one is born again, he cannot see the kingdom of God" (3:3).

The discourse which follows, punctuated by questions from an incredulous Nicodemus, reaches its climax in an allusion to the cross.[123]

"Red-letter" editions of the New Testament notwithstanding, John 3:16 seems clearly to mark a new beginning, where *John himself* "preaches," on the "text" of Nicodemus.[124] According to Beasley-Murray, John 3:16 is a "confessional summary" followed by "kerygmatic reflections" (3:17–21).[125] The "confessional summary" is John's own testimony, tying the incarnation, cross, and resurrection of the only begotten Son for the salvation of the world to the unfathomable love of God, a love which has grown more precious to John across the years. We must hear John 3:16 from the lips of an old man who has walked with Jesus, who "believed" at the empty tomb (20:8), and after these many years can still proclaim this simple message to sophisticated Greeks: "God so loved the world, that He gave His only begotten Son, that whoever believes in Him should not perish, but have eternal life."

CHAPTER

"AS ONE HAVING AUTHORITY": THE INSPIRED PREACHING OF JESUS

C. RICHARD WELLS

Brief and concise utterances fell from Him, for He was no sophist,
but His word was the power of God.

JUSTIN MARTYR

THE FIRST APOLOGY, 14.5

HE WAS NO SOPHIST

Have you ever wondered how the disciples of Jesus remembered so much of what he said? Jesus did not write books, articles, or study guides. He had no tapes, CDs, overheads, or PowerPoints. Jesus did not have a Web site. Yet his followers were able, years later, to recall not only what he did but what he said, so precisely that many modern scholars assume the Gospel writers essentially copied one another. Even more amazing, the disciples did not set out to *write* the words of Jesus at all. According to Eusebius, "They proclaimed the knowledge of the Kingdom of Heaven . . . giving very little thought to the business of writing books."[1] And yet, the apostle John says (if we may paraphrase), "There is a lot more I could tell you!"[2] All from an itinerant teacher with no tools but his voice. How can this be?

The Holy Spirit, the Teacher

The most obvious answer is that the Holy Spirit taught them, just as Jesus had promised: "But the Helper, the Holy Spirit, whom the Father will send in My name, He will teach you all things, and bring to your remembrance all that I said to you."[3] Should he have chosen to do so, the Holy Spirit could have given the disciples effortless verbatim recall of every word Jesus ever spoke (reversing the analogy of a college student who prays to remember answers from a textbook he has never opened!). But did he? From an exegetical point of view, the Lord's promise appears to emphasize the Spirit's role not in reproducing the *ipsissima verba* of Jesus, but in grasping their significance. Having spent the better part of three years learning from Jesus, the disciples already possessed a store of his teaching. The Holy Spirit would bring his teaching to life; and the Gospels testify that he did. After the resurrection, for example, the disciples "remembered" Jesus' teaching about destroying and rebuilding the temple [of his body],[4] "and they believed the Scripture, and the word which Jesus had spoken."[5] The Holy Spirit enabled the disciples to say, "Now I understand this word of the Master!"[6]

Regnum Dei Deus Est:
The Message of Jesus

Another obvious answer to our question is the extraordinary consistency of Jesus' message. Modern scholarship, which agrees on almost *nothing* else, "is quite unanimous in the opinion that the kingdom of God was the central message of Jesus."[7] In his cut-to-the-chase style, Mark so informs us. "Following his temptation and the arrest of the Baptist, Jesus launched his public ministry in Galilee," Mark says, "preaching the gospel of God, and saying, 'The time is fulfilled and the kingdom of God is at hand; repent and believe in the gospel.'"[8] The Gospels contain more than seventy-five different "kingdom of God" sayings,[9] in addition to innumerable allusions to "kingdom" themes. The disciples could scarcely forget that Jesus preached *the kingdom of God*.

As New Testament scholars are wont to note, the Bible never defines "kingdom of God" [Gk. *basileia tou theou*], nor does the phrase as such ever appear in the Old Testament. Yet Jesus spoke of the kingdom as if he expected his hearers to have some idea what he was talking about. Therefore, while it lies beyond our purpose to deal fully with the kingdom of God theme, we are bound to ask how the "kingdom" functioned *homiletically* in Jesus' ministry.

We begin by asking why Jesus took for granted that the "kingdom of God" would connect with his hearers. The answer may lie in the Jewish Targums. In the years after the Exile, it became customary to follow the reading of Scripture in the synagogue with an "interpretation" in the vernacular, on the order of Ezra's well-known "translation" of the law to the repatriated exiles in Jerusalem.[10] These interpretations tended to become fixed over time, thus serving as a kind of Jewish "amplified Bible." Bruce Chilton points out that while the phrase "kingdom of God" does not appear in the Old Testament, it does appear in the Targums, often as a substitute for the divine name. The following parallels from Zechariah and Isaiah will illustrate:

Zechariah 14:9

(text)   "And the LORD will be king over all the earth."

(targum)   "And the *kingdom of the Lord* will be revealed upon all the dwellers of the earth."

Isaiah 31:4

(text)   "so will the LORD of hosts come down to wage war."

(targum)   "the *kingdom of the Lord of hosts* will be revealed."

There are numerous such examples, especially in the prophets, suggesting that in later Judaism "kingdom of God" had become stereotyped vocabulary for the work of God. "*Regnum Dei Deus Est,*" says Chilton, "the kingdom of God *is* God!"[11] In preaching the kingdom of God, therefore, Jesus may simply have employed "a contemporary catch-phrase . . . to serve as the key term in his vivid assertion that God is active among us."[12] Jesus preached *the presence of God,* using *the language of the people.*

Like all good preaching, however, Jesus' preaching not only *connected* with his hearers; it also radically *confronted* them. In popular first-century Jewish consciousness, the "kingdom of God" portended a divine act of political deliverance (from Rome) and the restoration to David's golden age. The coming one, the Messiah, the Son of David, would usher in this new age as the king of the kingdom.[13] At "the centre of Jewish tradition," says Ulrich Wilckens, stood the kingdom of God as "the reward of righteousness for the righteous in their distress."[14]

Jesus turns that tradition on its head. He preaches about a righteousness that must surpass the righteousness of the "righteous."[15] He declares that he came not to call the "righteous" but "sinners."[16] He promises that the kingdom of heaven belongs to the "poor in spirit."[17] And what he *does* confirms what he *says.* Jesus spends himself on the hopeless and the helpless and the unwelcome. He opens blind eyes. He delivers demoniacs. He raises invalids. He touches lepers. He eats with publicans. He associates with the flotsam and jetsam. What Jewish tradition regarded as the pot of gold at the end of a rainbow of righteousness—*the kingdom of God*—Jesus proclaims as "God's ultimate salvation for those radically without salvation."[18]

So the preaching of Jesus entailed a fundamental contradiction to Jewish tradition. The power (the kingdom) of God proves itself not in apocalyptic visions but in the saving of the lost. The message had a familiar ring, but a strange sound. It fulfilled every human hope and unsettled every human heart. Even John the Baptist, we recall, languishing in prison, sent his followers to inquire of Jesus: "Are You the Expected One, or shall we look for someone else?" To which Jesus replies: "Go and report to John what you hear and see: the blind receive sight and the lame walk, the lepers are cleansed and the deaf hear, and the dead are raised up, and the poor have the gospel preached to them. And blessed is he who does not take offense at Me."[19]

Jesus did not preach a comfortable message for the comfortable pew. "He was no sophist," Justin declared.[20] He did not employ the clever tricks and rhetorical flourishes of those (then and now) whose only real objective was to win friends and influence people—the "persuasive words of wisdom" attributed by Paul to the sophists of Corinth.[21] Jesus came to preach the comforting affliction and the afflicting comfort of *the kingdom of God.*

JESUS—RABBI AND RABBONI

We are still left to ask about Jesus as teacher and preacher. How did the master preacher preach? We start with the testimony of that most famous Jewish historian, Flavius Josephus, half a century or so after Pentecost: "Now, there was about this time, Jesus, a wise man . . . a teacher of such as receive the truth with pleasure. He drew many over to him, both many of the Jews and many of the Gentiles."[22] Recent scholarship has tended to accredit his *testimonium;*[23] and we now have good reason to believe that while Josephus did not embrace Jesus as the Messiah, he did esteem Jesus as a teacher. At the very least, we may say with Rainer Riesner that "this was quite the way in which many contemporaries . . . looked at Jesus."[24]

The Gospels confirm the impression we get from Josephus. Jesus is addressed as "Teacher" (*Didaskale*) at least twenty-five times in the Gospels, often (though not exclusively) by those outside the band of disciples. Mark (4:1) and Luke (5:3) say that "crowds" gathered to hear him teach. Following the Sermon on the Mount, "the crowds were amazed at His teaching; for He was teaching them as one having authority, and not as their scribes."[25] Mark (1:22) documents a similar response in the synagogue at Capernaum. Luke is particularly fond of noting the impression Jesus left on others, as in the scribes' feigned compliment, "Teacher, we know that You speak and teach correctly, and You are not partial to any, but teach the way of God in truth" (20:21).

The fourth Gospel revolves around Jesus as teacher, beginning with the call of the first disciples who acknowledge Jesus as "Rabbi,"[26] the first of six instances in John, both by disciples and those outside.[27] The fourth Gospel reaches its climax in the resurrection garden when Mary exclaims, "Rabboni!" ("My Teacher!").[28] One might almost say that John tells the story of Jesus in terms of "Rabbi" and "Rabboni"; Jesus is *a teacher,* and he is *the Teacher.*

On Teaching and Preaching in the First Century

As a teacher, Jesus fell heir to a culture that valued teaching and teachers. The Greeks revered philosophers like Pythagoras, Plato, Aristotle, Epicurus, and Zeno,[29] who often gathered disciples and founded schools, such as Plato's Academy or Aristotle's Lyceum. Nearly all ancient cultures had their wise men, and especially so the Jews. We need only think of Solomon, whose "wisdom surpassed the wisdom of all the sons of the east and all the wisdom of Egypt."[30] The sages usually taught as well, and in many cases served as the principal educators for the ruling classes. Of course, the first century also had its share of what (in the twenty-first century) we would call "communicators," both Greek and Jewish, who turned their oratorical skills to a sometimes quite handsome living. These included lawyers, politicians, philosophers, religious sectarians, and the infamous Sophists who, according to Clement of Alexandria, cultivated their art of making "false opinions like true by means of words."[31]

But the culture Jesus inherited was decidedly Jewish, not Greek; and Jewish culture was also decidedly a "teach-and-learn" culture.[32] Even as a poor carpenter's son in out-of-the-way Nazareth, Jesus would have had the benefit of a synagogue school, as would almost any Jewish boy anywhere. He would have had as models the great prophets of the past and the rabbis of both past and present. As a child, he would have frequented the synagogue which, apart from its role in formal education, helped foster a biblically literate population, in Nazareth and elsewhere. (Josephus said that the synagogue fulfilled the Law as "every week the people should set aside their occupations and gather to listen to the Law and learn it accurately."[33])

The synagogue thus provided a ready-made preaching and teaching forum for Jesus,[34] as it would for Paul later on;[35] and the rabbinical tradition included certain standard preaching and teaching patterns that Jesus could use to great effect.[36] Not to mention that Jewish tradition extolled "the institution of preaching," using "the most extravagant terms."[37]

"Never Did a Man Speak the Way This Man Speaks"

The Gospels agree, however, that Jesus stood alone as a teacher. Quite simply, he baffles his hearers. He does not fit the stereotypical image of a rabbi, nor does he present any of the usual credentials, but he astounds those who hear him,[38] as when at the temple, the "Jews . . . were astonished, saying, 'How has this man become learned, having never been educated?'"[39] John's account of Nicodemus furnishes a case study on the effects of Jesus' preaching. Nicodemus addresses him as "Rabbi" and even acknowledges that he has "come from God as a teacher."[40] But Nicodemus comes to Jesus furtively,[41] doubtless desiring to hear him but fearing the censure of his peers whose minds are quite made up about this Galilean.

As Jesus' popularity grows, the chief priests and Pharisees send officers to arrest him (7:32), but they return empty-handed and offer as an excuse: "Never did a man speak the way this man speaks" (7:46). The Sanhedrin is livid: "You have not also been led astray, have you? No one of the rulers or Pharisees has believed in Him, has he? But this multitude which does not know the Law is accursed."[42] When Nicodemus protests that Jesus deserves simple fairness under the law (7:50–51), his peers turn on him (7:52). Jesus had unacceptable "credentials" but undeniable "authority."

The Gravamen against Jesus

It is precisely on the issue of Jesus' *authority as a teacher* that his death sentence will turn. In his account of the passion week, Matthew documents at least six "authority" encounters between Jesus and the accredited teachers: (1) the indignation of chief priests and scribes over Jesus' power and popularity (21:15–16); (2) the demand of chief priests and elders to know by what authority Jesus teaches (21:23); (3) the anger of chief priests and Pharisees over Jesus' parable of the vine-grower (which discredited their authority) and their subsequent plot, (21:45–46); (4) the curious alliance of the Pharisees and Herodians to trap Jesus with a politically charged question, a question set up by Shakespearean "faint praise" (22:15–17); (5) the Sadducees' question about a case of Levirite marriage (22:23–32); and (6) a lawyer's question (prompted by the Pharisees) regarding the great commandment (22:36). Interestingly, in the last three of these confrontations, Jesus' opponents address him as "Teacher" (*Didaskalē*), suggesting that the "professional" teachers, though forced to acknowledge Jesus as a teacher, are determined to discredit him—or, rather, to be rid of him.

Whatever other reasons the authorities may have had,[43] "the real reason for his being put to death," according to C. F. D. Moule, the "gravamen against Jesus,"[44] was his peculiar claim to authority. The Jewish leaders sought his life because they could not bear "Jesus' quiet assumption, unmediated by appeals to Scripture or tradition, that he knew God's mind and was doing God's work."[45] Either explicitly or by implication, Jesus claimed an authority greater than Moses,[46] Solomon,[47] and Abraham.[48] He never appealed to any human authority but claimed that his witness was true of itself: "Even in your law it has been written, that the testimony of two men is true," he declared, "I am He who testifies about Me, and the Father who sent Me bears about Me."[49]

Again, after he had healed on a certain Sabbath, Jesus answered his critics, saying, "My Father is working until now, and I Myself am working" (John 5:17). Those were fighting words! "For this cause," John adds, "the Jews were seeking all the more to kill Him, because He not only was breaking the Sabbath, but also was calling God His own Father, making Himself equal with God!"[50] Jesus preached with authority because he knew God; and in his preaching, he brought the "effect" of God "into disconcerting proximity."[51]

Jesus was a rabbi but most unlike the scribal authorities of his age, who coagulated their disciples into schools and sects to perpetuate scholarly distinctives. Jesus spoke in proverbs (as we shall see), but he was more than a sage and certainly no mere moralist. He was a prophet who consoled like a priest and a priest who thundered like a prophet. With Martin Hengel we can find no place for Jesus in the known paradigms of "teacher" or "leader" in the ancient world: "[Jesus] remains in the last resort incommensurable, and so basically confounds every attempt to fit him into the categories suggested by the phenomenology or sociology of religion."[52] A teacher like no other, a preacher par excellence—"Never did a man speak the way this man speaks!"

The Itineracy of Jesus

The uniqueness of Jesus extended also to what we might call his "teaching lifestyle." Everywhere he goes, Jesus teaches. Publicly and privately, indoors and out-of-doors, with multitudes and with individuals, with followers and with foes, on mountain slopes and in fishing boats—Jesus gives flesh and blood to Paul's charge thirty years later to young Timothy: "Be ready" to preach "in season and out of season."[53] The *sine qua non* of Jesus' preaching and teaching ministry is itineracy, which in and of itself raises two significant points.

The first is that Jesus had a "go and tell" rather than a "come and hear" approach to preaching. For example, while not unheard of, open-air preaching was rare in the first century, especially to large crowds.[54] But it was typical for Jesus, as for John the Baptist before him. From a theological point of view, Jesus' "go and tell" lifestyle suggests a sense of urgency. Like Dame Wisdom of Proverbs,[55] Jesus has "a message for all the people of Israel,"[56] which they ignore at their peril. In his second so-called "travel narrative,"[57] Luke recounts that "someone" posed the question—"Are there just a few who are being saved?"—which Jesus answers with a warning about the narrow way. In the judgment, some will "remind" the Lord that "You taught in our streets" (13:26), as if to substitute familiarity for faith. Yet the very fact that Jesus preached in the streets (rather than in synagogues or under shade trees) should have impressed them with the urgency of his message!

A second and related point is that Jesus taught and preached for everyone. "Many Jewish teachers had a limited audience," says Pheme Perkins. "They spoke to educated persons . . . who were seeking some higher insight . . . or 'wisdom.'" But Jesus "appealed to the crowds."[58]

"WORDS OF GRACE":
STUDIES IN THE SERMONS OF JESUS

We shall return to Jesus the preacher in the last chapter. Even so, we cannot hope in such brief compass to do justice to his preaching, let alone to be exhaustive. A vast literature exists on almost every utterance of his lips. (Robert Guelich, for example, cites almost three hundred works in his study of the Sermon on the Mount!) Having laid some groundwork for understanding the preaching of Jesus as preaching, the best we can hope to do now is to study some representative sermons, not theologically but homiletically, to hear more clearly the voice of Jesus.

The Sermon on the Mount

Is the Sermon on the Mount really a sermon? We can summarize in two sentences the problem we face in studying the Sermon on the Mount as "inspired preaching." First, the Sermon on the Mount is without question the most famous and influential sermon of any kind (or of any religion!) in human history. Second, almost no scholar today actually believes that the Sermon on the Mount is a sermon at all! This includes many evangelical scholars, who would be well-represented by Robert Guelich: "The Sermon on the Mount, as we know it, is ultimately the *literary product* of the first evangelist. Yet the evangelist himself did not 'write' the Sermon as such but composed it by combining various traditional units."[59]

Guelich is careful to say that "the traditional units . . . *reflected* [Jesus'] 'preaching,'" but "the actual 'Sermon' as such came into being . . . in the post-Easter community."[60] We may fairly say that modern critical scholarship is beyond doubting that the first Evangelist, popularly known as "Matthew," creatively compiled sayings attributed to Jesus so as to yield a "discourse" that served as the key to his theology. The only remaining questions have to do with particulars.[61]

It is true, of course, that not just in modern times but for centuries the *theological* significance of the Sermon on the Mount has far overshadowed its *rhetorical* or *homiletical* significance. Theologians from the second century onward have sweat drops of blood over its interpretation. Augustine called it a "perfect standard of the Christian life;"[62] but its radical demands and its ethical thrust have not yielded easily to his maxim. From Aquinas came the idea of two levels of righteousness, one the obedience necessary for salvation, the other a higher righteousness represented by the Sermon on the Mount. Luther saw in the Sermon an impossible ideal that the Christian should nevertheless embrace spiritually. For classic liberalism the Sermon on the Mount propounds the social agenda for the church. Radical theologians like Albert Schweitzer regarded the Sermon as a *Gesinnungsethik,* an ethics for the

"interim" between Jesus' announcement of the kingdom and its actualiza-
tion. Classic dispensationalism assigned the ethics of the sermon to the mil-
lennial kingdom, so that, in effect, they are not applicable today.

There are many other readings of the sermon,[63] and to paraphrase what
C. S. Lewis said of Jesus—that which calls forth so many theories must have
been a very great fact. The question we have to raise here is whether "the very
great fact" is not only *theologically* but *rhetorically* great, that is, whether the
Sermon on the Mount is really a *sermon* by the Son of God.

Amazed at his teaching. We may begin with the beginning of the
Sermon: "When Jesus saw the crowds, He went up on the mountain; and after
He sat down, His disciples came to Him. He opened His mouth and began
to teach them" (Matt. 5:1–2a).

A. M. Hunter remarks: "The ordinary church member, hearing these
words read in church, naturally enough supposes that Jesus delivered the substance of the following three chapters to his disciples on some Galilean hill-
side in one non-stop discourse." Though not a destructive critic, Professor
Hunter writes to disabuse the "ordinary church member" of that notion.
"Beyond doubt," he concludes, "the Sermon gathers together sayings of our
Lord uttered on many different occasions."[64]

But, of course, Hunter's "ordinary church member" regards the sermon
that way because the text of Matthew can hardly be read any other way. The
bookends of the sermon set it apart *as a unified whole* in a time-space context.
Jesus came to a specific place at a specific time. He sat down, his disciples
gathered around, and he opened his mouth, and began to teach. And when
Jesus finished, the crowd reacted (7:28–29).

The amazement of the multitude, in fact, provides an important clue that
the Sermon on the Mount really is a sermon. No one can help us here better
than Alfred Edersheim, an Oxford scholar who was, it will be remembered,
Jewish by birth and thoroughly conversant with rabbinical tradition. Edersheim
lamented that the modern reader, having only a fragmentary knowledge of the
Talmud, can hardly comprehend the "unspiritual" (even "anti-spiritual") thrust
of this tradition. Moreover, having breathed the atmosphere of Jesus' teaching
since birth, today's reader can scarcely imagine "the nameless feeling that starts
over a receptive soul when, in the silence of our moral wilderness, those voices
first break on the ear . . . . calling up echoes of inmost yet unrealised aspiration."[65] Christianized ears cannot fully appreciate the extraordinary effect of
Jesus' preaching on those who heard it for the first time.

While Edersheim allowed that Matthew might have edited the sermon to
some degree, he followed Eusebius[66] in treating Matthew's account as a substantially complete record of the Lord's actual teaching. Unquestionably,
Matthew intended the sermon to be heard that way. As we shall see, Luke
took care to record faithful summaries of the early preaching in Acts. David

Wenham has made essentially the same point about the discourses in Matthew. Based on an exhaustive analysis of the Olivet Discourse, he concludes that it must represent an elaborate pre-Synoptic tradition, perhaps derived from a "semi-official form of the apostolic teaching known and taught in Jerusalem at a very early date."[67]

According to George Kennedy, Matthew shared with most ancient cultures an assumption "that the ordinary form of presentation of important ideas was through continuous discourse, orally presented."[68] We could speculate that Matthew concocted such a speech or conflated bits of several speeches; but the evidence points to a dramatic sermon from the lips of the King.[69]

The rhetoric of the kingdom. The subject is the kingdom of God, of course, and, as such, the Sermon on the Mount belongs to that species of rhetoric known classically as "deliberative."[70] Compared with "judicial" (forensic) rhetoric and "epideictic" (praise and blame) rhetoric, "deliberative" rhetoric has to do with the future, and, in particular with what is good or bad for, or conducive or inconducive of, that future life or state which is thought to be best.[71] In the ancient world, deliberative oratory belongs especially to political decision-making. In the Sermon on the Mount, "political" vision gives way to issues of eternal significance. From the Beatitudes, with the repeated "blessed is," to Jesus' final approbation of the one who hears his words and does them,[72] the Sermon on the Mount holds out a vision for all of life—the life of citizens of the kingdom of God.

Rhetorically, the sermon naturally falls into four parts. The introduction, or *proem* (5:3–16), consisting largely of the Beatitudes, commands attention and "connects" Jesus with the audience.[73] This is followed (as in classical deliberative rhetoric) by a thesis, or *proposition* (5:17–20) that introduces, but does not explicate, two principles: (1) Jesus has come to fulfill the law; and (2) citizenship in the kingdom requires a higher righteousness. Jesus works out both principles in the *proof*, which constitutes the body of the sermon (5:21–7:20).

The first part of the proof (5:1–48) answers to the "fulfillment of the law" premise as Jesus examines the true spirit of the law, appealing to his own authority (in rhetorical terms, his *ethos*), as well as to the emotional responsiveness (*pathos*) of the hearers, through warnings about judgment.[74] The second part of the *proof* (6:1–7:20) corresponds to the "higher righteousness" of kingdom citizens.[75] In this section, Jesus appeals to the sense experience of his hearers by way of assertions followed by supporting reasons,[76] which he draws, in turn, from the world of ordinary human experience and observation. The *epilogue* of the sermon (again as in classical rhetoric), recapitulates the whole and "seeks to stir the audience to action."[77]

According to George Kennedy, himself a scholar of rhetoric, whether or not we accept Matthew's record at face value, it stands as a rhetorical unit and exhibits masterful technique. It has "unity of thought" together with "diversity of tone which gives it a sense of movement." Its "rhetorical devices . . . are not ornaments, but functional within the thought, creating audience contact and intensity." The "authoritative ethos is awesome, but [the sermon] repeatedly utilizes the form of logical argument with premises based on nature and experiences well known to the audience." Kennedy concludes, "Matthew says the original audience was astounded at the speech. It has continued to startle and challenge readers for two thousand years."[78]

"The Mystery of the Kingdom": A Parabolic Sermon

The ninth parable. With the publication of Adolf Jülicher's monumental study of the parables more than a century ago, New Testament scholarship more or less abandoned the long-standing allegorical interpretation of the parables. What made the parables of Jesus *"neu und wunderbar"* (Jülicher), in contrast to the dusty "parables" (allegorical stories) of the rabbis, was precisely that they went, so to speak, straight to the point.[79] It is nowadays a commonplace to say that the parables always teach a single truth. Craig Blomberg's recent *Interpreting the Parables* has rightly questioned this stock wisdom. While the parables are not allegories, per se, they certainly contain allegorical elements, and often (indeed usually) make more than one point.[80]

Helpful as it was in some ways, Jülicher's work tended to obscure not only the *theological* but also the *rhetorical* significance of the parables. Following Jülicher, C. H. Dodd defined a parable, for example, as "the dramatic presentation of a situation intended to suggest vividly some single idea."[81] In Dodd's view, a parable is little more than an apt illustration of some truth, usually a "moral." But as they come to us in the Gospels, the parables are manifestly more than cleverly devised paradigms.

Over half a century ago, T. F. Torrance described the parables as "sacramental." Jesus used them not merely to *illustrate* but in some sense, to *represent* the kingdom of God, that is, "to put a man into a situation in which he is confronted with God and can hear for himself the Word of the Kingdom which flesh and blood cannot reveal."[82]

This understanding is confirmed by Jesus' own words in Matthew 13 (= Mark 4) about the "mystery" of the kingdom and about the purpose of parables. The Matthew text, which scholars have long recognized as the third of Matthew's five discourses, is of special interest, however, for the light it sheds not only on the parables but also on the preaching of Jesus. For we meet here not a loose assemblage of the parables but a *parabolic sermon*.[83] Following the first parable, Jesus relates the purpose of parables to the mystery of the kingdom while the sermon as a whole exemplifies that purpose.

But why call Matthew 13 a *sermon*? We begin with the fact—now increasingly recognized—that these "parables of the kingdom" are carefully and thoughtfully arranged, so that the entire section functions as a rhetorical unit. It is often assumed that Matthew (or an anonymous redactor) did the arranging, deliberately combining seven parables,[84] doubtless to suggest some kind of completeness or fullness.[85] David Wenham has shown, however, that the account actually contains *eight* parables, arranged chiastically to form an *inclusio* between the "sower of the Word" at the front end and the "scribe who has become a disciple of the kingdom" (the eighth parable, v. 52) at the other end.[86]

The center of the chiasm is Matthew's statement that "Jesus spoke to the multitudes in parables, and He did not speak to them without a parable" (v. 34). Then follow the four remaining parables, *to His disciples* (v. 36). In the context, Jesus preaches, as it were, on the move, on the order of Aristotle's peripatetic pedagogy. But in this case, the movement itself becomes the *ninth parable* (!), as Jesus enacts the central message of the sermon—to wit, the mystery of the kingdom of God cannot be grasped by the dull ears and dim eyes of the "crowd," but only by those (few) who, like good soil, receive the Word.

How Do the Parables Preach?

The first half of the sermon (to the crowds) begins with the parable of the sower, which (as a good *proem* should do) prompts the disciples to question Jesus: "Why do You speak to them in parables?" (v. 10). In the last half of the sermon (to the disciples), Jesus poses a question to his followers: "Have you understood all these things?" (v. 51a). This question together with the eighth parable forms the *epilogue*, which (as a good *epilogue* should do), both recapitulates and sets the stage for future action. In both cases, parable is the rhetorical means to the "kingdom" end. But, we must ask, how *do* the parables function; or, in different words, how do the *parables preach*?

When the disciples ask why he speaks in parables, Jesus replies that parables differentiate between people, because parables simultaneously *reveal* and *conceal*, depending on the readiness of the hearer.[87]

But what is it about the *parable* that enables this to happen? The best answer we can give is that a parable draws the hearer into a real-life kind of experience, so as to confront him or her with a decision and, in doing so, to involve every dimension of the human personality—mind (cognition), heart (emotion), and will (volition). D. A. Carson helps us here. He demonstrates that the Greek comparative word-group *hōmoios* ("like"), used to introduce so many parables, has a nuanced meaning often lost in translation. In Matthew 13:24, for example, the NIV has "the kingdom of heaven is like." According to Carson, the translation should read "something like, 'the kingdom of heaven is like the case of. . . .'"[88] The NASB has "the kingdom of heaven may be compared to," which, while preferable, still misses the nuance, the significance of which lies precisely in the way it suggests *the real presence of the rule of God in human life.*

A fair contemporary analogy is the case study, which immerses a student vicariously in a real experience (albeit someone else's).[89] The difference, of course, is that the parable immerses the hearer in his or her *own* personal experience of confronting the claims of Christ. Turning again to the parable of the tares, Matthew uses the aorist passive of *hōmoiō* [*hōmoiōthē*] to say, in effect, "the kingdom of heaven *has* (already) *become like* this."[90] The "crowd" must decide! Am I a "weed" or wheat? What is to become of *me?*

The parables preach, therefore, by a kind of *indirection.* They immerse the hearer in a situation that confronts him with the reality of God's power and truth. But they leave the hearer free to decide. T. F. Torrance elaborated on this delicate balance between *confrontation* and *gentleness.* First, "the parable is chosen by Christ as a means of confronting man with Himself . . . in such a way that man can choose Him in love and yet not be over-whelmed by His divine majesty." Second, Jesus used parables not only for the moment, "but to keep the attention of the hearers awake until a more convenient time."[91] Third, Jesus "concealed" with the parables so that none "against their will should be forced to acknowledge the Kingdom, and yet He allowed them enough light to convict them and convince them."[92]

Jesus' parabolic sermon in Matthew 13 also brings to light what Philip Culbertson has called "the impact of cumulative parables." Culbertson documents the use of various kinds of rhetorical "strings" *(catenae),* used by the rabbis as aids to understanding. One form of catenae is a string of parables *(meshalim)* which the rabbis likened to "a journey toward truth." Just as Solomon arrived at the true meaning of Torah by stringing proverbs (the rabbis said), the master can guide the student to the whole of truth through its parts.[93] Culbertson calls the Matthew 13 discourse a "catena of the kingdom." These parables have a cumulative "emotional impact on [the disciples] that leads them to wonder, from wonder to philosophy, from philosophy to faith, and then on to the mysteries of the kingdom of God."[94]

"The Favorable Year of the Lord"
The Sermon in Nazareth (Luke 4:16–30)

At the conclusion of his essay, "Jesus as Teacher and Preacher," Rainer Riesner asks, "did Jesus succeed as a teacher?"[95] At one level, of course, history is answer enough. But at another level, the question makes perfect sense. What was the *effect* of Jesus' preaching? How did listeners respond to Jesus? Did he (or, rather, how did he) accomplish what he wanted to accomplish in his preaching?

Even a cursory look at the Gospels will show that the preaching of Jesus often had what we would nowadays call negative effects. We have only to remember the "disciples" who withdrew from him after his sermon on the "Bread of Life,"[96] or the several times he was threatened with stones after preaching,[97] or the way his (parabolic) preaching catalyzed the plot against his life during the passion week,[98] or, for that matter, we need only recall the questionings and doubtings by the Twelve when he preached.[99] If a good preacher is an effective "communicator," what are we to make of such strong, negative response to the Master Preacher?

It is precisely that question we meet in Luke's account of Jesus' synagogue sermon in Nazareth. Although Jesus often preached in synagogues,[100] this is the only record of an actual sermon.[101] This is also the only New Testament record of a synagogue *service* as such,[102] which service, in fact, presents one of four interpretative problems we must face: (1) why did Jesus read the text he read? (Isa. 61:1–2 with Isa. 58:6 inserted); (2) what was the occasion for the sermon? (3) where did the sermon end? and (4) how do we explain the congregation's reaction?

The reading of the prophet. The first problem arises because Isaiah 61:1–2 cannot readily be fit into any known scheme of readings from the prophets (though our knowledge is admittedly limited). The reading in any case is much too short for a *haftarah*,[103] but Luke seems to indicate that Jesus read precisely the verses recorded.[104] Further, while a *haftarah* reader might skip ahead to an appropriate "ending," he was not permitted to go backwards, as Jesus did by citing Isaiah 58:6. Thus Luke's account seems to hint that Jesus performed the *haftarah* for the day, but this seems unlikely.[105] An alternative is that, having been invited to speak in the very synagogue where he was "brought up" (4:16), Jesus had some liberty from the synagogue president to read (and expound) a text appropriate to the Torah reading (*seder*) and *haftarah* for the day. It is also conceivable, of course, that Jesus *was* handed the scroll *for the purpose* of reading the appointed *haftarah*, but that—against all "custom"—he read something else!

On the choice of Isaiah 61:1–2 (if it was not the *haftarah*), James Sanders offers a very plausible account. This particular text enjoyed wide currency among pious Jews, who interpreted it in terms of (a) blessings for themselves and (b) judgment upon their enemies.[106] If so, Jesus used the text as a *proem* to establish an immediate "connection" with his hearers and to prepare them, in a manner of speaking, for a radical reversal of their "tradition." This reconstruction makes good sense in light of Luke's telling observation that after the reading, Jesus "sat down; and the eyes of all in the synagogue were fixed upon Him" (4:20). Reading this text evidently created palpable expectancy.

The occasion of the sermon. As to the occasion for the sermon, Mark (6:1–6a) and Matthew (13:54–58) both mention Jesus' teaching in the synagogue in Nazareth (though without a sermon) but in what appears to be a different context. Most notably, in Luke, the synagogue sermon *precedes* the call of the disciples, while in Mark and Matthew, it *follows* the call. Most commentators, including some of the older authorities,[107] assume that the accounts are nonetheless parallel, and that Matthew/Mark simply transposed the account. William Walker hypothesizes that Matthew actually recognizes Luke's order in 4:13, but chose to elaborate on Jesus' rejection later.[108] Although his conclusion is inherently implausible, Walker may be on to something. Matthew 4:13 at least allows for the possibility that Jesus "left" Nazareth in the way Luke describes.[109]

If so, we have in Matthew a record of two visits to (and two rejections in) Nazareth, one at the beginning of the Galilean ministry, another at the end. In the first visit, Jesus refused to do any miracles and (in Luke's synagogue sermon) rebuked the congregation for demanding to see what "we heard was done at Capernaum."[110] Then, "after a long interval," says A. T. Robertson, Jesus gives "the Nazarenes another opportunity to hear his teaching, and to witness miracles."[111] First Jesus preaches "the Word" in his hometown; then he confirms the Word by his "works."

The end of the sermon. A more pressing homiletical question is where the sermon ends. Luke's comment in 4:22 that his townspeople were "wondering" might seem to imply the sermon had ended—with only a Scripture reading and a single (pregnant) sentence. But Luke may just as well have inserted the comment precisely at this point to show that even while Jesus was preaching, the congregation was already abuzz. The scene is utterly natural, especially given the astonishment so often associated with Jesus' preaching. On this interpretation, Luke 4:23–27 summarizes the closing part of the sermon, framed in response to the wonderment Jesus could observe with his own eyes! In popular language, Jesus read the body language of the congregation.

Acceptance or rejection. This brings us to the climactic question about this sermon—how do we explain the reaction of the people of Nazareth? It is often observed that the response *appears* to be positive, not negative. Luke says specifically that the crowd were "speaking well of Him" and that they "wondered" at his "gracious words." It has even been suggested that Jesus, in effect, overreacted and used a proverb[112] as a rhetorical weapon to "the effect of provoking offence, rather than a tactful handling of the situation."[113]

But Luke provides certain clues that this is not the case at all. The word translated "wondered" [*thaumazō*] expresses astonishment, but often has a *negative* connotation.[114] The "wonder," in any case, is over Jesus' "gracious words." In Greek, Luke's phrase is *tois logois tēs charitos*, "words of grace," apparently a reference to his *message* of salvation.[115] The Nazareth townsfolk, it seems, were ambivalent about Jesus—"impressed with his character . . . but astonished and critical . . . of his message."[116]

The basis of his message was the Old Testament law of the Jubilee year,[117] when debts were to be erased, leased land returned, slaves set free, in short, when *shalom* was to be restored. The "Jubilee" had long since fallen into neglect—if it was ever observed—and, on the strength of texts like Isaiah 61:1–2, had come to symbolize Israel's hope for her own eschatological deliverance. So Jesus announces that the "Jubilee" hope is fulfilled (4:21); but he knows that the crowd has no real taste for the Jubilee vision of salvation for the hopeless and the helpless.

Did Jesus *succeed* in his preaching? Every preacher must answer that question—together with Jesus in Nazareth.

"BEGOTTEN AGAIN TO A LIVING HOPE": PETER'S EPISTLES AS INSPIRED INCARNATIONAL PREACHING

C. RICHARD WELLS

When the Acts of the Apostles records that the sick used to be brought into the streets that "even the shadow of Peter passing by" might overshadow some of them (Acts 5:15), it is a figure of his subsequent influence on the Christian world, which for countless generations was dominated everywhere by "the shadow of Peter passing by."

F. J. FOAKES-JACKSON[1]

THE SCHOLAR'S STEPCHILD

Three-quarters of a century ago, Cambridge scholar F. J. Foakes-Jackson wrote of Peter's extraordinary significance: "From the very first Peter is, after Christ, the most prominent person in the story of our religion." He was "Prince of Apostles," and he has "captured the imagination of mankind."[2]

The "imagination of mankind," perhaps, but not of biblical scholars. To the obvious question, "Why not?" the most obvious answer is neglect by association. The prominence of Peter "in the story of our religion" is tainted for many evangelicals by his prominence in the Roman Catholic doctrine of papal succession. The Reformers, of course, summarily rejected that doctrine, even as they brought the doctrine of justification—and with it, Paul, the apostle of justification—to center stage. By the law of unintended consequences, the Reformation relegated Peter to the footnotes. It does not help matters that while we "are told more about him than about any of the twelve apostles in the Gospels and in the Acts,"[3] we still do not know nearly as much about Peter as we know about Paul.

To make matters still worse, Peter did not leave us an extensive written corpus as Paul did; and what he left has been endlessly controverted. The early church disputed 2 Peter until the late fourth century. Meanwhile, a sizable literature of more or less legendary material developed around Peter's persona, obscuring or confusing what might otherwise be known about him.[4] If ancient writers doubted the authenticity of 2 Peter, many modern scholars dismiss the letter out-of-hand, and 1 Peter as well. For most liberal scholars, and not a few conservatives, 1 Peter, to say nothing of 2 Peter, is the late product of a "Petrine circle," not the product of a fisherman's pen.

This history prompted J. H. Elliott to label 1 Peter the "exegetical step-child" of New Testament studies,[5] and the same might be said of Peter himself. Linked to a benighted doctrine and mocked by legends, overshadowed in his own lifetime by Paul as the gospel reached to the Gentiles, and displaced by Paul as the church returned to the doctrine of justification, his meager literary corpus always in dispute—Peter, the confessor of the Messiah, the preacher of Pentecost, the "Prince of Apostles," became a scholar's stepchild.

One suspects, however, that the Prince of Apostles might actually revel in the neglect accorded him. For the Peter we meet in the epistles and Acts is devoid of personal ambition. No—more than that—Peter is self-consciously self-effacing. He is a saved sinner, a beggar telling others where to find bread. Of all the apostles, Peter is the best representative of what nowadays we call "incarnational preaching,"[6] eternal truth mediated through the real human experience of a real human personality transformed by Christ. Phillips Brooks, of course, brought this idea into popular consciousness, with his famous 1877 Lyman Beecher Lectures on Preaching: "Preaching is the communication of truth by man to men. It has in it two essential elements, truth and personality. Neither of these can it spare and still be preaching. The truest truth, the most authoritative statement of God's will, communicated in any other way than through the personality of brother man to brother man is not preached truth."[7]

Peter preaches as "brother man to brother men." He is the "true-hearted man of God,"[8] an apostate turned apologist, begotten to a living hope (1 Pet. 1:3), a "witness" not only to the majesty of Jesus (2 Pet. 1:16), but also to his sufferings, sufferings Peter himself once vigorously resisted (Mark 8:32) but finally embraced (1 Pet. 4:1; 5:1).

In this chapter we will examine the incarnational preaching of Peter. We will begin with the life experience that shaped him; then we will attempt to analyze some of the incarnational elements of Peter's preaching as we find them in his epistles.

PETER THE PREACHER: FROM SIMON TO CEPHAS SIMON ROCK!

What's in a name? In the case of Simon Peter, we are tempted to say, almost *everything*. Shortly after the temptation in the wilderness, John the Baptist pointed to Jesus and declared him to be the promised "Lamb of God."[9] On the strength of that testimony, two of John's disciples[10] followed Jesus, and one of them, Andrew, "found first his own brother Simon[11] and said to him, 'We have found the Messiah.'"[12] Jesus seizes on Peter's *name* at first sight: "Jesus looked at him and said, 'You are Simon the son of John; you shall be called Cephas' (which is translated Peter)."[13]

Those who heard must have been slack-jaw astounded. Like "Peter" (*Petros*) in Greek, "Cephas" in Peter's native Aramaic denotes a "rock." But, to say the least, Peter was "not . . . a model of rock-like . . . firmness."[14] Oscar Cullmann suggests that "in order to understand what an impression the giving of a name to Peter must have made on him and on the other witnesses of this event, we would do well to translate the word *Kephas* not with the word Peter, which for us today is all too familiar and has become too rigidly fixed as a proper name, but with the English word 'rock,' and so call him Simon Rock."[15] The contrast between the character portrayed in the Gospels and the change prophesied by the Lord could scarcely be greater.

A Born Leader

To be sure, Simon Peter exhibits qualities and behaviors we commonly associate with a "born leader." "He is . . . at all times," says Cullman, the leading "*spokesman*" for the Twelve, "their *representative* in good as in bad action."[16] When Jesus directs a question to all the disciples, Peter invariably answers,[17] and Peter seems always ready to ask questions the other disciples apparently want (but are reluctant) to ask.[18] Peter is the first to confess Christ,[19] the first to run toward the tomb after the report of the women,[20] and the first to *enter* the tomb even though the "other" disciple arrived first![21]

In one sense, therefore, we are not surprised that Peter occupies the place of preeminence among the disciples. Just as the name of Judas Iscariot appears last in each list of the disciples, Peter's name always appears first.[22] Matthew (10:2) goes so far as to designate Simon "the first," using a term (*prōtos*) which implies special recognition, if not priority of rank.[23] Jesus directs Peter (together with John) to prepare his last Passover.[24] With the sons of Zebedee, Peter accompanies Jesus to the Mount of Transfiguration and into the Garden of Gethsemane. There, even though all the disciples sleep, the Lord directs his rebuke to Peter.[25] Outsiders apparently considered Peter a spokesman for the disciples as well, if not for Jesus himself.[26] And after the resurrection, an angel instructs the women, "Go, tell His disciples and Peter, 'He is going before you into Galilee.'"[27]

On the one hand, then, Peter seems a natural leader and stands first among the disciples. But on the other hand, Peter seems most unsuitable for leadership. The prophecy of "Simon Rock" belies a phalanx of character flaws that conspire to produce a substantial career of failure. The Gospels call attention to three such flaws in particular. Peter is *impetuous, ambiguous,* and *presumptuous.*

The most memorable instance of Peter's *impetuosity* is his walking on the water,[28] which follows "an almost boyish request to Jesus to prove his identity: 'Lord if it be thou, bid me come unto thee upon the water.'"[29] But we meet that same impetuousness at every turn—whether rushing to the tomb,[30] swearing loyalty unto death,[31] jumping into the sea to swim to Jesus,[32] proposing to build tabernacles at the transfiguration,[33] or cutting off the right ear of Malchus in Gethsemane.[34] Peter embodies the adage about acting in haste and repenting in leisure.

The Gospels also picture Peter as curiously *ambiguous.* He confesses Jesus as Messiah at Caesarea Philippi, apparently in genuine faith.[35] But he recoils from the implications of messiahship, as Jesus began to unfold them: "From that time Jesus began to show His disciples that He must go to Jerusalem, and suffer. . . . Peter took Him aside and began to rebuke Him, saying, 'God forbid it, Lord! This shall never happen to You.'"[36] Perhaps Peter feared for himself. The Gospels provide evidence enough that Peter shrank from the disapproval of authority figures.[37] Perhaps Peter only wanted to protect Jesus, a thought suggested by Peter's own words: "This shall never happen *to You.*"[38] Certainly Peter failed to understand the character and the cost of messiahship, as Jesus made clear in his rebuke.[39]

No doubt Jesus' call to suffering draws from Peter a whole complex of motives and emotions, that together bespeak sensitivity to spiritual truth ("You are the Christ"), mixed with a weak will ("This shall never happen to You"). Peter's ambiguity surfaces again—less obviously, perhaps, but no less strikingly—in his infamous denials. All four Gospels tell the story. Following the arrest of Jesus, Peter rallied somewhat and followed "at a distance . . . to see the outcome."[40] Peter resolved to follow, but his very resolve would bring him face to face with his own cowardice, which for the moment would triumph as resolve wilted under pressure. Jesus had analyzed Peter already in Gethsemane: "The spirit is willing, but the flesh is weak."[41]

Finally, the Gospels call attention to Peter's *presumptuous* self-confidence. Again, we have a notable instance in the "sad story of Peter's downfall,"[42] which (as we noted) all four Gospels relate in excruciating detail,[43] against the backdrop of Peter's sworn allegiance to Jesus. "Even though all may fall away because of You," Matthew has it, "I will never fall away."[44] Mark notes that all the disciples "were saying the same thing also," but Peter "kept saying insistently, 'Even if I have to die with You, I will not deny You!'"[45] Only hours later, his confidence evaporated, and "All his boasting rushed back into his mind and added bitterness to his salty tears."[46]

The Grim Abyss

Anton Boisen founded the clinical pastoral education movement out of his own tortured experience. Boisen came to believe that emotional distress can often prepare the way for (what Boisen called) religious "creativity,"[47] especially for those who "go down to the grim abyss" of personal failure.[48] In the grim abyss, of course, is just where Peter found himself. The Synoptics are one in their poignant telling of it. After the "cock crowed," according to the prophecy of Jesus, Peter "went out and wept bitterly."[49]

The Gospels probe more deeply into the significance of Peter's grim abyss than we might first imagine. Luke tells us that in the upper room a dispute arose among the disciples "as to which one of them was regarded to be greatest."[50] It was an argument they had had before.[51] Peter may have stated his own claims forcefully, for after calling them all to servanthood, Jesus addresses the "leader" of the Twelve: "Simon, Simon, behold, Satan has demanded permission to sift you like wheat; but I have prayed for you, that your faith may not fail; and you, when once you have turned again, strengthen your brothers."[52] "Simon" (note the old name) is not yet "Cephas." Hours later—in the courtyard of the high priest, under the provocations of menial servants, betrayed by his own impetuous chatter,[53] giving the lie to his brazen boast in the upper room and his brandished sword in the garden—Simon is being sifted and prepared to preach.

But the Gospel record takes us deeper still, to the very nadir of Peter's abyss. All three Synoptics tell us that when the cock crowed, Peter "remembered the word which Jesus had said."[54] The word for "remembered" is theologically loaded. For example, after the resurrection, the women "remembered" (*emnēsthēsan*) Jesus' words about dying and rising again the third day,[55] and the disciples "remembered" (*emnēsthēsan*) the prophecies concerning Jesus.[56] In each of these cases, to "remember" the words of Jesus is to have them "come alive." Now his words come alive for Peter, and prepare "the ground for *metanoia*."[57]

But Luke adds a critical bit of information that allows us a glimpse into the worst moment of Peter's life. Just as the rooster crowed, Peter had eye contact with Jesus. J. B. Phillips captures the intensity of the Greek [*eneblepsin*] this way: "The Lord turned his head and looked straight at Peter."[58] Peter had not merely *failed*; he had *betrayed*. And at this moment, like a disobedient child reading unspeakable hurt and disappointment in his father's face, Peter reads his own shame in the eyes of unutterable love. And he *remembered* the words of Jesus. His best intentions, his most solemn promises, his most earnest resolve have all failed. Tried and found wanting, "sifted like wheat," he goes outside to weep bitterly.[59]

"Feed My Sheep"

The New Testament writers only mention; they do not give details of Simon's emergence from the "grim abyss," his *metanoia*, and his transformation into the "Rock." Remarkably Peter's failure does not seem to have estranged him from the other disciples. Perhaps the other disciples did not yet (fully) know about Peter's denial. Perhaps because all had scattered, Peter's failure was greater only in degree. In any case, on Easter morning we find Peter in company with John when Mary Magdalene brings news of an empty tomb,[60] though "as yet [the disciples] did not understand the Scripture, that He must rise again from the dead."[61] Mark tells us that the angel singled out Peter when he instructed the women to tell the disciples.[62] Luke mentions an appearance to Peter,[63] and so does Paul.[64] But none of the writers gives particulars.

Only John gives us anything like a formal account of Peter's restoration. The scene is all too familiar now, but it is full of high drama. The disciples had returned for the moment to their fishing, and they had fished all night without success. At dawn, unrecognized, Jesus calls to them from the beach: "Children, you do not have any fish, do you?" "No," they reply. Again he calls to them: "Cast the net on the right-hand side of the boat, and you will find a catch." And they do. John recognizes instantly that this is a reprise of that morning some three years earlier when Jesus originally called the disciples to be "fishers of men."[65] So John turns to Peter and says to him, "It is the Lord."[66] Impetuous always, Peter dives into the water and swims to Jesus. The stage is now set for his transformation from *Simon* to *Cephas*.

Following breakfast, Jesus questions Peter: "Simon, son of John, do you love Me?"[67] The address is significant, for to "call him *Peter*, a *Rock*, in the face of conduct which seemed to prove him fickle, would be fearful irony," but to "call him *Simon, Son of John*, was sincere reproof."[68] Just as Peter's boast had dissolved in three denials, Jesus pressed the question three times, and three times called for proof ("feed my sheep"). Simon understands only too well. He answers each question the same way—"You know that I love [*phileō*] You"—deliberately, so it seems, understating the terms of his affection.[69] And when Jesus asked the third time, John informs us, "Peter was grieved."[70]

All the props are knocked out. "Simon Rock" has a future, indeed; but not of his own doing or even his own choosing.[71] Simon has been "sifted," but Cephas will strengthen his brothers.[72] Simon *professed* his loyalty; Cephas will *prove* his love by feeding the sheep.[73] Simon fell into the "grim abyss"; Cephas will emerge to preach.

The story of the disciples in the fourth Gospel begins and ends the same way. Both in the first chapter and in the last, Jesus singles out Peter from the others and draws a sharp contrast between what he is by nature ("Simon") and what he shall become by faith ("Cephas"). In John, therefore, as in the Synoptics, Peter proves to be the representative disciple on a grand scale. He possessed notable strengths, but his "human weakness was very striking,"[74] and that very weakness became, in Christ, the source of his strength and the foundation for his leadership of the early church. "Peter," writes Foakes-Jackson, "is always the same—impulsive, affectionate, easily disheartened, failing, yet always returning to his allegiance to the Master. He is the type of the church militant with its many shortcomings, not of the church triumphant. But it is through failure and inconsistency, repentance and a return to loyalty that the great triumphs here on earth are won."[75]

"Failure and inconsistency, repentance and a return to loyalty" is also a formula for great preaching. If it is true that "preaching by its very nature is autobiographical,"[76] then the most authentic preaching will always be mediated through the most genuinely transformative life experience. This is incarnational preaching, and this is Peter's preaching, which we hear in the epistles that bear his name, where Simon Rock proves his love for Jesus by feeding the sheep.

THE PETRINE EPISTLES AS INCARNATIONAL PREACHING

1 and 2 Peter as Preaching

In the year 1911, R. Perdelwitz published *Die Mysterienreligion und das Problem des I. Petrusbriefes*[77] and touched off a minor modern scholarly debate. Perdelwitz argued that 1 Peter was essentially a baptismal sermon. A number of scholars followed his lead, including B. H. Streeter[78] and F. W. Beare,[79] but for a number of reasons, his theory did not win the day. What has won the day—somewhat inchoately—is the idea that 1 Peter is more *sermonic* than literary. Some have suggested that the letter consists of "homiletical fragments."[80] Others have simply noted certain homiletical features in 1 Peter, such as, for example, his tendency to use the Old Testament in proof-text fashion.[81]

C. F. D. Moule thinks that 1 Peter may contain two different sermons, "one for those not yet under actual duress (i.1–iv.11 and v.12–14), and the other—terser and swifter—for those who were in the refining fire (i.1–ii.10, iv.12–v.14)." The "messengers were bidden to read the appropriate part to each community according to the situation,"[82] on the analogy of Paul's letter "coming from Laodicea," which he instructed to be read in Colossae.[83] Donald Guthrie says simply, "The homiletical form of the Epistle is fairly plain . . . [as] might be expected from a man whose vocation was preaching not writing."[84] Perdelwitz may have missed the tree, but not the forest.

We are arguing throughout this book that the New Testament, in whole and in part, consists mainly of preaching. On that theory, we should not be surprised to find "homiletical elements" at every turn. But the Petrine letters offer a particularly striking illustration of our thesis. They read like sermon manuscripts, and on the assumption that we hear Peter's voice behind them, they offer striking evidence that Peter's preaching was truth "transmitted into life" through an "incarnation of the truth."[85]

The Petrine Epistles: Orality and Genuineness

But is it *Peter's* voice we hear? As we noted earlier, 1 and 2 Peter have suffered violence at the hands of critics—2 Peter in ancient times, and both letters in modern times—despite the fact that both claim apostolic authority.[86] Our primary concern here is not with higher critical questions as such, but with the homiletical character, form, and content of the Petrine letters. We cannot, however, ignore the critical questions entirely,[87] because at least two bear directly on our thesis.

One question has to do with the undeniable similarities between 2 Peter and Jude.[88] Many modern scholars believe the parallels are best explained on the assumption that 2 Peter borrowed from Jude.[89] On the further assumption that Jude was written some time after Peter's death, it follows (the argument goes) that Peter could not have written the epistle. A second question concerns the relationship of 1 and 2 Peter to each other. Both claim Peter as author, but the Greek of 1 Peter is noticeably more polished than that of 2 Peter. Critical scholars cite other differences as well, including vocabulary, use of the Old Testament, links with the Pauline epistles, even doctrinal differences. Many critical scholars have concluded (a) that the same person could not have written the two letters and, more seriously, (b) that the language and style of 1 Peter are too elevated for an undereducated Galilean fisherman.[90] If the critics are right, then the voice of Peter the apostle, if we can detect it at all in either of these letters, is but a faint, indistinct echo.

But we have no compelling reason to believe the critics are right. There are alternative explanations that not only make good sense but highlight the original orality of the letters. First, the relationship of 1 and 2 Peter. As early as the fifth century, Jerome attributed the differences between the letters to Peter's use of a different amanuensis for each.[91] A. T. Robertson theorized that while Peter probably used Silvanus as an amanuensis for his first letter,[92] he may have written the second letter himself.[93] Either theory is plausible, but in either case, the problem of hearing Peter's voice in 1 and 2 Peter is no different from the problem of hearing Paul's voice on Mars Hill. As we will see in the next chapter, Luke does not give us full sermon transcripts in Acts but "condensed accounts of speeches actually made,"[94] true in form and substance to the original. There is no reason to doubt that Silvanus could have recorded Peter's preaching in a similar way, but cast them in epistolary form to meet the needs of the moment. Another amanuensis could easily have produced 2 Peter in the same way, if Peter did not do it himself.

On the relation of 2 Peter and Jude, most older writers maintained the priority of 2 Peter. Both Cyril of Alexandria (d. 344) and Theophylact (d. about 1181) thought that Peter's letter *anticipated* the full flowering of heresies just beginning to appear in his lifetime.[95] Luther agreed and suggested that what Peter *anticipated*, Jude actually *experienced*. Jude then adapted the preaching of Peter to his special situation.[96] In fact, many of the earliest writers paid almost no attention to the similarities between 2 Peter and Jude, except as indicators that the first-century church cared deeply about truth and false teaching, which is the concern of the letters.

It is certainly not impossible, of course, that Peter borrowed from Jude, nor, we think, would Peter himself chafe at the suggestion. Did he not freely admit that Paul wrote "some things hard to understand"?[97] Humility is one of the recurring themes in the Petrine letters, and we have no trouble imagining that Peter would practice what he preached, even if that meant borrowing from a lesser-known preacher.

Nevertheless, a better solution to the problem lies close at hand. Norman Hillyer suggests that Peter and Jude drew on common preaching sources.[98] In 1 Peter, for example, we detect a number of striking parallels with Paul, as well as with James. Such "closeness of thought," says Hillyer, "suggests that the body of teaching . . . was traditional in the Christian circles" of the day.[99] It is certainly not hard to imagine that the close working relationship of the apostles and others (including Jude) in preaching and teaching missions would result in a shared store of preaching material from which any and all would draw—adapting, reshaping, contextualizing as needed.

In summary, these critical questions not only fail to undermine but may indeed help confirm the thesis of a homiletical (oral) origin for the Petrine letters. Stated another way, if we treat the Petrine epistles essentially as sermons, the critical questions tend to fade into insignificance.

The Petrine Epistles: Biography as Theology

Peter never got over his descent into the "grim abyss" and his subsequent restoration. That experience wafts through his preaching like a melody through an overture. In 1 and 2 Peter, biography becomes theology.[100] This is what we mean by "incarnational preaching." The major doctrinal (preaching) themes of the Petrine letters elaborate the apostle's conscious awareness of his own transformation from *Simon* to *Cephas*. We can discern at least six such "incarnational" themes in 1 and 2 Peter.

1. Begotten to a living hope. Above all, Peter preaches that *our hope is in Christ alone, not in ourselves.* Many commentators regard "living hope" as a major theme, if not the central theme, of the first letter. The primary text for that theme (1 Pet. 1:3) reverberates with allusions to Peter's own experience, generalized to all believers: "Blessed be the God and Father of our Lord Jesus Christ, who according to His great mercy has caused us to be born again to a living hope through the resurrection of Jesus Christ from the dead."

Note the following "biographical" links: (1) Peter's own life was transformed ("born again"); (2) Peter's new life was characterized by "living hope" (as opposed to his dead hope after the denials and the crucifixion); (3) "through the resurrection" refers not only to the triumph of the crucified Lord, but hints at the Lord's special post-resurrection appearances to Peter; and (4) God's "great mercy" through Christ restored Peter out of his abjection.

Peter's self-confidence as a disciple eventually gave way to Christ-confidence; and now he urges that same Christ-confidence upon distressed believers. They should "fix [their] hope completely on the grace to be brought to [them] at the revelation of Jesus Christ" (1:13). "Through Him," they "are believers in God" (1:21). He reminds them that they "were continually straying like sheep, but now [they] have returned to the Shepherd and Guardian of [their] souls" (2:25). He exhorts them to live faithfully amid their sufferings and reminds them that "though you have not seen [Christ], you love Him, and though you do not see Him now, but believe in Him,[101] you greatly rejoice with joy inexpressible and full of glory" (1:8).

2. Clothed with humility. Peter urges believers to *walk humbly with their God.* One of the strongest evidences of Peter's voice in the letters is the theme of humility that recurs so frequently and so resoundingly. In the first epistle, Peter exalts humility as a Christian virtue. Believers must conduct themselves "in fear" (1:17). They must behave excellently, even though slandered, for the glory of God (2:12). They must submit to human authority (2:13), even slaves to unreasonable masters (2:18). They must follow Christ's example of suffering unjustly for what is right (2:20–21; 3:14–18; 4:13–16). They must be "humble in spirit; not returning evil for evil, . . . but giving a blessing instead" (3:8–9). Even elders must not lord it over the flock (5:3). The "younger men" must subject themselves to the elders, and all must "clothe [themselves] with humility toward one another" (5:5).

In the second letter, humility is a corrective to false teaching. Thus, for example, "entrance" into the kingdom of Christ will be "abundantly supplied" as faith is actualized in virtue, culminating in brotherly kindness and love (1:5–11). Again, Scripture is not "a matter of one's own [prideful] interpretation" (1:20), but false teachers arrogate just such prerogatives to themselves. Because of "greed" (2:3), "corrupt desires," and "daring self-will" (2:10), they "despise authority" (2:10) and "do not tremble when they revile angelic majesties . . . reviling where they have no knowledge" (2:10, 12). These "mockers . . . following after their own lusts" (3:3) "distort" the Scriptures "to their own destruction" (3:16) and carry others away in their error (3:17).

While we should not expect Peter to tout his own humility, we do find striking indirect testimonies, the most remarkable of which appears at the end of 2 Peter. Liberal critics almost universally regard 2 Peter as the work of a much later (probably second-century) author, seeking either to legitimate his own work with Peter's moniker or to contemporize Peter's teaching.[102] But Donald Guthrie remarks how strange it would be that a pseudepigraphist should use the name "Simon Peter," where the first epistle has only "Peter" (the name by which he would long since have been known).[103] Why would someone trafficking on the elevated name of the preeminent apostle use "Simon," with all its unflattering associations, instead of "Peter"?

But "Simon" (or "Symeon") makes perfect sense in the mouth of Peter himself, as he seeks to expose those who deny "the Master who bought them" (2:1). For "the Master who bought them" is Jesus, who prophesied that "Simon" would become "Peter" and whom "Simon Peter" now serves as a "bond-servant" (1:1).

To that same spirit of humility we must attribute Peter's shockingly frank acknowledgement that Paul wrote "some things hard to understand" (3:16). Again, we can scarcely conceive why anyone intent on lionizing Peter would suggest such an unfavorable comparison, especially considering Paul's rebuke of Peter's lapse into Judaizing![104] But all of it accords perfectly with Peter's transformation from the braggadocious Simon to the "Rock" who walks humbly with his Master.

3. Becoming a living stone. Peter preaches that *steadfastness in Christ is the norm of Christian living.* If Peter is a "Rock," Jesus Christ is the "living stone."[105] "And coming to Him," Peter declares, "you also, as living stones, are being built up as a spiritual house" (2:4–5). What Jesus had said to Peter on their first meeting, Peter now proclaims that to all that they are to become "rocks" in Christ.

Though the words *stone* and *rock* are absent, the theme of steadfastness recurs in 2 Peter: "Therefore, brethren, be all the more diligent to make certain about His calling and choosing you; for as long as you practice these things, you will never stumble; for in this way the entrance into the eternal kingdom of our Lord and Savior Jesus Christ will be abundantly supplied to you."[106] The second letter also mentions heretics who, "denying the

Master . . . [are] bringing swift destruction upon themselves" (2:1), a warning that vividly recalls Peter's own denials.

4. Walking "in His steps." Peter preaches that *the way of Christ is the way of the cross.* At the crossroads of Caeserea Philippi, Peter confessed his faith but recoiled from the implications of messiahship, and received the Lord's stern rebuke.[107] Chrysostom reminds us, however, that Jesus "was by no means satisfied with the mere rebuke." Rather, desiring to show both the rashness of Peter and "the benefit of His passion," Jesus says, "Thy word to me is, 'Be it far from Thee' . . . but my word to thee is, 'Not only is it hurtful to thee, and destructive, to hinder me and to be displeased at my Passion, but it will be impossible for thee even to be saved, unless thou thyself be continually prepared for death.'"[108] The Peter of the letters, especially 1 Peter, is "continually prepared for death." He has (now at last) "taken up the cross." Indeed, it is not too much to say that Peter's experience of first disavowing, then embracing, the cross unlocks the meaning of 1 Peter, where suffering is "the central concern."[109]

Anyone familiar with today's Christian youth culture recognizes the "WWJD" emblazoned on T-shirts, ball caps, and bracelets. Not everyone knows that "WWJD" comes indirectly from 1 Peter. In 1896, Congregational pastor Charles Sheldon wrote a book challenging Christians to live like Christ by asking in every situation, "What would Jesus do?" Sheldon entitled the book, *In His Steps,* a phrase he took from 1 Peter 2:21: "For you have been called for this purpose, since Christ also suffered for you, leaving you an example to follow *in His steps*" (emphasis added).

Whatever WWJD means today, for Peter, following "in His steps" meant taking up the cross as a way of life. He wrote not only to console, encourage, and sustain Christians in their trials but to urge them to embrace trials as the way of authentic followership. The steps of Christ lead to the cross, and Christians "have been called for this purpose."[110]

They are to "arm [themselves] also with the same purpose" as Christ, "who has suffered in the flesh" (4:1). Recalling the Beatitudes, Peter declared Christians "blessed" when they "suffer for the sake of righteousness" (3:14)[111] or when they "are reviled for the name of Christ" (4:14).[112] Peter bids them rejoice if they "share the sufferings of Christ" (4:13), if they suffer not as evildoers but "as a Christian" (4:16). And he exhorts the elders to faithfulness as a "fellow elder" and as a "witness of the sufferings of Christ, and a partaker also of the glory that is to be revealed" (5:1).

5. Feeding the sheep. Peter preaches that *ministry is caring as a shepherd for the flock that belongs to Christ.* Thomas Oden writes that, even though there are other images both in Scripture and in culture, "shepherding" is "the pivotal analogy" for Christian ministry.[113] We confirm Oden's thesis with our use of the term *pastor,* the Latin form of the Greek *poimēn*, which denotes a "shepherd."[114] Certainly the Lord characterized his own ministry—and ministry in general—as "shepherding."[115] In doing so he adapted an Old Testament "figure so widely imprinted on the minds of the people of biblical times that it needed no elaboration."[116] Among New Testament writers, Paul employs the image at critical points.[117] From Peter, however, we gain insights into the ministry as shepherding, derived from his own experience.

Peter's charge to the elders (1 Pet. 5:1–4) sets forth a strikingly comprehensive model of what we might nowadays call "servant leadership." First, he urges them to cultivate *pure motives for leadership*, warning them against motives of mere professionalism ("not under compulsion, but voluntarily, according to the will of God") or material gain ("not for sordid gain"). Second, he calls them to *reject authoritarian styles of leadership* ("nor yet as lording it over [them]"). Third, he reminds them that their *leadership is not a status but a stewardship*, not power over, but responsibility for, "those allotted to your charge." Fourth, he calls them to base *their authority on godly character* ("proving to be examples to the flock").

In one sense, of course, Peter is simply adapting the familiar shepherd image to the life of the body in the context of a hostile environment. But in doing so, he echoes the teaching of Jesus and the threefold commission Jesus gave him beside the Sea of Galilee: "Tend my lambs."[118] Peter writes now as a "fellow elder," or, as Gregory the Great put it, "the first pastor," called by Christ to prove his loving by "the care of feeding."[119] Now, Gregory said, he "anxiously admonishes" the elders to "glow with ardor in regard to the inward affections of those they have the charge of."[120]

Even if the shepherds must reject authoritarianism, they must not neglect their responsibility to protect the flock. In 2 Peter, the "shepherd" language does not appear; but the entire letter *illustrates* this quality of ministry, as Peter exposes the "false prophets" (2:1),[121] and endeavors to establish his hearers in the truth (1:12).[122]

6. **Born again by the word.** Finally, Peter preaches that *lives are transformed by the Word preached*. Peter had long before embraced this truth. John tells us that when "many of His disciples withdrew" because of His teaching about the "true bread," Jesus asked the Twelve whether they had misgivings: "You do not want to go away also, do you?"[123] As we would expect, Peter answers for everybody and confesses perhaps more than he knows: "Lord, to whom shall we go? You have words of eternal life."[124] But it is a confession, nonetheless, a turning point in John's Gospel, says Bruce, similar to Peter's confession at Caesarea Philippi in the Synoptics (and occurring about the same time).[125] Early on, it seems, Peter grasped the significance of Jesus' life and of his *teaching*. Jesus had said, "The words that I have spoken to you are

spirit and are life."[126] And Peter hangs on every one, however imperfectly and incoherently at the time.

His letters show that Peter was saturated with the very words of Jesus.[127] Peter echoes Jesus' teaching about shepherds and sheep,[128] the new birth,[129] the indestructible inheritance,[130] the threats of Satan and firmness in faith,[131] among many, many others. Peter alluded to the Beatitudes,[132] and repeated the Lord's citations of Old Testament Scripture.[133] In addition, even though the exact words do not appear, Jesus' call to "love your enemies" recurs throughout the letter.[134]

Second Peter echoes the Jesus tradition as well. Peter speaks of the believers' "entrance into the eternal kingdom of . . . Jesus Christ," an expression that recalls the "kingdom" theme of Jesus' preaching,[135] but with a nuance—that the kingdom belongs to Christ.[136] Peter recalls the transfiguration (1:16–19) with a reference to his own death as a "departure," using the exact word (*exodos*) Luke used for the death of Jesus as it was being discussed by Moses and Elijah.[137] Peter indicates that his own death is imminent, as "our Lord Jesus Christ has made clear to me" (1:14). With Nero on the throne and Christians "becoming increasingly unpopular," Peter no doubt "has in mind Christ's prophecy that his end would be a violent one."[138] In both letters, Peter expressed his transformation from self-confidence to Christ-confidence in Christ-language. Peter breathed the words of Jesus in his preaching.

He breathes Old Testament language the same way, "and consistently brings to it a Christian, often Christological interpretation." He cites the Old Testament at many points, but he also frequently "weaves into his argument the words of Scripture" or "alludes in passing to the biblical history generally . . . or to specific passages or stories from the Scripture."[139]

Edward Lohse has argued that, at least in 1 Peter, both the Old Testament sources and the sayings of the Lord "stand side-by-side and are adduced according to the specific needs of the moment," a method that suggests oral development of a paraenetic tradition rather than written sources lying behind the letter.[140] Further, according to Lohse, the author of 1 Peter typically supports parenesis with kerygma, that is, the author links his admonitions, directly or by allusion, to "the will and acts of God," proclaimed either from the Old Testament or from the sayings of Jesus.[141] For example, Peter exhorts believers not "to be conformed to the former lusts which were yours in your ignorance" but to be holy [*parenesis*] like the Holy One who called them, "because it is written, 'You shall be holy, for I am holy'" [*kērugma*].[142]

The same pattern recurs in 2 Peter, where, however, kerygma takes the form of judgment oracle. Peter calls his readers to holy living [*paraenesis*], for example, recognizing that "the day of the Lord will come like a thief,"[143] an explicit teaching of Jesus [*kērugma*].[144] Peter's exposé of false teachers (2:1–22) is likewise undergirded by Old Testament references and allusions.

Lohse has shown that the attempt to link 1 Peter (and, we maintain, 2 Peter as well) to specific written sources or fixed liturgical forms is highly questionable. The letters are rather compiled from oral material. We do indeed hear a voice in 1 and 2 Peter. The voice belongs to one whose life has been transformed by, and is now steeped in, the Word of God and the testimony of Jesus Christ. The voice that "preaches" these letters into existence belongs to "Simon Rock."

CHAPTER

THE INSPIRED PREACHING OF ACTS: THE FIRST THEOLOGY OF PREACHING

C. RICHARD WELLS

> *On the day of Pentecost a band of peasant evangelists faced the world with a new religion. They were furnished with neither prestige nor earthly power; they had neither a priesthood, nor temple, nor learning, nor formulated creed, nor even organization or visible leadership. They had only a Gospel and the testimony of personal experience. But their word was with power. With that weapon of fire they attacked the iron fortresses of Antiquity, Superstition, Philosophy, Skepticism, Luxury, Pride and Political Despotism, and everywhere prevailed. They confounded the wise, convinced the infidel, converted the depraved and reared the fabric of Christianity on the ruins of every false faith.*

> J. Spencer Kennard[1]

INTERPRETING ACTS HOMILETICALLY

The first "act" of the apostles was a sermon. Following the ascension and prior to Pentecost, Peter stood before the nascent church to preach on the fall of Judas Iscariot (1:15–16a). The sermon had an introduction and a conclusion, a text, application, and "points" (though no poem!). The sermon provided a biblical rationale for ecclesial organization, and as a result, the disciples cast lots to replace Judas with Matthias.

The last "act" of the apostles was also a sermon. Several days after his arrival in Rome, Paul preached to a large number of Jews. Luke records only the conclusion, but he informs us that Paul was "testifying about the kingdom of God, and trying to persuade [the Jews] concerning Jesus, from both the Law of Moses and from the Prophets, from morning until evening."[2] And

75

Acts leaves off with Paul in the Imperial City, "preaching the kingdom of God and teaching concerning the Lord Jesus Christ."[3]

Between Peter in the "upper room" and Paul in Rome, Luke records at least eighteen other (a total of twenty) evangelical speeches—eight by Peter, ten by Paul, and one each by Stephen and James—plus four non-Christian speeches.[4] In addition, Luke makes reference to more than twenty-five other preaching episodes;[5] not to mention that Paul's "missionary journeys" were simply large-scale preaching missions. Preaching is the tie that binds Acts together.

Preaching and the Story of the Acts

Scholars have often observed that we can analyze the Book of Acts from several different points of view.[6] Luke was an evangelist, writer, historian, theologian, and apologist, all in one;[7] and he was able to weave various interests and themes into a multiform but harmonious whole. So one strand of Acts tells the stories of Peter and Paul. Another strand leads to strategic cities—Jerusalem, Antioch, Athens, Corinth, Ephesus, and Rome. Yet another strand brings to light the encounter of Christ with culture. Still another displays the power of the Holy Spirit against forces of opposition without the church and within. And, of course, no one can ignore the apparent correspondence between the flow of the Acts' history and Luke's Great Commission (1:8).

We may also interpret Acts homiletically; and for that purpose, the ascension provides a key. Luke's "first account" (the Gospel of Luke) concerned "all that Jesus began to do and teach, until the day when He was taken up."[8] According to John Stott, Luke implies that in Acts he will tell how the disciples *continue* what Jesus *began to do and to teach,*[9] beginning in Jerusalem, then to all Judea and Samaria, and finally to the remotest parts of the earth, symbolized, no doubt, by the Imperial City of Rome. The outworking of that mandate is "the story of The Acts."[10] At every critical point in the story—which unfolds in four major movements—preaching plays not merely a role but the primary role.

1. The church is born. Luke begins with the nascent church in an upper room, waiting and praying (1:12–14). The first sermon readies the church for Pentecost by restoring its apostolic leadership to full complement.[11] (Not without reason does Luke say that at Pentecost Peter took his stand to preach "with the eleven."[12]) And, of course, preaching creates the New Testament church at Pentecost.

2. Christ confronts culture. Peter's sermon at Solomon's Portico[13] represents the first of several transitions effected by preaching. As a result of this sermon, the infant church grows—now to more that five thousand men. This sermon also brings the growing church into conflict with the culture—conflict that Luke traces thematically throughout Acts. Peter's defenses before the Sanhedrin,[14] together with a number of subsequent defenses, enable Luke to show that while (authentic) Christianity will always clash with culture, Christ overcomes the world through the foolishness of preaching!

3. **From Jerusalem to the world.** Stephen's sermon[15] undoubtedly represents the single most significant transition point in the Book of Acts. This one sermon affected the early church and its mission in at least four critically important ways. First, Stephen's sermon intensified the early church's conflict with culture. Like Peter's defenses, Stephen's was occasioned by a culture clash that forced the early church to face the distinction between the gospel *message* and its (Jewish) cultural trappings.[16] Both Stephen and his antagonists, however, were hellenistic Jews, suggesting that the conflict had spread. The martyrdom of Stephen indicates further that Christianity was now considered a legitimate threat. Second, Stephen's preaching incited a persecution against Christians, which in turn forced the gospel to move beyond Jerusalem, reaching eventually to Gentiles.[17] Third, Stephen's preaching played a crucial role in the conversion of Saul, the apostle to the Gentiles.[18] Fourth, Stephen's preaching brought trained rhetorical skills into the service of the gospel for the first time. This, too, as we shall see, became an issue for the early church. The preaching of Stephen thus creates the first stirrings of what will eventually become the universalization of the Christian faith and the worldwide missionary enterprise of the church.

The missionary enterprise first develops *programmatically*, then *theologically*; and again, largely through preaching. Programmatically, Philip[19] and Peter and John[20] preach in Samaria and Judea, and after his conversion, Saul begins preaching in Damascus.[21] Luke then follows Peter to the fringe of the uttermost parts,[22] where God prepares him for yet another turning-point sermon— to the household of Cornelius in Caesarea.[23] Peter's subsequent sermon in Jerusalem quells opposition to this revolutionary new direction and furnishes the beginnings of a missionary theology.[24] Finally, sermons by Peter and James before the Jerusalem council help prepare the church to establish theological and methodological parameters for the missionary enterprise.[25]

4. **Preaching as "systematic" theology.** Immediately after his conversion, Saul began to preach Jesus to the Jews, first in Damascus then in Jerusalem.[26] "As one learned in the Law," says Chrysostom, "he stopped their mouths. . . . They thought they were rid of disputation in such matters, in getting rid of Stephen, and they found another, more vehement than Stephen."[27] Paul was already a theologian when he met Christ. Now he was a theologian on fire. As we shall see in chapter 8, Paul's sermons are case studies in proclaimed theology. Whether to Jews in Antioch Pisidia, pagans in Lystra, or philosophers on Areopagus, Paul proves the maxim of Karl Barth that "theology . . . ought to be nothing other than sermon preparation."[28]

Paul not only *proclaimed theology*; he also entered the Christian faith with a ready-made *theology for proclamation*, the outline of which he later set forth in Romans: The gospel "is the power of God for salvation . . . to the Jew first and also to the Greek."[29] As Luke tells the history, Peter's preaching seems episodic, occasional, almost serendipitous. Paul's preaching, by contrast, is *systematic*—with planned preaching journeys, criteria for selecting sites, and a methodology for preaching ministry.[30] It is no coincidence that the extension of the gospel to "the remotest part of the earth" coincides with the preaching ministry of the church's first systematic theologian.

Types of Sermons in Acts

Even from such a brief survey, it is clear that, for Luke, preaching is dynamic not static, catalytic not inert. When preachers preach, things happen. But, we may ask, "what things?" Our best answer to that question is that the sermons in Acts fall into three more or less discreet categories. These categories not only enable us better to understand the first preaching and the first preachers; they also help fill in Luke's theology of preaching.

The paraenetic sermons. Five of the twenty sermons in Acts are preached *to believers* for purposes of encouragement, edification, and/or instruction. These sermons are critical to the building up of the body of Christ, and Luke's accounts indicate the importance he attached to this function of preaching.

Luke records only one *paraenetic* sermon by Paul, to the Ephesian elders at Miletus (20:18b–35), though Luke often casts the apostle in the role of exhorter.[31] In any case, Paul's sermon to the elders is extremely important in its own right as a virtual pastoral theology.[32] In recording only one such sermon, Luke may only be reflecting Paul's own sense of calling for missionary work over settled ministry.[33]

By contrast, three of Peter's sermons are paraenetic: (1) in the upper room;[34] (2) before Jewish believers in Jerusalem;[35] and (3) to the Jerusalem council.[36] These sermons highlight Peter's role as a shepherd of the flock, a theme which Luke develops through much of the first half of Acts. In "every case," writes Oscar Cullmann, "[Peter] presides over the believers."[37] He is not only the most visible figure, he takes the lead in "binding and loosing,"[38] as when he exercises discipline in the case of Ananias and Sapphira,[39] lays hands on believers in Samaria,[40] or rebukes Simon Magnus.[41] Luke's portrayal accords well with Jesus' commission to "tend My sheep,"[42] and foreshadows Peter's own self-identification: "I exhort the elders among you, as your fellow elder . . . shepherd the flock of God."[43]

James preaches the only other paraenetic sermon, before the Jerusalem council.[44] As "Bishop of Jerusalem"—so-called by later writers—James "sums up the whole debate of the Council" and "proposes the decree" which sets a new course for the church.[45]

Missionary sermons. Seven of the sermons have evangelization as their primary purpose, including three by Peter: (1) At Pentecost (2:14b–39);

(2) in Solomon's Portico (3:12b–26); and (3) before the household of Cornelius (10:34b–43). Peter is the "first preacher" at Pentecost, and the "first missionary" at Caesarea. We hear echoes from the Gospels in these sermons, particularly the prophecy of Jesus (recorded only by Luke) that Simon would "be catching men."[46] Luke portrays Peter in the role of evangelist through his account of the apostle's travels to Samaria (8:14, 25), Lydda (9:32–35), and Joppa (9:36–43), his preaching to the household of Cornelius, and through the sermons of both Peter[47] and James[48] before the Jerusalem council. As Chrysostom puts it, by the mouth of Peter, "the door of faith opened thenceforth to the Gentiles."[49]

But Paul is the missionary preacher *par excellence*—preaching to Jews in Damascus (9:20, 22) and Jerusalem (9:28–29) immediately after his conversion, and from there to Cyprus (13:5), Iconium (14:1), Thessalonica (17:2–3), Corinth (18:4), Ephesus (19:8), and Rome (28:30–31). Luke records four missionary sermons of Paul: (1) At the synagogue in Pisidian Antioch (13:16b–41); (2) before the pagans in Lystra (14:15–17); (3) at the Areopagus in Athens (17:22b–31); and (4) before Jews in Rome (28:24–28).

Luke's record calls special attention to Paul's practice of preaching to "the Jew first and (only) then to the Greek."[50] We may therefore regard Paul's first recorded sermon—at the synagogue in Pisidian Antioch—as a case study both in Paul's missionary *method* and his *message*. At Antioch, as elsewhere, Paul goes to "the Jew first," and he preaches what he preaches everywhere—"the Good News of the promise made to the fathers, that God has fulfilled this promise . . . in that He raised up Jesus" (13:32b–33a). Not surprisingly, we hear in Paul's letters many echoes of the sermons in Acts, which indicates that Luke faithfully represented Paul's theology of mission. Paul's "custom" had its roots in a theological conviction that "the gospel . . . is the power of God for salvation . . . to the Jew first and also to the Greek."[51]

Apologetic sermons. Surprisingly, almost half of the sermons in Acts are *apologetic*,[52] and others have apologetic elements. Peter's two speeches before the Sanhedrin[53] are defenses, of course, but his sermons to the disputants in Jerusalem[54] and at Pentecost also have the flavor of *apologia*. Stephen's sermon, the longest in Acts (7:2b–53), is a defense.[55] The bulk of Paul's preaching consists in five apologetic sermons: (1) Before a hostile crowd in Jerusalem;[56] (2) before the Sanhedrin in Jerusalem;[57] (3) before Felix in Caesarea;[58] (4) before Herod Agrippa in Caesarea;[59] and (5) before Jews in Rome.[60] The Mars' Hill sermon is in part *apologia* as well.

From the "preaching as defense" motif we may suggest at least four qualities Luke ascribed to preaching.

First, preaching is *witness*. True preaching can never be separated from the person of the preacher. Thus, when commanded "not to speak or teach at all" in Jesus' name, Peter and John reply that their witness will not, *cannot*, be silenced.[61]

Second, preaching is a *bridge* between theology and culture. The Christian faith is inherently countercultural, and yet the gospel is for all. Preachers must face squarely the inevitable oppositions of culture and take "every thought captive to the obedience of Christ."[62] Paul's defense before the mob in Jerusalem[63] is a good example. Accused of attacking cherished traditions,[64] Paul counters that his zeal for God—which was comparable to their own!—has found its true home in Jesus.

Third, preaching has *power*. As we shall see, Luke takes pains to document certain effects of preaching, as when the Sadduccees are disturbed by Peter's preaching of Jesus and the resurrection, then silent before Peter's defense.[65]

Fourth, preaching is the *God-approved means* for effecting real change. At several critical points, Luke juxtaposes Christian preaching with non-Christian speeches to highlight the qualitative difference between them. In Ephesus, for example, Paul's preaching results in miracles, large-scale conversions, and the beginnings of social change.[66] In response (and blind to the potential of a city turned right side up), Demetrius delivers what amounts to a political speech,[67] the effect of which is a near riot, to be quelled by yet another political speech, from the city clerk.[68] Politics may effect temporal change. Preaching effects both temporal and eternal change.

Species of rhetoric. The three categories of speeches in Acts correspond roughly to the three "species" of classical rhetoric. The *paraenetic* sermons resemble *deliberative* rhetoric, the purpose of which is either to exhort or to dissuade. Deliberative rhetoric concerns the "useful," that is, what will bring about a desirable (or undesirable) state of affairs. Deliberative rhetoric, therefore, always points to the *future*. The speeches of Gamaliel (though in a judicial context), Demetrius, and the Ephesus city clerk are more or less pure examples of deliberative rhetoric.

The *missionary* sermons are analogous to *epideictic* rhetoric, which has to do with "praise and blame" and therefore, with whether a person is due "honor" (or "dishonor") in the *present*. The early preachers, of course, proclaim Jesus as worthy, not merely of honor, but of worship.

The *apologetic* sermons correspond to *judicial* rhetoric. (The speech of Tertullus is also judicial.) As the name implies, judicial rhetoric belongs to the law court, as concerning right or wrong actions in the *past*.[69]

While each sermon exhibits dominant features of one of the classical species, each also combines elements of the other two species. To use modern jargon, the sermons in Acts are more holistic than classical oratory. Paul's speech before Agrippa[70] will illustrate. It classifies as *judicial* rhetoric because Paul is defending his actions. But Paul quickly makes the resurrected Jesus the real point of issue (*epideictic* rhetoric), and weaves that theme through his message. He closes with an appeal to Agrippa and "all who hear me this day"[71] to become as he is (*deliberative* rhetoric).

LUKE'S BREVIARY OF PREACHING

Luke's Four Theses

If Paul was the first preaching theologian, Luke is the first theologian of preaching. Luke's argument in Acts, as we have seen, is that what Jesus "began to do and teach" before the ascension, he continues to do now by the Spirit, through the church, in the world,[72] *primarily and strategically through preaching*. We do not overstate the case to say that Acts is a theology-of-preaching-in-brief, a "breviary," if you will, which we may summarize in five theses.

1. **Preaching creates the church.** First, Luke shows that preaching *creates the church*. Peter's preaching on the day of Pentecost is only the beginning. Even persecution resulted in more preaching and more churches.[73] Under the preaching of Paul, churches are born in Lystra, Pisidian Antioch, Iconium, Lystra, Derbe, Philippi, Thessalonica, Berea, Corinth, Ephesus, and (in all probability) in Damascus, Cilicia, Cyprus, Perga, Phyrgia, and elsewhere, not to mention churches born when Barnabas and John Mark preach in Cyprus.[74] Then there is Philip in Samaria, Azotus, and along the coast to Caesarea,[75] later Peter and John as well in "many villages of the Samaritans."[76] No preaching, no church.

2. **Preaching establishes and strengthens the church.**[77] Second, Luke shows that preaching *enables the church to fulfill its calling*, to become what, through the grace of God, she already is.[78] Preaching is the appointed means for guiding, shaping, establishing, strengthening, and building the body of Christ in conformity to the Word of God. In his upper room sermon, for example, Peter not only explained the fall of Judas, but he also gave the church-about-to-be-born a biblical rationale for its leadership structure. Of course, Paul routinely encouraged the churches he founded through preaching,[79] and his sermon at Miletus (as we shall see) is a virtual pastoral theology,[80] calling the elders to counter false preaching by truth, lest the flock should suffer harm.

3. **Preaching interprets the present reality in terms of biblical reality.** Luke considers preaching a means by which *biblical reality interprets present reality.* Ian Pitt-Watson is well known for his "two texts" of preaching, "the text of Scripture" and "the text of life," whereby "the great conceptual truths of the Christian faith are pictured and storied in the commonplace of human experience."[81] The Acts sermons, like the parables of Jesus, do indeed "picture" and "story" biblical truth "in the commonplace of human life," as when Paul uses "rain" to explain the goodness of God the Creator to pagans (14:14–17).

Just as often, however, the preachers of Acts work in reverse, reading every condition and culture through the lens of biblical revelation. Peter's upper room sermon explains the demise of Judas. His Pentecost sermon explains the phenomena of tongues. Paul explains the religiosity of Athens in terms of inchoate human longings for the "unknown God." The preachers of Acts not only use human experience to illustrate biblical truth and gain a hearing; they employ biblical truth to demythologize human experience and gain a soul.

4. The gospel is the heart of preaching. For Luke, *the heart of all preaching is the Good News of Jesus Christ.* In his groundbreaking work, *The Apostolic Preaching and Its Development*, C. H. Dodd argued that the speeches in Acts "afford a comprehensive view of the content of the early *kerygma*." By *kerygma*, Dodd meant the *message*, the theological parameters of the (so-called) "primitive preaching."[82] Even though not every sermon contains every point of the *kerygma*, Dodd argued, every sermon contains some points, and each follows a similar pattern of presentation. (Dodd discerned the same pattern throughout the New Testament.)

According to Dodd, the ancient *kerygma* consisted in six affirmations.[83] First, "the age of fulfillment has dawned." What the prophets had promised has now come to pass in human history. Thus Peter at Pentecost: "This is what was spoken through the prophet Joel."[84]

Second, this fulfillment has taken place through the ministry, death, and resurrection of Jesus, the Son of David. When invited to say "a word of exhortation" at the synagogue in Pisidian Antioch, Paul recounts the history of Israel up to King David in order to declare that "from the offspring of this man, according to promise, God has brought to Israel a Savior, Jesus." He then recounts the ministry of Jesus from the annunciation of John the Baptist to his resurrection "on the third day."[85]

Third, by virtue of the resurrection, Jesus is now exalted at the right hand of God. This is a major emphasis of Peter's second Sanhedrin defense: "We must obey God" who "raised up Jesus . . . the one whom God exalted."[86]

Fourth, the coming of the Holy Spirit is the sign of Christ's present power and glory. Peter's Pentecost sermon is virtually an exposition of this theme. The new age has dawned in Jesus, who "having been exalted to the right hand of God, and having received from the Father the promise of the Holy Spirit, He [Jesus] has poured forth this which you both see and hear."[87]

Fifth, the messianic age will soon reach its consummation in the return of Christ. This idea is often expressed indirectly, as when Peter refers to Jesus as the "Judge of the living and the dead" at Caesarea.[88]

Finally, according to Dodd, "The *kerygma* always closes with an appeal for repentance, the offer of forgiveness and the Holy Spirit, and the promise of 'salvation,' that is, of 'the life of the Age to Come.'"[89] At Pentecost, "Repent, and let each of you be baptized in the name of Jesus Christ for the forgiveness of your sins; and you shall receive the gift of the Holy Spirit."[90] At Solomon's Porch, "Therefore repent and return, so that your sins may be wiped away, in order that times of refreshing may come from the presence of the Lord."[91] In the synagogue at Pisidian Antioch, "let it be known to you, brethren, that through [Jesus] forgiveness of sin is proclaimed to you."[92] And even on Areopagus, Paul declares, "Therefore having overlooked the times of ignorance, God is now declaring to men that all people everywhere should repent, because He has fixed a day in which He will judge the world in righteousness through a Man whom He has appointed, having furnished proof to all men by raising Him from the dead" (17:30–31).

"Preaching the Kingdom": Luke's Theology of Preaching in a Phrase

The earliest preaching, Dodd argued, "follows the lines of the summary of the preaching of Jesus as given in Mark 1:14–15; 'Jesus came into Galilee, preaching the gospel of God, and saying, "The time is fulfilled, and the kingdom of God is at hand; repent and believe in the gospel."'"[93] In other words, the Acts *kerygma* is contained within the three main points of Jesus' preaching: (1) the prophetic promises have now come to *fulfillment*; (2) this new age of fulfillment is nothing other than the "*kingdom of God;*" and (3) the appropriate response to kingdom preaching is *repentance.*

The apostles elaborate each of those themes—*fulfillment, kingdom, repentance*—in their preaching, but they pay special attention to the kingdom of God. This kingdom, as we saw in chapter 4, is the rule of God, bringing the powers (and the blessings) of the "Age to Come" into this present age.[94] In preaching the kingdom the earliest preachers stood, as it were, in an unbroken line of homiletical tradition. The prophets had proclaimed the kingdom of God as a hope, looking forward to the day when God would set His anointed "on the throne of David and over his kingdom, to establish it and to uphold it with justice and righteousness from then on and forevermore."[95] Jesus announced the kingdom, brought the kingdom through his ministry, death, resurrection, and exaltation, and then, according to Luke, Jesus prepared his disciples for preaching by teaching them "the things concerning the kingdom of God."[96] It is no accident, therefore, that as Acts draws to a close, Luke has Paul "preaching the kingdom of God" in Rome.[97] The "kingdom of God" captures Luke's theology of preaching in a phrase.

The earliest preaching was Christ-centered, but in a special way. Sidney Greidanus rightly says that true preaching must always be "Christocentric." But Greidanus also rightly warns that preaching does not magically become Christocentric simply because the sermon "somehow" makes "reference to Jesus of Nazareth."[98] Sermons can be "Jesucentric," Greidanus concludes, without being "Christocentric," when they ignore the fact that the kingdom constitutes "the central message of Jesus."[99]

TOWARD A THEOLOGY OF RHETORIC

"Witness"—The Other Side of Kerygma

Valuable as it has proved to be, Dodd's *Apostolic Preaching* missed something vitally important about the early preaching, indeed, about preaching as such. What he missed we can demonstrate from Paul's famous one-line theology of preaching: "God was well-pleased through the foolishness of the message preached to save those who believe."[100] The English language requires two words, "message" and "preached," to express the pregnant Greek word which lies at the heart of that theology (and of Dodd's thesis)— the word *kērugma*. For the ancients, a *kērugma* was a *message*, an inviolable message, entrusted to a "herald" (*kērux*) for "heralding" (*kērussō*); in short, a "message . . . heralded." In Christian terms, *kērugma* integrates *theology* and *rhetoric*. On the one hand, it is a message, a word, a truth, sacred and inviolable. On the other hand, it is an act of communication, of proclamation, of persuasion. Dodd did the "theology" side of the *kerygma*, but he left the "rhetoric" side undone.

To be fair, Dodd did not leave rhetoric entirely undone. The earliest preachers regarded themselves primarily as "witnesses who were chosen beforehand by God" (10:41), not wordsmiths. The very consistency of the kerygma suggests that like the ancient *kērux*, the earliest preachers felt themselves constrained by the gospel message. As witnesses,[101] they had no creative license—rather, a sober responsibility to proclaim what they had seen and heard.[102] As Paul reminded the Thessalonians, "Our exhortation does not come from error or impurity or by way of deceit; but just as we have been approved by God to be entrusted with the gospel, so we speak."[103]

And yet, as witnesses, the apostles did *not* testify only to bare facts—as in, "Yes, I saw the defendant running from the house just as I pulled into my driveway at midnight." They testified also to the *significance* of the facts—as when Paul dares to tell the Areopagites that the resurrected Christ is the answer to their soul's question.

It is here that we begin to discern the outline of another dimension to Luke's theology of preaching in Acts; namely, a theology of communication, a "spiritual rhetoric," if you will, an understanding not only of *what* the disciples preached, but *how they preached it*; not only of the kerygma as a "*message* preached," but a "message *preached*." The early preachers felt themselves constrained by the "facts" of the gospel, but they also felt themselves constrained to "persuade men,"[104] about its "significance." For Luke, true preaching combines *theology* and *rhetoric*.

Toward a "Spiritual Rhetoric"

Luke makes it clear that the early preachers did not simply intone the bare facts of the gospel without regard to culture or context. At Pentecost, for example, Peter answers a charge of public drunkenness; and his answer segues into a message about the fulfillment of prophetic hopes. Stephen charges his accusers with complicity in killing the prophets, a massive calculated risk, sure to evoke a response. In Caesarea, Peter confesses his bigotry, not in order to win friends, but to correct a possible misconception. Before the Sanhedrin, Paul takes advantage of known antagonisms between Sadducees and the other Pharisees to focus attention on the theological heart of the gospel. Luke furnishes example after example in Acts that the earliest preachers use rhetorical means to connect with their hearers. To say they preached the kerygma does not imply that their sermons all sounded alike, that they ignored context, paid no attention to the audience, or settled for orthodox dullness. Quite the contrary.

In the following two chapters, we want to see how the earliest preachers "connected" with their hearers. In the process, we hope to discern the outline of Luke's theology of communication; or better to say, his theological or "spiritual" rhetoric. Before turning to those sermons, however, we must frankly face two questions, the answers to which will largely confirm or inform the hypothesis of such a rhetoric in Acts.

1. Are the sermons really sermons? We must deal first with the fact that the sermons as we have them are clearly not verbatim transcripts. They are uniformly brief,[105] and we have every reason to believe that in every case the preacher preached much longer. Luke says as much about Peter's Pentecost sermon: "And with *many other words* he solemnly testified and kept on exhorting them."[106] Nor can we forget that in Troas, Eutychus fell asleep as Paul "prolonged his message until midnight."[107] Anyone might be forgiven for asking whether the "sermons" of Acts qualify as sermons at all.

Many modern scholars, regarding the sermons as little more than pious fabrications intended to serve narrow theological interests, would answer in the negative.[108] Luke observed the literary conventions of his day, the argument goes, according to which an author would re-create (or, create) a speech, imagining what such and such speaker might say on such and such an occasion. Is that what Luke did in *Acts*?

Clearly not. In the first place, contrary to some scholarly opinion, most ancient writers did *not* simply invent speeches. Rather, they reconstructed as best they could what a speaker actually said, *summarizing* (on the basis of available knowledge), but not *inventing*.[109] In the second place, we must take seriously Luke's claim to be a thorough and careful historian.[110] There is no doubt, Sir William Ramsey declared, that Luke "claims to state throughout what is perfectly trustworthy."[111] "Luke is a real historian," he concluded, "and the first and the essential quality of the great historian is truth."[112] So we must allow that, however abbreviated, the speeches of Acts faithfully represent the speeches as delivered.

We should consider the speeches in Acts, therefore, as sermons in summary. Luke has handed down to us synopses of actual sermons which preserve both the form and substance of what the preachers actually preached,[113] and which, in turn, Luke sets accurately in context. Brief though they be, they serve as reliable guides to the "rhetoric" of Peter, Paul, Stephen, and James.

2. Did Luke care about rhetoric? Should we regard the sermons merely as *illustrative*, or also (in some sense at least) as *normative*? Do they lay the foundation for an authentically Christian rhetoric, or only drop hints about the "preaching styles" of the disciples, if anything? To the degree we can detect rhetorical emphases in the sermons, are they *descriptive* or *prescriptive*? A fuller answer to this question must await our study of the speeches themselves; but even at this preliminary stage, four observations are in order.

First, Luke presupposed that *the early preachers preached by the power of the Spirit*. That fact might seem to foreclose on the use of rhetorical strategies. Does not the empowerment of the Spirit render all human means equally effective (or equally superfluous)? To be sure, much of the preaching in Acts is impromptu (and presumably unpremeditated). Of what value would rhetorical strategies be under those conditions? In addition, did not Jesus tell his disciples to take no thought when hailed before authorities, since he himself would give them "utterance"?[114] But "the power of the Spirit" surely applies to *means* as well as *ends*. The Spirit not only effects supernatural results of preaching and hearing, but also gives the preacher the "ability in each case," as Aristotle defined *rhetoric*,[115] "to see the available *means of persuasion*." We need only recall here Paul's asking the Colossians to pray "in order that I may make it clear in the way I ought to speak" (Col. 4:4), where "it" is the "mystery of Christ" (4:3). The context suggests the "removal of all internal impediments to preaching."[116]

A second observation: Luke's record leaves no doubt that the early preachers *intentionally used means of persuasion* (*rhetorical strategies*). No less than five times, for example, Luke explicitly states that Paul "reasoned" in the synagogues and elsewhere, "trying to persuade Jews and Greeks."[117] This, even though Paul vigorously rejected the sophistical rhetoric so popular in first-century Greek culture.[118] As we will see, not only Paul but all the preachers of Acts were keenly attuned to context—audience, setting, purpose, and the like—and tailored their messages accordingly.

Third, Luke is at pains to demonstrate certain *"persuasive" effects of preaching*. Interestingly, Luke analyzes these effects most thoroughly in those cases where the audience is unsympathetic. Following the mission to Cornelius, for example, Peter faces Jews in Jerusalem who "took issue with him" because (they said) "You went to uncircumcised men and ate with them."[119] As we shall see in the next chapter, Peter crafts his defense in order to put the ball in the court of the naysayers: "If God gave therefore to them the same gift as He gave to us . . . who was I that I could stand in God's way?" The conclusion is foregone: "When they heard this, they quieted down, and glorified God, saying, 'Well then, God has granted to the Gentiles also the repentance that leads to life.'"[120]

Fourth, while Luke does not unpack the dynamics of homiletical "effects" systematically, he clearly indicates that *transformed character is the preacher's most powerful rhetorical resource*. When Paul reminds the Thessalonians that his life authenticated his message,[121] he illustrates a theme that Luke weaves through the Acts. The early preachers did not always "persuade," in the classical oratorical sense; but they always had impact.

We shall return to the concept of "spiritual rhetoric" in the final chapter, and in the following two chapters, we will trace the concept through the Acts sermons. For now we need only to say that the early preachers were concerned, as all "communicators" are concerned, with being heard and understood. But Luke also took for granted the filling of the Spirit in the preaching of the first preachers; and he seems to have presupposed a kind of synergy of Holy Spirit and human means. The result was dynamic, as in the case of those who heard Stephen preach: "They were unable to cope with the wisdom and the Spirit with which he was speaking."[122] Rejected, maybe; never ignored.

FOUR NOTES ON METHOD

Before turning to the Acts sermons, we should explain our methodology. First, because "rhetoric" always follows "context,"[123] we will adopt Luke's homiletical order in Acts. We have already seen that Luke uses sermons strategically to unfold the story of the church in four "movements": (1) establishing the church; (2) engaging the culture; (3) clarifying the missionary calling of the church; and (4) preaching as systematic theology. We will utilize these rubrics to analyze the speeches in Acts.

Second, since our focus is on *rhetoric*, we will not examine the sermons in detail theologically. (For that see chapters 5 and 9, and the commentaries.)

Third, in this chapter and the next, we will rely heavily on Chrysostom, the fabled preacher of Constantinople, who delivered a series of homilies on Acts in the late fourth century. The reason is simple. Chrysostom studied classical rhetoric under the far-famed Libanios of Antioch.[124] With his professional eye, he adds fresh insight to our understanding of the underlying "orality" of Acts.

Fourth, while the sermons of Peter and Paul constitute the bulk of the Acts sermons, we will also treat the sermons of Stephen and James (and even the non-Christian speeches), but in the context of Paul and Peter. As we will see, these connections follow naturally from Luke's own method.

CHAPTER

THE INSPIRED PREACHING OF PETER IN ACTS

C. RICHARD WELLS

"A damsel," it is written, "came out unto him, saying, 'Thou also wast with Jesus of Nazareth.'" And, says he, "I knew not the Man." And being again questioned, "he began to curse and swear." But see here his boldness, and his great freedom of speech.

CHRYSOSTOM

THE ACTS OF THE APOSTLES, 5[1]

WINSOME CREDIBILITY

Have you ever read a letter from a friend and thought to yourself, "That sounds just like him"? You mean of course that his personality is stamped on his writing. Just so, we hear the voice of Peter through the eight sermons attributed to him in Acts.[2] Luke has stamped Peter's personality on these sermons. They "sound just like him."

Despite their brevity, Luke's sermon records give us a surprisingly complete picture of Peter as a communicator of God's Word. Or, perhaps, *because of* their brevity! While we might wish for a video of Peter preaching, Luke more or less forces us to pay attention to what matters most—not body language, voice inflections, gesticulation, and the rest of what passes for "preaching style," but Peter's "homiletical character," what Aristotle would have called his *ethos*.

As we have seen, C. H. Dodd traced a *theological* pattern through the sermons of Peter in Acts;[3] but we can discern a *rhetorical* pattern as well. Luke has Peter preaching to believers and nonbelievers, to hostile audiences, curious audiences, excited audiences, and expectant audiences, to Jews, and to Gentiles. He preaches for salvation, for edification, and in defense of the faith. But in all of these preaching contexts, Peter preaches as a

Christ-actualized personality. His *character* (*ethos*) adorns the gospel[4] with winsome credibility. We have said that Luke tells the "story of Acts" in "four movements." Peter's sermons figure most prominently in the first three of these movements: (1) establishing the church; (2) engaging the culture; and (3) clarifying the missionary calling of the church. In keeping with his portrayal in the Gospels, Peter leads the way in each movement *through his preaching*.

INSPIRED PREACHING AND THE BIRTH OF THE CHURCH

The First "Act" of the Apostles:
Peter's Sermon in the Upper Room (1:16–22)

About a month has passed since the disciples gathered for Passover in an upper room, where Peter had led the others in swearing fealty to Jesus.[5] Peter failed ignominiously, as we know; but in that very Passover night, Jesus had prophesied Peter's restoration, adding, "When once you have turned again, strengthen your brothers."[6] Peter has now "turned again." He is finally "Simon Rock"[7]; and his first recorded act, the first "act" of the apostles, is a *sermon*—to strengthen the brothers and sisters.

The setting was unlike any other in kingdom history. The Messiah had come, as the prophets foretold but in such a strange fashion that many, even his closest followers, could scarcely understand. He served, and suffered, and died, and he rose again. He commissioned his disciples for their mission and promised to empower them by the Spirit. Then he left! For the moment, the disciples could only wait for "what the Father had promised."[8] At this point, said John Calvin, the ascension had all "the appearance of contradiction."[9] How much sense does it make that the Messiah would accomplish his kingdom purposes by *leaving*?[10] Yet he did just that and in fact told his disciples so beforehand.[11]

One can easily imagine that the ten days from ascension to Pentecost would give rise to wondering, if not distress.[12] Such is the context for Peter's first sermon: Peter has been (a) restored and commissioned (b) to strengthen the disciples during the ambiguous days of waiting after the ascension.

The rhetoric of the sermon shows that Peter understood the situation well. He begins with a two-part *proem* that connects him with the context: "Brethren, the Scripture had to be fulfilled, which the Holy Spirit foretold by the mouth of David concerning Judas . . ."[13] The vocative "brothers"[14] (the first New Testament use of the term for "Christians")[15] shows that Peter intentionally identifies himself with the community of the believers. In the second part of the *proem*, as Chrysostom says, the apostle comforts the disciples by an appeal to "the prophecies."[16] Perhaps some were troubled by the fall of a *chosen* disciple. Perhaps some worried about a leadership vacuum. Whatever unease they may have felt, Peter "shows . . . that no strange thing had happened, but what had already been foretold."[17] God was not surprised by Judas!

The sermon is structured around two different Greek words for "must." The first (Gk. *edei*) appears in the *proem* and expresses a *moral* or *divine* necessity—"the Scripture *had to be* [*edei*] fulfilled" (v. 16). The second (Gk. *dei*) appears in the proposition and expresses *logical* necessity—"it is therefore necessary [*dei*]" to replace Judas (v. 21). In the *proem*, therefore, Peter *interprets the present situation;* but in the body of the sermon, he *draws out logical implications.*[18] In short, Peter employs Scripture, first to comfort, then to guide, the nascent church.

Because he uses Scripture to guide, Peter allows the church to assume responsibility for responding. Chrysostom again: Peter did not simply "appoint" a replacement for Judas, lest he appear to dispense ecclesial office as a "favor." Rather "he . . . introduced the proposition to that effect, at the same time pointing out that even this was not his own, but for all time by prophecy; so he acted as expositor, not as preceptor."[19] Peter proclaims a biblical mandate, but the "brothers" must act on it.

"This Is As That": Peter's Sermon at Pentecost (2:14b–36)

Taking Peter seriously. Other than the Sermon on the Mount, no sermon ever preached has attracted more attention than Peter's message at Pentecost. The reasons are not hard to see. For many Catholics, the sermon virtually installs Peter as the papal "Rock" upon which Christ built his church. For others, the sermon provides a proof text[20] for baptismal regeneration. For many in all traditions, including most evangelicals, the Pentecost sermon marks the birth of the church.[21] Most critical scholars consider the sermon a test case for rhetorical, source, and form-critical analysis. (This even though many of these scholars regard the Acts speeches as little more than pious fabrications.) Almost everyone is drawn to Peter's preachment at Pentecost.

Yet the Preacher of Pentecost himself is conspicuously absent from many of these discussions. New Testament scholar John Kilgallen writes, for example, about the "problem" of Acts 2:33, where the resurrected Jesus is said to have "poured forth this which you both see and hear." Like most scholars, Kilgallen assumes that, using literary sources, *Luke* put these words in Peter's mouth for theological reasons. The "problem of Acts 2:33" is thus a *literary* problem; to wit, since the statement occurs in the context of Luke's argument that Jesus is "Lord,"[22] it seems to be a digression, or even a "distraction." Kilgallen thinks the saying *could* have been formulated as an answer to the wonderment of the Jews at Pentecost (2:12); but if so, why did Luke place it here rather than at the *beginning* of the sermon?[23] Kilgallen answers that the

"Lucan style" is to "explain the present moment . . . by virtue of a rehearsal of past deeds prophetically understood."[24]

The "problem" vanishes, however, if we define the problem *rhetorically* and take Peter seriously. Peter's habit, as we shall see, is to hold off on more difficult or potentially offensive matters until he has prepared his audience to hear them.[25]

Pentecost in context. Luke takes pains to help us visualize Peter's audience, whose wonderment he pictures in three different ways. At first, they "were bewildered" at hearing their "own language" (2:6). Then they "were amazed and marveled" that the preachers were Galileans (2:7). Finally, hearing "the mighty deeds of God," they "all continued in amazement and great perplexity" (2:12). Note that the audience was prepared for Peter's sermon *by preaching* (vv. 4, 6–8, 11) that perplexed them completely—the *message*, the *messenger*, and the *method!* No wonder they ask, "What does this mean?" (2:12).[26] While all marveled, some, looking for a simple explanation, were "mocking," Luke says, accusing the disciples of public drunkenness (2:13).

Chrysostom carefully analyzed Peter's strategy for preaching in this highly charged and severely conflicted atmosphere. While he did not enumerate them systematically, Chrysostom returned time and again to four rhetorical keys to the apostle's preaching. First, Peter preached communally—he took "his stand with the eleven" (2:14a). The apostles "expressed themselves through one common voice, and [Peter] was the mouth of them all."[27] Luke does not elaborate further; but the remark suggests mutual support, theological agreement, and perhaps accountability, and may point, in fact, to a corporate "composition" of the earliest preaching.[28]

Second, Peter managed to "connect" with both factions in the crowd at a personal, emotional level. First, Peter wins the ear of the majority, who "accounted it a high encomium to dwell in Jerusalem," by addressing them as "men of Judea, and all you who live in Jerusalem" (2:14). Next he soothed the scoffers with a "soft answer."[29] Significantly, Peter made no attempt to answer the charge specifically. He dignified *them*, but not their accusation. "Hence we learn," says Chrysostom, "that on unessential points one must not spend many words."[30]

Third, Peter relies on Scripture throughout to make his case. He begins by taking "refuge with the prophet [Joel]."[31] The prophecy contains both grace and "something terrible," says Chrysostom, both the ineffable blessings and the unspeakable terrors of "the last days."[32] By using this text in his introduction, Peter prepares his hearers for repentance. And by using Scripture as the connecting link with his hearers throughout the sermon, Peter is able to lead them sequentially from their experience of perplexity (2:12, 14–15), to an understanding of that experience (2:22–31), then to the truth that Jesus is the Messiah (2:32–36), and finally, to "a horrified realization of their culpable participation in the killing of the Messiah (2:37)."[33]

Scripture enables Peter to argue a difficult case and yet stay connected with his hearers. For example, Peter calls King David (revered by all) as a witness to the Messiah.[34] Because David "was a prophet," he himself looked forward to the fulfillment of God's promise of an everlasting throne (2:30)[35] in "the resurrection of the Christ" (2:31);[36] and he acknowledged the Messiah as Lord (2:34–35).[37] Knowing that the Scriptures would be accepted by all, Peter had only to apply them at critical points to Jesus: (1) the "signs and wonders" of Jesus fulfill the prophecy of Joel and prove that God sent him (2:22);[38] (2) the resurrection of Jesus fulfills the prophecy of David's everlasting kingship (2:32); and (3) the exaltation of Jesus fulfills David's prophecy that the Messiah is Lord (2:36). The rhetorical effects were powerful. Through the prophet Joel, Chrysostom observes, Peter offered his hearers "excellent hopes if they would have them;"[39] and by "his reverential expression towards the blessed David, he awed them."[40]

Fourth, Chrysostom detects a rhetorical pattern in Peter's preaching that we might characterize as "lower to higher," combined with cycles of "soft to hard to soft." By "lower to higher,"[41] we mean that Peter typically began with the familiar, the easily understood, the readily accepted, and progressed to the unfamiliar, the uncomfortable, the more difficult: "Setting out from facts notorious . . . [Peter] then comes to the things hidden."[42] By "soft-hard," we mean alternating extremes of confrontation and comfort—as from "soothing" to "shocking." We can trace both strategies through the sermon.

For example, since "the name of Jesus would have given offence,"[43] Peter does not speak at first "of the things relating to Christ," but only *explains the Pentecost experience.* Only gradually does Peter introduce Jesus—initially saying only that "Jesus the Nazarene" (2:22a) was "attested . . . by God" (2:22b), later asserting that "God raised Him" (but without mentioning Jesus' name or calling him "Messiah," 2:24), then tying Psalm 16 to "the resurrection of the Christ" (but without mentioning the name "Jesus," 2:31), then, at last, identifying "Jesus" with "the Christ" whom God raised (2:32).

Only then does Peter progress to the ascension/exaltation, but, again, without mentioning the name Jesus—having "been exalted to the right hand of . . . the Father . . . He has poured forth" the Spirit of Pentecost (2:33). Finally, at long last, after the David prophecy of Psalm 110:1, Peter declares *for the first time* that Jesus is both Lord and Messiah (2:36)!

Peter's "low to high" rhetoric addresses difficulties inherent in the *message* itself. "Soft-hard" rhetoric, on the other hand, has to do with the *hearers;* and Peter employs it from the very beginning. His *proem* takes the form of the familiar rabbinical *pesher* ("this is that") interpretation of Joel, to the effect that the events of Pentecost were harbingers of the "last days!"[44] In citing the text of Joel, Peter alternates between large-hearted, nonconfrontational ("soft") rhetoric (2:17–18) and a full frontal ("hard" rhetoric) assault of eschatological crisis (2:19–20) before returning to the ("soft" rhetoric) promise of salvation (2:21). In short, the *proem* of Peter first soothes ("soft"), then shocks ("hard"), then soothes ("soft") again. First he sets at ease, then sets on edge, and sets again at ease.

The cycle recurs throughout the sermon. At two critical points, for example, Peter renews his introductory vocative. Of the first (2:22), Chrysostom says, "As [Peter] has borne hard on them [with the Joel prophecy], he relaxes a little . . . that they may not become excited, now that he is going to make express mention to them of Jesus."[45] Likewise, in introducing Jesus, Peter cycles from his miracles, which "you yourselves knew" ("soft"), to the role of his hearers in Jesus' crucifixion ("hard"), to the resurrection, which put "an end to the agony of death" ("soft").[46] The second vocative (2:29) follows Peter's recitation of David's messianic prophecy ("soft"), and introduces the "hard" rhetoric that David is dead! But David foresaw his eternal descendent (2:30–31; "soft"), who is Jesus (2:32; "hard"). A similar pattern recurs in connection with David and the Messiah.[47]

Significantly, Peter ends the sermon with "hard" rhetoric: "Therefore let all the house of Israel for certain know that God has made Him both Lord and Christ—this Jesus whom you crucified" (v. 36). At one level, this *epilogos* simply recapitulates (a) the "theocentric horizon" of Jesus' life and work,[48] (b) the culpability of the Jews in Jesus' death, and (c) the theme that Jesus the exalted Lord fulfills the ancient prophecies. But the hard rhetoric of the ending also appeals directly "to the heart and the conscience of [Peter's] hearers."[49] In this, says Chrysostom, Peter "does well . . . [for] when he has shown how great [the work of God] is, he has then exposed their daring deed, . . . to possess them with terror . . . [for] men are not so much attracted by benefits as they are chastened by fear."[50]

CHRIST CONFRONTS CULTURE

Preaching and Politics

Luke reports that in the afterglow of Pentecost "many wonders and signs were taking place through the apostles;"[51] and once again, as at Pentecost, a miracle creates an audience. One late afternoon, in the course of their worship routine, Peter and John encounter "a man . . . lame from his mother's womb" (3:2), who, asking only a handout, receives instead new legs (3:6). Those who see him "walking and leaping and praising God" (3:8) are "filled with wonder and amazement" (3:10). Once again, Peter seizes on the "wonder" of a crowd to preach Jesus the Messiah.

But in many ways, the setting here is quite different. For one thing, the *audience* at Pentecost was international. Here, Luke seems to imply (the feast now ended), the hearers were temple regulars (3:10a). Second, at Pentecost the hearers experienced the miracle. Here, they only witnessed its result. Third, Pentecost began in a "house" and spread from there, probably to the temple precincts. Here the healing occured at a busy temple gate,[52] and a crowd snowballed to Solomon's Portico as the news spread (3:11). Fourth, at Pentecost the disciples "preached" before Peter preached. Here, the healed man testifies. Fifth, Peter preached at Pentecost "with the eleven," here only with John. Finally, even the crowd's "amazement" was different this time. At Pentecost, we observe incredulity mixed with mockery, here a nearly reverential awe. At Pentecost, the crowd asked, "What does this mean?" (2:12). The unspoken question at Solomon's Portico is, "How can this be?"

But there is yet more to the story. Randall Webber argues that Peter's sermon at Solomon's Portico and his subsequent defense before the Sanhedrin constitute the first round of an orchestrated series of conflicts with the Sadducees over control of the temple and the right to define orthodoxy. According to Webber,[53] Peter *intended* to provoke the Sadducees by preaching the resurrection, then refused a saducean "settlement that would allow both sides to save face," because "the Christians" stood "to gain prestige . . . in continued conflict."[54] What this power-politics hermeneutic lacks in plausibility it makes up with imagination. And yet, without intending it, Peter's preaching clearly did offend the political and cultural sensibilities of the Jerusalem power class. Thus at Solomon's Portico, the infant church undertakes the epic struggle of "Christ and culture."[55] As always in Acts, preaching plays the key role.

"The People Saw Him Walking and Praising": The Sermon at Solomon's Portico (3:12b–26)

Peter's immediate problem, however, is not political. Chrysostom says that at Pentecost Peter "took occasion to speak" from (unjust) "accusations," but at Solomon's Portico, Peter is prompted by the (mistaken) "supposition"[56] that the disciples are faith healers! To say the least, this crowd is "not in a state of indifference."[57] How does Peter establish credibility when he has become suddenly famous? That he saw a problem is evident from Luke's remark that he began to speak when he "saw this."[58] Fame is no substitute for credibility. So Peter begins immediately "by rejecting the glory which was to be had from them." For "nothing is so advantageous," says Chrysostom, "and so likely to pacify the hearers, as to say nothing about one's self of an honorable nature, but, on the contrary, to obviate all surmise of wishing to do so." By "rejecting the glory," Peter also connected with his hearers. Chrysostom says it elegantly: Peter chose "to join with them in admiration [of God's work], rather than to receive it."[59]

No further introduction is necessary, so Peter moves without delay to interpret the miracle. Stott comments that "the most remarkable feature" of this sermon "is its Christ-centredness."[60] Or, rather, "God-centeredness," for *"God* is throughout *the central subject* who performs these mighty acts *with and through Christ."*[61] The body of the sermon is organized around three mighty acts of "God in Christ," each one set off by a vocative. Part one has the opening address[62] and *proem* (3:12b), followed by Peter's declaration that "God . . . has glorified His servant Jesus . . . whom you . . . disowned" (3:13). Peter elaborates by using covenant language (3:13–16). God is the "God of Abraham, Isaac, and Jacob, the God of our fathers." Jesus is the "servant of God," an unmistakable allusion to the "Servant" of Isaiah, who "will be high and lifted up, and greatly exalted."[63] Jesus is also "the Holy and Righteous One" (3:14), a title with many Old Testament (and specifically messianic) applications.[64]

The "low to high" and "soft-hard-soft" rhetorical pattern recurs here, but with a subtle change.[65] Peter transitions much faster in this sermon, probably because the audience is well disposed to him. From his self-effacing *proem,* Peter moves breathlessly from the covenant God ("low" and "soft") to the ("high" and "hard") core of his message, that the hearers *disowned their covenant God* by rejecting Jesus![66]

A second vocative ("And now, brethren" [3:17a]) introduces part two. Peter returns to "soft" rhetoric ("I know that you acted in ignorance, just as your rulers did," [3:17b]), and transitions to a *second* mighty act of God-in-Christ: What "God announced beforehand by the mouth of all the prophets, that His Christ should suffer," he has fulfilled through their rejection and disavowal (3:18).

The third vocative returns to "hard" rhetoric ("Therefore repent and return," [3:19a]). But Peter quickly cycles again to "soft" rhetoric with the *third* mighty act: Though rejected, the covenant God yet promises "times of refreshing" through Jesus the Messiah (3:19b–24).

The *epilogos* (3:25–26) of the sermon recalls the language and themes of the first proposition. These "temple regulars" disowned their God, but he did not disown them! They are still "sons of the prophets, and of the covenant," who have lived to see God keep his promises to Abraham.[67]

Peter's rehearsal of the mighty acts of God in Christ has rhetorical as well as doctrinal significance. Peter "assiduously . . . thrusts himself upon the fathers of old," says Chrysostom, "lest he should appear to be introducing a new doctrine."[68]

"By What Power?":
Peter before the Sanhedrin (4:8b–12)

Peter had scarcely finished the sermon (if at all) before temple authorities, led by the Sadducees, placed him and John under arrest (4:1). The next day they are hailed before the Sanhedrin, and the council president demands to know, "By what power, or in what name, have you done this?" (4:7b). So it is that the prophecy of Jesus comes to pass. His followers have been delivered up to the authorities, by which means they have an opportunity to bear witness.[69] Peter and John are placed in the center of the Sanhedrin, and the healed man is with them. Perhaps he was "held partly responsible for the commotion . . . or else . . . summoned as a witness."[70] In any case, he becomes, unwittingly, a witness for the defense.

Peter begins with a pointed response that establishes his credibility on different grounds than at Pentecost or Solomon's Porch. First, he counters the council's disparagement with respectful address.[71] Second, he answers the emphatic "you" (humeis) in the demand-question with an equally emphatic "we" (hēmeis [4:9]) in the defense. Peter hints thereby that the trial is illegitimate and that he is incredulous over it.[72] Finally, Peter restates the vague "this thing" (touto) of the demand-question. For the Sanhedrin, the antecedent of "this" was doubtless Peter's preaching; but Peter refers it to the "benefit [euergesia] done a sick man,"[73] and thus reframes the case, from "Peter" to "Jesus," from power-politics to the life of God, from the council's preoccupation with status and authority to Peter's confidence in the power of Jesus. Peter gains a hearing by commanding the moral and theological high ground. The Sanhedrin has positional authority; Peter enjoys moral authority.

Having reframed the debate, the defendant turns prosecutor. Citing Psalm 118:22—which Jesus had quoted to many of these same men just a few weeks earlier![74]—Peter charges them with rejecting the promised Messiah. He concludes (epilogos) with an asyndeton, a rhetorical device that naturally calls for a decision: "And there is salvation in no one else . . ." (4:12).[75] The judges must "judge."

"We Must Obey God":
Peter's Second Defense
before the Sanhedrin (5:29b–32)

After the first defense, the Sanhedrin released Peter and John with a command "not to speak or teach at all in the name of Jesus."[76] But the Word continued to multiply, especially in the area near Solomon's Portico. "Filled with jealously," Luke says, the authorities mass-arrested the apostles. After a miraculous release and further preaching, they were arrested once more and hailed before the body a second time.

The stakes now are higher than before, as indicated by the Sanhedrin's two-part indictment of (a) insubordination and (b) malicious intent. And the charges are highly personalized: "*We* gave . . . orders . . . *you* have filled Jerusalem with *your* teaching, and *intend* to bring this man's blood upon *us.*"[77] The charges were also unreasonable, for as Chrysostom wisely observes, Peter had already avowed that he and the apostles *could not* stop speaking![78] Peter, however, utters not a word. Instead, Chrysostom observes, "he [refers] the whole [matter] to the Father . . . showing [his] own unassuming temper, and intimating the greatness of the gift."[79] Says Peter, "we must obey *God* rather than men,"[80] again deflecting attention from himself to God—for the "*God of our Fathers* raised up Jesus," who is "the one whom *God exalted,*" to which the Holy Spirit bears witness, "whom *God has given* to those who obey *Him.*"[81]

With those words, Peter strikes again the theme of "obedience" with which he began this defense; and once more he calls the judges to judge, specifically, to judge of Christ by judging of the apostles themselves. As if to say: "God gives the Spirit to those who obey him. We claim to obey him. So judge—do we speak by the Spirit or not?"

THE GOSPEL TO THE GENTILES

Cornelius "Over and Over Again"

The centrifugal God. It has been said that the God of the Bible is "centrifugal." Certainly in Acts he is. The outbreak of persecutions following the martyrdom of Stephen (8:1–4), forced the disciples out of the Jerusalem ghetto. The gospel invades Samaria through the preaching of Philip (8:5–13) and Peter and John (8:25). Luke then relates the conversion of the "apostle to the Gentiles" (9:1–30), and he follows both Philip (8:26–40) and Peter (9:32–43) to the fringe of the "uttermost parts." Philip evangelizes an African. Peter evangelizes outlying districts west of Jerusalem and spends "many days" with Simon the Tanner in Joppa. Because "tanning" was an "unclean" occupation, some scholars imagine a discrepancy here, since (presumably) a man with Peter's scruples would scarcely have defiled himself. Knowling counters that "mention of the trade seems to show that St. Peter was already in a state of mind which would fit him for . . . further revelation."[82] Certainly Peter is being prepared to preach as he has never preached before.

In doing so, he will launch the world mission enterprise of the "centrifugal God." At Caesarea, Peter will break down cultural barriers by preaching to Gentiles as previously he had preached to Jews (10:34b–43). In Jerusalem, Peter's preaching will quell opposition to this new development (11:5–17). And when the apostles and elders assemble in Jerusalem to set theological parameters for a world mission, Peter will warn them not to bury God's truth in human traditions (15:7b–11). In short, God will use Peter's preaching to *inaugurate, defend,* and *confirm*[83] his plan for global missions.

The last three recorded sermons of Peter thus belong together. All three share a historical, cultural, and theological context, connected specifically with Cornelius and his household, of course, but also related to broader questions about the inclusiveness of the gospel, the clash of faith and culture, and orthodoxy and orthopraxy. The sermons also share a common *rhetorical form,* in that all are confessional. In studying them, therefore, we stand to learn a great deal about the *preacher* in preaching.

Peter's third conversion. Luke's narrative of events leading to the sermon at Caesarea is dominated by two outstanding characters—Cornelius, a devout proselyte, and, of course, Peter—"unknown to each other and seemingly both doing God's will in their lives."[84] God appears to each in a vision[85] that exposes a need. Put bluntly—Cornelius needs conversion, and Peter needs "conversion."[86] The story is familiar and need not detain us, except to highlight the impact of Peter's transformation on his preaching. Peter's "conversion" at Joppa is his third life change: (1) from disciple of John the Baptist to disciple of Jesus; (2) from "Simon" to "Simon Rock"; and now, (3) from "culture Christian" to "kingdom Christian." If the human personality consists in thinking (cognition), willing (volition), and feeling (emotion), we can trace Peter's development psychologically through his life-changes—from the intellectual faith (cognition) of Peter the confessor, to the strong-willed confidence (volition) of Simon Rock before the Sanhedrin, and finally to the mature changed heart (emotion) of the Peter who presents himself at Caesarea as "just a man."[87]

Peter's experience at Joppa and Caesarea transformed his preaching— from *rash* truth (Caesarea Philippi), to *bold* truth (Pentecost), and now, to *gracious* truth (Caesarea). Peter is now enabled to preach outside his comfort zone (cf. 10:27–29). Furthermore, Peter now preaches more experientially. Before Joppa, Peter certainly knew intellectually that "the awesome God . . . does not show partiality."[88] But listen to him at Caesarea: "I most certainly *understand* now that God is not one to show partiality."[89] Peter, we might almost say, now *feels* his theology. This experiential preaching emboldens Peter. A familiar principle of group psychology holds that a position taken publicly tends to strengthen the underlying conviction. Luke does not traffic in psychological explanations, of course, but Peter's subsequent preaching certainly suggests that the sermon at Caesarea marked a turning point for him. Having crossed the line by preaching to the Gentiles as a matter of theological conviction, Peter takes a firm stand later with the disputants in Jerusalem and in the Jerusalem council.[90]

The Cornelius corpus. Half a century ago, Martin Dibelius argued that Peter's Cornelius sermon and his sermon to the objectors in Jerusalem contradicted each other and could not have come from the same source.[91] Dibelius attributed the Cornelius speech to Luke's sources and the Jerusalem speech to Luke, but neither of course to Peter himself. Recent scholarship has by and large dismantled the textual basis for these claims,[92] but we must still ask about the relationship between the two sermons.

Ronald Witherup argues that the three last sermons of Peter in Acts manifest "functional redundancy." According to Witherup, Luke used repetition rhetorically "to ensure a full and unambiguous reception of the message."[93] Luke told the Cornelius story "over and over and over again" to drive home the point that the extension of the gospel to the Gentiles was no happenstance, nor was it culturally or politically motivated; rather, it was the plan of God from the beginning. Witherup focuses specifically on Luke's (supposed literary) rhetorical strategy, of course, but as we are about to see, his analysis touches on Peter's rhetorical strategy at many points.

"Now I Know": Peter's Sermon at the House of Cornelius (10:34b–43)

Luke sets the stage by showing that God orchestrated Peter's preaching at Caesarea—Peter's stay with Simon the Tanner, the visions, first to Cornelius (10:1–8), then to Peter (10:9–16), and (yet another preliminary sign of Peter's openness to non-Jewish associations) hospitality to the men sent from Cornelius (10:17–23).[94] Peter's arrival at Caesarea occasions a rehearsal, first by Peter (10:28–29), then Cornelius (10:30–33), of God's preparatory work. God has indeed prepared everything specifically for *preaching;* so that Cornelius is able to say to Peter: "Now then, we are all here present *before God* to hear all that you have been commanded by the Lord" (10:33, emphasis added).

Following the rhetorical pattern we have observed in his other preaching, Peter begins with "low matters" (vv. 36–37) and transitions to "high matters," in this case, a rather straightforward presentation of the *kerygma:* (1) Jesus of Nazareth "went about doing good" by the power of the Spirit (v. 38); (2) "they" [the Jews in Jerusalem] put him to death on a cross (v. 39); (3) God raised him (vv. 40–41); (4) the disciples are called to testify that Jesus is Messiah (v. 42a); (5) as Messiah, Jesus is coming as judge (v. 42b); and (6) the prophets call everyone to faith in him for the forgiveness of sins (v. 43).

What distinguishes this sermon is the *proem,* which takes the form of a theological confession: "I most certainly understand now that God is not one to show partiality, but in every nation the man who fears Him and does what is right, is welcome to Him" (vv. 34b–35). Peter admits that his faith and understanding have matured, or, rather, that God has opened his eyes.

Rhetorically, Peter's confession functions in three ways. First, it establishes Peter's *credibility*, through identification with his audience. Even though he is a Jew, Peter takes his place among those "in every nation" who are "welcome" to God (v. 35).[95]

Second, the confession properly establishes Peter's *authority*. In one sense, words like *credibility* and *authority* seem out of place in this context. Recall that when Peter arrived in Caesarea, Cornelius "fell at his feet and worshiped him" (10:25). Peter had "authority"! But like the crowd at Solomon's Porch, Cornelius and his household thought more of Peter than they ought; and in both cases, the apostle deflects attention from himself to God. At Solomon's Porch, Peter disclaimed responsibility for the mighty work of God. Here he confesses just such a mighty work *in his own life*. So he preaches as one without authority, or, rather, as one whose authority is a life transformed and being transformed by the power and mercy of the God of all the nations.

Third, Peter's confessional *proem* fosters *authentic receptivity*. We must remember that, while Cornelius and his household were eager to hear Peter, they did not know what he would say. Of Jesus they had some knowledge (vv. 37–38). But Peter is about to proclaim him, not as religious leader, but as the crucified, resurrected, exalted *judge*, before whom all must bow! By confessing his own sin and need, Peter helps prepare his hearers to confess their sin and need.

"Who Was I?":
Peter before the Disputants (11:5–17)

"The news of Peter's revolutionary behavior . . . reached Jerusalem before he himself did."[96] Upon his arrival, certain Jewish believers, zealous for the law, "took issue with him" for going to Gentiles and even eating with them (11:2–3). Chrysostom calls it a "frigid objection," which Peter does not "stop to notice."[97] Instead, Peter repeats the Cornelius story. As we have seen, Martin Dibelius argued that this sermon and the previous one could not have a common source, since they represent the Cornelius encounter so differently. We argue that the *very differences* indicate not only that the sermons have a common source, but that the source is none other than Peter.

Like the sermon in Caesarea, Peter's sermon in Jerusalem is confessional. And as in all of his recorded sermons, Peter deflects attention from himself and takes refuge in the mighty acts of God. Thus the *epilogue*: "Therefore if God gave to them the same gift as He gave to us also after believing in the Lord Jesus Christ, who was I that could stand in God's way?" (11:17). Peter reaches this conclusion *inductively*, however, whereas at Caesarea, he *begins* with a proposition and works it out *deductively*. Put differently, Peter's confessional *emphasis* changes from Caesarea to Jerusalem. In Caesarea, he emphasizes God's transforming work in his own life and the inclusiveness of the gospel. In Jerusalem, he emphasizes the irresistibility of God's sovereign power and purpose.

There are other differences. In Acts 10, for example, Luke relates the vision of Cornelius first (*chronologically*), then Peter's vision in Joppa. But Peter reverses the order in Jerusalem, thereby emphasizing that God had orchestrated these revolutionary events. In addition, Chrysostom calls attention to the fact that in Jerusalem Peter nowhere mentions the name of Cornelius, or hints at the "approbations of his fitness," so as not to offend Jewish sensibilities unnecessarily.[98] Finally, in Jerusalem, Peter adds that as the Holy Spirit fell on them at Caesarea, he "remembered" the post-ascension prophecy of Jesus (11:16)[99]—a further indication that God was at work.

This sermon exudes the character of the Peter we have met time and again in Acts. Sensitive to the peculiarities of audience and context, he deflects attention from himself to the theocentric horizion, and proceeds from "low matters" to "high."

"Saved through Grace": Peter's Sermon before the Jerusalem Council (15:7b–11)

"At every step of the right progress of the Gentiles," observes Chrysostom, "the *beginning* is brought in as matter of necessity."[100] In the Jerusalem council, the early church took another step toward worldwide missionary enterprise. In doing so, they returned to first principles, and again, primarily through preaching. Luke's account of the council includes two sermons—by Peter (15:7b–11) and James (15:14–21)—and alludes to at least one other, by Barnabas with (or, in addition to) Paul (15:12). James preaches last, doubtless reflecting his position not only as leader of the church but as putative "champion" of the circumcision party.[101] Unlike the others, he had no experiences to share,[102] which may have cloaked him with a certain perceived objectivity.

James brings keen sensitivity[103] to bear on what, in effect, is an oracle in three movements: (1) Scripture itself authenticates Peter's report of God's work among the Gentiles (15:14–18); (2) the gospel should not impose cultural burdens on Gentile believers (15:19); and (3) the gospel does not liberate Gentile believers to run roughshod over Jewish sensibilities (15:20–21).

The "text" of James's sermon is in fact the last recorded sermon of Peter. At issue, of course, was the gospel itself; to wit, whether Gentiles who believe must also be circumcised *in order to be saved* (15:1, 5). The council called to deliberate the matter included members of the Antioch church, along with the apostles and elders of Jerusalem, as well as a number of judaizing Christians.[104] Not surprisingly, the atmosphere was highly charged.[105] At this critical point, Peter returns to first principles. He repeats "Cornelius" yet again, but—ever adaptable—he speaks to the need of a different and dangerous moment.

While the sermon as such conforms to the special pattern we have traced through the "Cornelius" sermons, we also observe distinctive applications of the pattern here. First, the sermon exhibits a distinctive "theocentric syntax."[106] In Caesarea, Peter emphasizes *confession* (God's work in his own life) and *kerygma* (God's work through Jesus). With the Jerusalem objectors, Peter related his *vision* (11:5–10) and its *confirmation* (a) by the Holy Spirit (11:15) and (b) by the words of Jesus (11:16). Before the council—assembled, we recall, to settle a theological question—Peter emphasized God's *purpose* and God's *salvation*: (a) God made a sovereign "choice" that through Peter, the Gentiles should hear the gospel (15:7b) and (b) "God who knows the heart" (15:8a) gives salvation to all the same way, by "cleansing their hearts by faith" (15:8–9).

Second, Peter deflects attention from himself in a paradoxical way. We might suppose that Peter is blowing his own horn when he says that God chose to preach to the Gentiles "by my mouth." But the statement actually is a masterful double entendre. While it alludes to Peter's preeminence among the disciples and his role as the first preacher, it also alludes to Peter's personal reluctance to preach among the Gentiles! *To the Judaizers*, Peter says, in effect, "God himself used me, contrary to my own inclinations, to accomplish his purposes among the Gentiles." *To the apostles and others*, Peter says, in effect, "Whatever preeminence I have as a preacher of the gospel, it is for God's saving purpose to the Jew first (Pentecost) and also to the Greek (Cornelius)."

Finally, Peter appeals to his audience by interpreting salvation in human terms. The judaistic tendency represents an unattainable economy of salvation—"a yoke which neither our fathers nor we have been able to bear" (15:10). "But"—one can almost feel the breath of blessed relief in Peter's voice!—"we believe that we are saved through the grace of our Lord Jesus, in the same way as they also are" (15:11).

Here in brief compass is the preaching of the kingdom of God. The longings of the human heart are met in the Messiah, foretold by the prophets, and now proclaimed by his witnesses. Why, Peter wants to know, should we want to return to the dead hope of works when we have been begotten again to a living hope through the Messiah?[107]

CHAPTER

8

"TO THE JEW FIRST": THE INSPIRED PREACHING OF PAUL IN ACTS

C. RICHARD WELLS

What is intriguing, even mysterious about Paul is this:
Why did he come to say what he did?

BRUCE CHILTON

"THE MYSTERY OF PAUL"[1]

"PASSION WITH HIGH MOTIVES": ON THE MAKING OF A PREACHER

Paul had come back to Jerusalem for what will be the last time (Acts 21:20–32). On the advice of James, he tried to allay suspicions that he encouraged Jewish converts "to forsake Moses"; but, alas, his best intentions come to naught. Certain Jews from Asia whipped up a mob, charging Paul with desecrating the temple and subverting Jewish culture with his preaching. The mob wanted blood.

A Sidebar and a Sermon (Acts 21:32–22:15)

Rescued by a centurion, Paul now faces two very different audiences—the frenzied mob and a Roman tribune perplexed by these bizarre events. In a sidebar conversation, Paul sets the commander at ease. Does Paul speak Greek (21:37)? Yes—and more, he is a Roman citizen, a native of Tarsus in Cilicia, "no insignificant city" (21:39). Paul is a civilized man, not a cult figure (21:38). With the centurion's permission, Paul speaks to the mob, quieting them, Chrysostom says, "by the sound of their . . . mother tongue."[2] He reminds them that though he was born in the Greek lands, he was brought up in Jerusalem and studied under the revered Gamaliel. Paul has gained a hearing and has begun to preach on the work of God in his life.

First, he affirms his Jewish heritage. He had been "zealous for God, just as you all are today" (22:3), so much so that he had persecuted the Christian Way "to the death" (22:4), until God arrested him, appointed him to see "the Righteous One" (22:14), and commissioned him to be "a witness" (22:15). Paul testified that the "change in him was of God's doing," said A. T. Robertson, "and no one should charge him with being a turncoat."[3] Thus from a sidebar and a sermon on the steps of the tower of Antonia, we learn the education and enculturation that prepared Paul to bear the name of Christ "before the Gentiles and kings and the sons of Israel" (Acts 9:15): (1) the Hellenism of Tarsus; (2) education under Gamaliel; and (3) zeal for the law.

Tarsus: no mean city. Next to Athens and Alexandria, says James Stalker, Tarsus was the third great university city of the Roman Empire;[4] and clearly Paul considered his birth there a distinct advantage. It has been suggested that Paul's strict pharisaic upbringing[5] would preclude substantial hellenist influence. A century ago, however, Sir William Ramsey proved beyond reasonable doubt that Paul could have been a Roman citizen "by birth" (Acts 22:28) only if his family belonged to the Tarsian aristocracy.[6] His father would have been a hellenist, though not a hellenizer, sympathetic to the best of Greek culture, but a "real Jew" at heart.[7] Thus while we must not make Paul a "real Greek," warns Robertson, he certainly felt at home in the Greek world. He could engage and hold the attention of Athenian philosophers.[8] He could cite pagan Greek writers to bolster an argument,[9] one of whom, Aratus (Acts 17:28), hailed from Paul's native Cilicia. And he could impress the Roman Festus with his immense learning (Acts 26:24). For Peter, the culture of the Gentiles was *terra incognita*; for Paul, it was homefield advantage.[10]

Educated under Gamaliel. According to a long and strong (though technically undocumented) tradition, Gamaliel was the grandson of the far-famed Rabbi Hillel, whose moderating influence had largely won the day in mid-first-century Judaism. Gamaliel, however, outshone even Hillel. He was the first to bear the honorific title "Rabban" ("our Master," or "our Great One") rather than "Rabbi" ("my Master"). And it was said that when "Rabban Gamaliel the Elder died, the glory of the Law ceased and purity and abstinence [*separateness*] died."[11] Gamaliel had counseled tolerance at the second trial of Peter (with the apostles) before the Sanhedrin (Acts 5:35–39); and Luke does not exaggerate when he informs us that Gamaliel was "respected by all the people" (5:34). Gamaliel, Paul says with understandable pride, had been his teacher.

Scholars have debated the Rabban's real influence on Paul. How can we reconcile Gamaliel's putative liberal spirit with Paul's "threats and murder" against Christians?[12] Robertson warns us not "to get too extravagant an idea of Gamaliel's breadth of view and sympathy."[13] True, he had urged caution in the Sanhedrin; but when Stephen is stoned and persecutions erupt against the Christians, Gamaliel is nowhere to be found. Furthermore, the two examples cited by Gamaliel involve political movements quashed by the Romans! His advice, therefore, may amount to little more than prudent politics— "leave this alone; the authorities will deal with it soon enough!"[14] We have no reason to think that Gamaliel would necessarily have objected to Paul's campaign against the church.

So what *did* Paul get from his mentor? Robertson offers us three answers.[15] First, Paul "gained a thoroughly trained mind." The rabbinical methods of question and answer, disputation, debate, and distinguishing "things that differ"[16] would have honed his native intellectual gifts. Second, Paul "won familiarity with the letter of Scripture." However thick the encrustations of rabbinical tradition, an able rabbi like Paul would have the Scriptures at his fingertips. Third, building on Paul's hellenistic background, Gamaliel would help Paul acquire a "really cosmopolitan" education. In addition to the teaching of the rabbis, Gamaliel would have allowed (perhaps required) Paul to read some Greek authors, as well as Jewish Alexandrian philosophy. Under Gamaliel's tutelage, "a certain amount of Greek and Roman culture," would augment his Jewish learning to make Paul "a real citizen of the world and a fit vessel to bear the Gospel to the Gentiles."[17]

"THE SON OF A PHARISEE": PAUL'S ZEAL FOR THE LAW

There is a telling bit of psychology in Paul's defense in Jerusalem, the *proem* of which (22:3) contains at least six different "connections" with the crowd. Paul is (1) a Jew, (2) brought up in Jerusalem, (3) educated under Gamaliel (4) strictly according to the law, and (5) he is zealous for God, (6) just as the mob is. The last statement amounts to a massive and charitable understatement! But it also fairly represents Paul's life before Christ. As the mob is, Paul was!

Paul frequently mentions his zeal for the law. He is a Pharisee and the son of a Pharisee,[18] and he was advancing over his peers in zeal for the "ancestral traditions" (Gal. 1:14). Paul inherited his pharisaism, and he felt it in his bones. Thus to Herod Agrippa, he acknowledges a compulsion "to do many things hostile to the name of Jesus of Nazareth" (Acts 26:9), being "furiously enraged" at his followers (26:11). Luke himself employs the striking figure of "breathing" [*empneuō*] to plumb the psychology of this vehemence (Acts 9:1)—as if Paul's very personality was all rage against the Way. Paul does not hesitate to own this blood lust. It is a theme of his preaching in Acts[19] and his letters,[20] serving as proof both of his former zeal and God's lavish grace.

By all indications, Paul's zeal for the law resulted from strong convictions combined with an intense personality. In our modern vernacular, Paul was fanatically purpose-driven. Unlike Peter, who could speak now and think later, Paul seems almost obsessively premeditated. Peter was impetuous; Paul was vehement,[21] and his zeal for the law knew no bounds.[22] Robertson points out that an ordinary man would have been satisfied to drive Christianity out of Jerusalem. But Paul was no ordinary man. He went to Damascus "determined to finish the business while he was at it." In Paul, "passion was linked with high motives."[23]

Jesus Christ himself purified Saul's zeal, which we meet everywhere in Acts and the epistles. Paul reminds the Thessalonians, for example, that his preaching was not "in word only, but also in power and in the Holy Spirit and with full conviction" (1 Thess. 1:5). Festus seems almost overwhelmed by Paul's learned passion (Acts 26:24). Sir William Ramsey observes that Luke's brief characterizations of Paul's body language—his gestures,[24] his eye contact,[25] tearing his clothes and rushing into a pagan crowd (Acts 14:14), crying with a "loud voice" in the Philippian jail (Acts 16:28)—all testify to character qualities that fed Paul's "impassioned oratory."[26] Paul "was not a man to do things by halves,"[27] either as the son of a Pharisee or as the apostle to the Gentiles. Paul's preaching was passion with high motives.

The story of Paul's conversion begins when his zeal for the law met its match. As in Chicago or New York one might find a Haitian Baptist church, or Presbyterians from Laos, first-century Jerusalem boasted synagogue congregations of expatriates from all over the world,[28] among them the so-called "Synagogue of the Freedmen" (Acts 6:9).[29] Paul may well have attended this synagogue, since (Luke tells us) it included "some from Cilicia." Doubtless he followed with great interest the controversy that had arisen in that synagogue, involving a brilliant, outspoken Christian named Stephen. Stephen, like Saul, was a hellenist, one of the seven chosen to administer the early church's food distribution program for widows (Acts 6:1–6). "He was also," said John Foxe, "an able and successful preacher," whose boldness caught the attention first of the synagogue, then the Sanhedrin itself (Acts 6:12, 15; 7:1), and at last earned Stephen the first place in Foxe's *History of the Christian Martyrs*.[30]

Paul was complicit in these doings. He likely took part in the disputations with Stephen and found himself, with the other rabbis, "unable to cope with the wisdom and the Spirit with which [Stephen] was speaking" (Acts 6:10). Like the rest, Paul was "cut to the quick" by Stephen's sermon, and while he cast no stones, Luke informs us that Saul "was in hearty agreement with putting him to death" (Acts 8:1). Stephen had the measure of Saul.

More than twenty years later, Paul alludes to the influence of Stephen on his life. He recalls to Herod Agrippa what Jesus spoke to him on the Damascus road: "Saul, Saul, why are you persecuting Me? It is hard for you to kick against the goads" (Acts 26:14). "Kicking against the goads" was a proverb (familiar to Greeks, Romans, and Jews alike) signifying self-destructive stubbornness.[31] John Stott suggests that the "goads" must have included at least three experiences working like abrasives on the hard shell of Paul's heart: (1) doubts about Jesus; (2) a "bad conscience"; and (3) Stephen.[32] In reality, of course, Stephen was the "goad" personified. His preaching catalyzed Saul's rage against Christians and plunged him into profound moral dissonance—a Pharisee, of all people, committing heinous crimes, against even women (Acts 9:2)! At the same time, Stephen was a true *martus*, whose very life testified that the Nazarene Saul so vehemently repudiated was really alive (Acts 22:20). Thus, in the words of Richard Rackham, "Stephen and not Gamaliel was the real master of St. Paul."[33]

Stephen's Preaching

What was it about Stephen that so deeply affected Saul? Luke's account furnishes three answers: (1) Stephen knew the "spirit" of Scripture not just the letter; (2) he combined eloquence and power; and (3) he embodied grace.

1. The spirit of the Scripture. The charges against Stephen came first as a public accusation from witnesses suborned against him: "We have heard him speak blasphemous words against Moses and against God" (Acts 6:11). They later appeared as an indictment before the Sanhedrin: "This man incessantly speaks against this holy place and the Law" (6:13). The charges come to the same thing, since "Moses" corresponds to the "Law," just as the temple ("this holy place") corresponds to God himself.[34] Stephen was accused of blasphemy, because (supposedly) he spoke against the house of God and the law of God.

The very fact that witnesses were bribed proves that the charges were spurious; but how did they arise in the first place? Henry Alford thinks that Stephen was the "first who plainly set forth the transitory nature of the law and the temple, [compared with] the permanence of the later and better covenant."[35] In doing so, Stephen merely echoed Jesus, who spoke of his own coming as "something greater than the temple" (Matt. 12:6). Jesus vigorously affirmed the permanence of the law (Matt. 5:18), but he did not hesitate to challenge traditional interpretations.[36] Early in his ministry, Jesus had created a stir when he declared, "Destroy this temple, and in three days I will raise it up." Even though, John said, "He was speaking of . . . His body" (John. 2:19, 21), false witnesses twisted the words into a formal charge before the

Sanhedrin (Matt. 26:61), just as they were now doing with Stephen's words. To all intents, Jesus was "back on trial again."[37]

For John Calvin, Stephen's experience is a lesson for all who preach. We need not wonder, Calvin said, that what we "teach godly, well, and profitably" should be "so falsely misconstrued," for "the doctrine of the gospel can never be handled so warily and moderately, but that it shall be subject to false accusations." For that very reason, when we see the gospel "corrupted, deformed, and torn in pieces with false reports, we must not repent that we have begun." Rather, "it is our part and duty to dash and put away those lies wherewith the truth of God is burdened."[38]

According to Calvin, that is just what Stephen did. With many modern scholars,[39] Calvin agrees that "Stephen's answer may seem at first blush absurd and foolish," consisting as it does, of "a long narration [with] no mention . . . of the matter at hand."[40] Stephen did indeed rehearse a long, well-known history to the Sanhedrin, but "in such a way as to draw lessons from it which they had never learned or even noticed."[41] He "put away the lies" which burdened the truth of God.

Stephen wastes no time putting them away. With his *proem* (7:2), Stephen seeks to gain a hearing in three different ways: (1) a respectful address;[42] (2) a theological first principle—"the God of glory"; and (3) telling the story of the Jews.[43] Chrysostom observes that Stephen's reference to "the God of glory" struck at the heart of the Council's "conceit," because it implies "that [God] needs not the glory which comes from us, which comes by the Temple. . . . Think not, he would say, to glorify Him [by Temple service]."[44] Like Peter at Pentecost, Stephen created a theocentric horizon. He shifted attention away from the human to the divine—in this case, from the glory of the *house* of God, to the glory of the *God* of the house.

The body of the sermon elaborates that opening thesis in four particulars, each drawn from great figures in Israel's history. First, the God of glory called *Abraham* out of Mesopotamia and made a covenant with him, when as yet Abraham had no inheritance (let alone a temple) in the land (7:2–8). Second, the God of glory protected and preserved Israel through *Joseph* (the very one his brothers had disowned) in Egypt, not in the land of promise (7:9–19). Third, the God of glory, "the God of Abraham and Isaac and Jacob" (7:32), delivered Israel through *Moses*, even though the people of God rejected him both before (7:28–29, 35) and after (7:39–43) the Exodus. Moses received the law (7:38) and the pattern for the tabernacle (not *temple*, 7:44–45), but he also prophesied that God would raise up another prophet like himself (7:37; cf. Deut. 8:18). Fourth, even though David found favor in God's sight and asked to build a temple (7:46), God did not allow it, showing that the God of glory "does not dwell in houses made by human hands" (7:48).

Stephen's discourse on Moses (7:20–45) not only answers the charge of speaking against the law; it prepares for the *epilogos*. The Israelites rejected Moses. The Council rejected the "Righteous One" prophesied by Moses (7:51–53). Recalling his very language,[45] Stephen charges the Council directly. They have resisted God's Spirit (7:51), betrayed and murdered the Righteous One, and finally, although they received the law (cf. 7:38), they "did not keep it!" (7:53).

In short, Stephen's defense exposes the negative, narrow, truncated, proof-texting, culture-bound, and hide-bound hermeneutics of the scholars. In the spirit of the prophets, Stephen proclaims instead the "God of glory" and his mighty works that climax in Christ, the great prophet like Moses. And all without ever once mentioning the name "Jesus"!

2. Eloquence and power. Stephen appears before the Council alone. It is entirely possible, of course, that the apostles were otherwise occupied, were unaware what was happening, or (given their own recent engagements with the Council!) had no opportunity to intervene. But it has also been suggested that, while there "is no evidence that the twelve felt any jealousy of Stephen," it is true that "Stephen was a new type of preacher."[46] Perhaps some of the disciples "thought Stephen too bold and aggressive."[47]

Stephen was unquestionably a different kind of preacher. The charges leveled against him implied "an insulting and blasphemous manner"[48] and suggest that Stephen's message had struck a nerve. As a Jew, Stephen knew that the new wine of Christ would burst the old wineskins of Judaism. And as a hellenist Stephen was already preaching "the spiritual nature of worship irrespective of nature or place,"[49] long before Peter would venture to the home of a Gentile. Stephen's *message* was ahead of its time.

So was his *method*. The Jews who accosted Stephen hailed from Cyrene, Alexandria, Cilicia, and Asia—all centers of Hellenism.[50] In Greek style, as Luke's language shows, these Jews intended to engage Stephen in a "full-dress debate;"[51] and Stephen meets them on their own turf. Later on Paul himself will debate (*suzēteō*) hellenistic Jews in Jerusalem (Acts 9:29) and both hellenist Jews and Greeks in Athens (Acts 17:17); and Apollos, an "eloquent" Alexandrian, will refute hellenistic Jews in Ephesus (Acts 18:24, 28).[52] But Stephen is the first, it seems, to employ hellenistic tools of rhetoric in the service of the gospel.

He did so effectively, for his antagonists "were unable to cope with the wisdom and Spirit with which he was speaking" (Acts 6:10). Luke does not mean, of course, that the Jews acquiesced, only that "they could adduce no arguments [against him] possessing any force."[53] Just as the "confidence" of Peter and John left the Sanhedrin speechless (Acts 4:14), the hellenists had no answer for Stephen.

Stephen is a case study in what we have dubbed "spiritual rhetoric,"[54] which Paul will later describe as "divinely powerful" weapons for "destroying speculations and every lofty thing raised up against the knowledge of God, and . . . taking every thought captive to the obedience of Christ" (2 Cor. 10:4–5). Eloquence incorporates *fluency*, *power* (or *forcefulness*), and *appropriateness*, each of which is manifest in the "wisdom and Spirit" of Stephen. He (a) knows the Scriptures thoroughly (*fluency*) as both *Geschichte* (history) and *Heilsgeschichte* ("salvation-" or "holy-" history). He (b) grasps the similarity between rejection of Moses "then," and rejection of the prophet like Moses "now" (*appropriateness*). And he speaks (c) in the *power* of the Spirit.

3. Christlike personality. The most lasting impression young Saul got from Stephen's preaching, however, he must undoubtedly have got from the extraordinary personality of the man, which Luke characterizes in four ways. First, Stephen *walked by the Spirit*. Stephen is named first among "the seven" chosen to serve tables (Acts 6:2–3), all of whom were "full of the Spirit and of wisdom." Luke says specifically that Stephen was "full of grace and power" (6:8); and, as the rage of the Council begins to erupt, Stephen is said to be "full of the Holy Spirit" (Acts 7:55).

Second, Stephen *walked with Christ*. Chrysostom thinks that Stephen displayed extraordinary boldness in his preaching because he knew from the outset what his fate would be. He preached "at the point to die."[55] This would give new meaning to Stephen's vision of Christ "standing at the right hand of God" (Acts 7:55–56), whether to plead his case, as some say, or to welcome him home. On any reading, the vision testifies to Stephen's walk with Christ.

Third, Stephen *had a gracious bearing*. In modern vernacular, Stephen "came across" as a man of grace and goodness and love. Luke says that the Council "saw his face like the face of an angel" (Acts 6:15), using language reminiscent of Moses, whose face reflected the glory of God (Exod. 34:29–35). Luke's point seems to be that Stephen reflected Christ in his face. He *affected* those who heard him, even if he did not *persuade* them.

Finally, Stephen *preached from pure motives*. Scholars have frequently observed that the last words of Stephen (Acts 7:59b) echo like Jesus on the cross. "Lord Jesus, receive my spirit" (cf. Luke 23:46), he cries, and again (with a loud voice), "Lord, do not hold this sin against them!" (7:60a; Luke 23:34). Chrysostom explains that Stephen prayed for his accusers in order "to show that he forgave their wrath and rage in murdering him, and that his own soul was free from all passion," in order perhaps (even now) "to win them over."[56] By "passion," Chrysostom means impure motives, particularly anger. (Stephen was hardly dispassionate about the gospel!) Stephen was free of anger, because he was "clear of all feeling for [himself]."[57] Stephen lost his "self" in the gospel[58] and grew bold! Chrysostom makes an application here to all preachers. "Boldness," he says, is not "wrath"; for "no matter how just your words may be, when you speak with anger, you ruin all."[59]

The Forerunner of Paul

The "real master" of Paul was not Gamaliel, indeed, but Stephen.[60] His grasp of Scripture, his rhetorical power, his personality all left their mark. We know too little of Stephen to do more than speculate what might have been had his life not come to an untimely end. Our best guess is Paul himself. A. T. Robertson called Stephen the "forerunner of Paul"[61] for this very reason. Prior to his conversion, Paul wages war against Stephen's ghost; and after his conversion, he takes up Stephen's mantle.

As we shall see in the studies of his sermons, Paul extends the ministry of Stephen in almost every particular we have named. He preaches the kingdom of God in Christ as the true prophetic message of the Scriptures. He seeks to take every thought captive to Christ by the power of the Spirit. And if Stephen could pray for his murderers, Paul—who never forgot that he had been "in hearty agreement" with them (Acts 8:1) and thus deserved to be called "the chief of sinners" (1 Tim. 1:15)—Paul could "wish that I myself were accursed . . . for the sake of . . . my kinsmen according to the flesh" (Rom. 9:3). Just as Peter recalls Cornelius "over and over and over," Paul recalls Stephen.

In examining Paul's sermons in Acts, we will adopt the same procedure as with Peter's sermons,[62] but we should add a couple of explanatory notes. First, given the limitations of space and scope, we will not examine every sermon of Paul in detail but in representative fashion. (We note that Luke himself records only one major sermon to the Jews, another to the Gentiles, and a group of apologetic sermons.)

FROM DAMASCUS TO ROME: THE MISSIONARY PREACHING OF PAUL

Paul was converted and commissioned all at once in Damascus and "immediately," so Luke informs us, "began to proclaim Jesus in the synagogues" (Acts 9:20). Some three years later, Paul is in Jerusalem, among the hellenistic Jews (9:29), including, no doubt, many with whom Paul had colluded in debates with Stephen and in his death, and who now sought Paul's life as well (9:30). From Damascus and Jerusalem, to Galatia and Greece, and finally, to the Imperial City itself, Paul will travel eleven thousand miles over the next twenty-five years, preaching the Good News—to the Jew first and also to the Greeks.

"To the Jew First":
The Synagogue Sermon at Pisidian Antioch
(Acts 13:16b–41)

Although he records only two missionary sermons to the Jews—in Pisidian Antioch (Acts 13:16b–41) and Rome (28:25–28)—Luke provides ample evidence not only that the apostle to the Gentiles customarily preached "to the Jew first,"[63] but that his preaching to the Jews had its own special character. Not to put too fine an edge on it, Paul had (a) a theologically shaped *vision* for preaching to the Jews, (b) a theologically shaped *message* to the Jews, and (c) a theologically shaped *rhetoric* for communicating with the Jews. Luke captures the *vision* in his record of Paul's mission strategy. As to *message* and *rhetoric*, Luke's notes provide a fairly clear picture.

Paul's synagogue sermon in Pisidian Antioch furnishes the only extant model of this preaching—though the sermon is important for other reasons as well. Lawrence Wills points out that the sermon typifies not only the preaching of Paul, but early Christian preaching in general.[64] Furthermore, as one of only two examples of synagogue sermons in the New Testament,[65] this sermon gives us a glimpse into the Jewish background of Christian preaching. Still further, its affinities with Peter's sermon on Pentecost suggest that the early preachers employed "a common stock of *testimonia* or Old Testament selections."[66]

And like Peter's sermon at Caesarea, this sermon comes at a critical juncture historically, viz., the commencement of the first missionary journey, as the church begins *strategically* to penetrate the Gentile lands. As always, Paul goes to the Jew first; but now to hellenistic Jews living in Greek culture, remote from the events in Jerusalem, events which, nevertheless, fulfilled their prophetic hopes.[67] Luke intends, no doubt, to capture the heart of Paul's preaching to Jews in this sermon.

Beginning in Antioch of Syria, Paul, Barnabas, and John Mark cross over to Barnabas's native Cyprus (Acts 5:36; cf. 15:39), preaching their way across the island before sailing to the mainland of Asia Minor. At Perga, John Mark forsakes the mission (Acts 13:13), which however presses northward into the mountains, to Antioch of Pisidia, the civil and military center of the region and (like Philippi) a Roman colony. On the first Sabbath, Paul and Barnabas make their way to the synagogue. Perhaps because they had already attracted some attention in the city as men of biblical learning,[68] the "rulers" [*archisunagogoi*] of the synagogue—who could appoint a qualified person to bring a message of comfort, consolation, or encouragement—invite them to speak (13:15).

Apparently the rulers expected a traditional synagogue sermon, as indicated by the (more or less technical) phrase "word of exhortation" (13:15).[69]

Luke provides two clues to the form and substance of that sermon. First, the synagogue sermon followed immediately on the reading of the Law (*seder*) and Prophets (*haftarah*). As at Pentecost,[70] Paul's Pisidian sermon follows the *proem* pattern, whereby a third text bridged the two readings.[71] Second, the *archisunagogoi* ask if Paul and Barnabas have a message "for the people" (13:15), indicating that the sermon was expected to *apply* the Scripture texts.[72] The synagogue sermon was to be *biblical* and *hortatory*. According to Luke, Paul had already proclaimed Jesus as "the Son of God [or Messiah]" in Damascus and Jerusalem. In Pisidia he preaches the same message (cf. Acts 9:20; 13:33; 17:3), but tailors it to the need of the moment.

Clifton Black contends that the peculiarities of Jewish context notwithstanding, the "word of exhortation" in Pisidia does not exhibit "any significant deviation from the conventions of Greco-Roman rhetoric."[73] According to Black, Paul follows the standard rhetorical pattern: (1) an *exordium* or *proem* (v. 16b); (2) a *narratio* (statement of the facts of the case), here a recital of God's salvific work in Israel's history (vv. 17–25); (3) a *propositio* (thesis), that the climax of God's saving work, Jesus, has been sent to the Jews and God-fearers present (v. 26); (4) a *probatio* (demonstration or proof), to the effect that the significance of Jesus has been vindicated by the resurrection (vv. 27–37); and (5) an *epilogos*, which satisfies the four requisites established by Aristotle.[74]

Furthermore, according to Black, the sermon conforms in a number of details to traditional emphases in classical rhetoric. For example, Paul's narrative (vv. 17–25) is brief, plausible, and vivid,[75] satisfying Quintilian's criteria for effective *narratio*.[76] If Black is right, Paul's sermon at Pisidian Antioch not only links Christian preaching to the traditional synagogue sermon but to the canons of rhetoric as well.

We have previously called attention to Paul's cosmopolitan education, and his use of rhetoric in Pisidia might merely reflect his own (and his hearers') hellenistic background.[77] On the other hand, we should remember that Paul had theological reasons for using means (rhetoric) to communicate the gospel as effectively as possible—reasons which Paul himself summarized in his well-known determination to "become all things to all men, so that [he] may by all means save some" (1 Cor. 9:22b). Aristotle said that rhetoric is *not* the art of persuasion, but the "ability . . . to see the available means of persuasion,"[78] to observe the givens of a situation, to enter empathetically into the phenomenology of the hearers, and to tailor the message accordingly.

For Paul, "what is at stake [in his ministry] is not simply the failure or success of human persuasion, . . . but man's eternal destiny."[79] To the end of winning persons eternally, Paul used rhetoric, not to manipulate, but (as Aristotle had it) to empathize. Or, to cite Augustine—Paul sought to liberate people "with so great [love], as if he were himself in that evil from which he wished to make them whole."[80]

"And Also to the Greek":
An Impromptu Sermon in Lystra (Acts 14:15–17)

A few days after his sermon in the Pisidian synagogue, Paul preaches (perhaps for the first time) to a Gentile audience, one hundred miles southeast, in Lystra, the home of Timothy. As at Solomon's Portico, the healing of a man lame from birth (14:8) provided the occasion. Perhaps owing to a familiar legend that Zeus and Hermes once visited Lystra incognito,[81] the residents conclude that the gods have come again (14:11) and rush to honor them with sacrifices (14:13). Because the crowd spoke the Lycaonian dialect, Paul and Barnabas did not at first realize what was happening. When they did (14:14a), they tore their clothes in protest and rushed into the crowd— preaching![82]

As it stands, the sermon contains only an *exordium* (*proem*) (14:15b), a *propositio* (14:15c), and a three-part *probatio* (14:15d–18). The absence of an *epilogos*[83] suggests either that the apostles lacked opportunity to complete the sermon, or, more likely, that Luke intended to juxtapose Paul's preaching to Jews (in Pisidia) and pagans (in Lystra), and highlight the differences by recounting only the most salient points of comparison.

Paul's opening "Men" (14:15a) contrasts with "Men of Israel" in Pisidia (13:16b); after which follows a longer and more developed *exordium*, where Paul (a) questions the Lycaonians' action[84] on the ground that (b) Paul and Barnabas are indeed only men, as they are, and that (c) their coming is to turn the Lystrans from "vain things."[85] The *exordium* passes almost imperceptibly into a *propositio* (thesis), to the effect that there is one and only one true and living God (14:15c). As proof (*probatio*), Paul offers three affirmations about God: (1) he is the Creator of all (14:15d);[86] (2) he has shown mercy by not judging the nations in their ignorance (14:16); and (3) he has displayed his goodness in giving gifts to all (14:17). As compared with his sermon to the Jews in Pisidia, Paul's preaching to the pagans emphasizes the nature of God (monotheism), the human experience of the Lycaonians ("vain things"), and the witness of God in creation, especially of his goodness.[87]

Tō Agnō Theō:
The Sermon on Areopagus (Acts 17:22b–31)

Those same emphases recur in Paul's sermon on Mars' Hill.[88] It is sometimes supposed that the Areopagites had put Paul on trial. Bruce Winter has shown, however, that the proceedings constituted a step in the process by which the city of Athens sanctioned the worship of new deities, a process in which the Council of Areopagos played a leading role.[89] Paul's "reasoning in the synagogues . . . and in the market place every day" (17:17b) had effected two quite different responses. Some dismissed him as an "idle babbler," but others took him to be a "herald" (*kataggeleus*) of new deities,[90] for which reason Paul was taken for a formal inquiry to determine whether (a) he was actually heralding new deities[91] and (b) if so, to judge whether his claims satisfied criteria for admission to the Greek pantheon.[92]

To use Aristotle's categories, the context called for *deliberative* rhetoric, since the questions at issue were cultural and political, having to do with what is advantageous or harmful[93]—in this case, to the culture of Athens. We should expect Paul to observe the conventions of rhetoric in such a setting.

He does so in an almost classical style.[94] The speech begins with an *exordium* (17:22–23a) that establishes rapport with the audience by means of a *captatio benevolentiae*.[95] Paul "seizes the good will" of the Athenians by observing (complimenting?) their piety in order to allay their suspicions about his "new religion." Paul then moves deftly to his real interest by using the Athenians' own experience as a point of contact. For all their religiosity, the Athenians worship at an altar *tō agnō theō* ("to an unknown god"; 17:23a). The *propositio* follows immediately: "Therefore what you worship in ignorance, this I proclaim to you" (17:23b).

Mark Given has argued that Paul's rhetoric on Areopagos had an almost Socratic flavor, in that he apparently intended to set the members of the council thinking, by using words with ambiguous or double meanings. For example, the word *deisidaimōn* (v. 22) might connote either "very religious" or "very superstitious." Which does Paul intend? In keeping with the conventions of rhetoric, the council would *expect* Paul to mean "religious"; but the word is ambiguous enough to plant a seed of doubt.[96] It is likewise with other terms. Is *agnountes* (v. 23b) "unknowingly" or "improperly"? Are the "times of *agnoia*" (v. 30) times of "misconception" or "[culpable] error"? Is *pistis* (v. 31) "proof" or "faith"? We can well imagine the unsettling cumulative effect of so much double entendre, by which Paul manages to be culture-sensitive and countercultural at the same time.

This culture/counterculture dynamic recurs throughout the *probatio* (17:24–29), as Paul moves back and forth between the philosophers' traditions and biblical revelation. So pronounced is Paul's willingness to accommodate that Martin Dibelius thought Luke formulated this speech (as a paradigm for preaching to cultured Gentiles) in terms more stoic than biblical.[97] But that ignores both the biblical heart of the speech[98] and the rhetorical strategy behind it.

But according to Dean Zweck, Paul did indeed adapt a stoic *line of argument*. Beginning with the nature and existence of God (vv. 24–25), he moves on to God's providential governance of the world and humanity (vv. 26–27b), and finally, he addresses humanity's relationship to God

(vv. 27c–29).[99] At each point, Paul seizes on a tenet of Greek philosophy and moves quickly to draw out the implications of a biblical corrective, usually in a way that even some of the philosophers could acknowledge.

For example, Paul begins with a concept most familiar to the Greeks, the *kosmos*, where (in stoic pantheism) "God" is found. But, no, Paul says, God "*made* the kosmos" (v. 24, emphasis added). By implication—and even Plato and Zeno would have agreed—God cannot be contained in temples or served with human hands. Paul deals with concepts like the *providence of God* and *relationship with God* in the same way.[100] Paul's conclusion (*peroratio, epilogos*) reprises the Athenians' ignorant worship of the "Unknown God" (17:30–31).

As he did in Lystra, Paul again emphasizes God's mercy. The Athenians have attempted to worship God in a way that does sacrilege to his nature; but he has "overlooked the times of ignorance" (v. 30a). Yet this God now commands repentance inasmuch as he has determined judgment according to the righteousness of Jesus—the man approved (proved) by the resurrection.

Paul's teaching of the resurrection had been the catalyst for these proceedings, and now it becomes the watershed for response. Though the question is endlessly debated, it seems probable that the division followed party lines. The Epicureans (v. 18), with no conception of an afterlife, "began to sneer" (v. 32a); while the Stoics (v. 18), who allowed for the survival of the soul, said, "We shall hear you again concerning this" (v. 32b).[101] It is instructive for every preacher to recognize in Paul's experience that despite our best efforts to make the gospel intelligible, in the end many people will reject the greatest hope as the sheerest folly.

Apologia Pro Vita Sua:
The Defense Speeches of Paul

Of the twenty Christian speeches in Acts, more than one-third—fully half of the ten speeches attributed to Paul—qualify as "defenses." These statistics confirm the hypothesis that Luke wrote the Book of Acts, among other things, to show that neither the Jewish nor Roman authorities had anything to fear from the preaching of the gospel. As Pilate had found no fault in Jesus, none of those who accused Peter or the apostles could make their charges stick. Throughout Acts, Luke "produced evidence to show that Christianity was harmless, . . . innocent . . . and lawful."[102] The apologetic speeches in Acts, however, document the beginning of what will become a long history of Christians' having to defend themselves against the baseless charge that they subvert culture.

The history begins for Paul almost as soon as he is converted; but the formal history begins when certain "Jews from Asia" stirred up a mob in Jerusalem, claiming that Paul preached against "our people [the Jews], and the Law, and this place [the temple]."[103] Paul will find himself answering that charge all the way to the Imperial City, to "the leading men of the Jews" in Rome (Acts 28:17a). "Brethren," he says to them, "though I had done nothing against our people or the customs of our fathers, yet I was delivered as a prisoner from Jerusalem into the hands of the Romans" (28:17b). The road from Jerusalem to Rome passed of course through Caesarea, where Paul must plead his case before Felix the governor (24:10b–21) and later before Herod Agrippa II (26:2–23).

"A Ringleader of the Nazarenes": The Speech of Tertullus (Acts 24:2b–8)

A certain Tertullus prosecuted the case before Felix, doubtless retained by Ananias the high priest and his collegues. He specified three charges: (1) Paul stirred up dissension "among all the Jews throughout the world" (24:5a); (2) he was a "ringleader of the sect of the Nazarenes" (24:5b); and (3) he attempted to desecrate the temple (24:6)—charges which Paul categorically denied (24:11–13), but which Tertullus adroitly turned to his advantage. Contrary to a good deal of popular and scholarly opinion,[104] Tertullus actually presented a formidable case in a skillful way. Not only did rhetorical handbooks recommend using "sedition" in the prosecution of criminal cases, but Tertullus cleverly linked Paul to known agitations among Jews in certain parts of the Roman Empire during the early years of Nero.[105]

Indeed, according to Bruce Winter, the speeches of both Tertullus and Paul before Felix conformed precisely—as we should expect—to the pattern of forensic rhetoric in Roman courts. Each includes a *captatio benevolentiae* in the *exordium* (*proem*), intended to secure the judge's goodwill, attentiveness, and readiness to learn.[106] Each contains a statement of the facts of the case (*narratio*), proofs (*probatio*, or *confirmatio*), and a *peroratio*, or set of conclusions. In addition to showing that Christianity was no threat either to Jerusalem or Rome, Luke's record of the speeches before Felix show that Christian preaching may make use—indeed, must make use—of rhetorical forms.

"Almost Persuaded": Paul's Defense before Herod Agrippa (Acts 26:2–23)

Felix, of course, delayed his promised decision on Paul's case (24:22b–23) and left Paul imprisoned for his unfortunate successor Festus (24:27). Forced (as he thought) to reopen the case and (like Felix) hoping to curry favor with the Jews (25:6–9), Festus left Paul with no choice but to appeal to Caesar (25:10–11). Having no intelligible report to send to Rome, however, Festus in turn appealed to Herod Agrippa II, before whom Paul delivers his *apologia pro vita sua*.

Rhetorically, Paul's defense before Agrippa (26:2–23) follows the conventions of the law courts. The *exordium* (26:38) includes the now-familiar *captatio benevolentiae* (vv. 2–3), appealing to Herod's familiarity with Jewish customs and theology, and setting forth in brief (a) his Jewish heritage (vv. 4–5) and (b) his contention (*propositio*) that the charges against him are actually *theological*, not *civil* (vv. 7–8). A *narratio* follows (vv. 9–18) in which Paul recounts to Herod his testimony of God's call. In his *probatio* (vv. 19–21), Paul contrasts his obedience with the persecution of the Jews. Finally (*peroratio*), Paul reiterates the proposition (vv. 7b–8) by asserting that he has done nothing more than to proclaim the fulfillment of God's promise through Moses and the prophets (vv. 22–23).

The *captatio* provides a vital clue to the interpretation of this speech, and, indeed, to all of Paul's apologetic preaching. Paul expressly mentions his gratitude for a hearing with Herod, inasmuch as the king is "an expert in all customs and questions among the Jews" (26:3). Not only does Paul expect to be heard; he expects Herod to grasp (as Festus could not grasp) what is really at stake in Paul's case. For while the Jews have accused Paul of civil misdeeds, the real issue is theological. Paul is forced, as a matter of legal necessity, to answer the civil charges; but, as a matter of conviction, he also addresses the theological issue—which is, in a nutshell, the resurrection hope of Israel. Thus Paul's *propositio* before Herod: "I am standing trial for the hope of the promise made by God to our fathers" (26:6). And thus Paul's question to Herod and those in attendance: "Why is it considered incredible among you people if God does raise the dead?" (26:8).

What Herod knows, all Israel knows. The central hope of the people of God is the resurrection. Paul preaches that God has fulfilled that very hope in Christ—but rather than receive the message as *Good News*, God's people put the messenger on trial. In a bizarre twist on the ancient practice of executing the bearer of bad tidings, the Jews would execute the bearer of good!

Implicitly or explicitly, the juxtaposition of culture and theology runs like a thread through the apologetic sermons of Paul. Which is to say that each of the speeches operates on two levels simultaneously. First, it answers the charge that the Christian faith is anticultural. Second, it exposes the real objection to the Christian message—which is the resurrection!

C. S. Lewis once wrote, "Amiable agnostics will talk cheerfully about man's search for God."[107] But Lewis knew from his own experience how threatening an encounter with the living God could be. Man's search for God? One might just as well speak of the mouse's search for the cat! From Paul to the present, Christians have been tried, convicted, tortured, and executed, as enemies of culture, by people who claimed they were seeking God, when in truth, they were just afraid of the cat!

CHAPTER

PAUL'S EPISTLES AS INSPIRED PREACHING

A. BOYD LUTER

> *Paul and his letters have fascinated readers for generations. Scholars have analyzed his theology, his missionary practices, the chronology of his life, the sociology of the churches he planted, the epistolary structure of his letters, the rhetorical structure of his letters, and many other features. Most of this analysis, however, has treated Paul's letters as purely literary compositions and has, by and large, ignored an important aspect of Paul's culture: its orality.[1]*

> *The flow of narrative and argument was circular rather than linear.[2]*

> *[In regard to] the letter of Paul to the Philippians . . . what in a text shaped for the eye, with its structural changes indicated by paragraphing, could be taken as indications of compositional sources, in a text shaped for the ear may well have been intended as oral/ aural signs of structure.[3]*

> *See with what large letters I am writing to you with my own hand (Gal. 6:11).*

> *I adjure you by the Lord to have this letter read to all the brethren (1 Thess. 5:27).*

In our day, there is no widespread consensus on the preparation and delivery of sermons. Different pastors prepare and present their sermons in very different ways. For example, some employ full manuscripts. By contrast, others work with outlines, though the outlining approach may range from extremely detailed to very sketchy. And there are some who champion "preaching without notes," though that wording does not really clearly communicate what is taking place. It is hardly ever the case that no notes at all are used in the process. Rather, it is that no notes are taken into the pulpit. In fact, many who preach without notes actually prepare full manuscripts in the study.

To further complicate this picture, some preachers prepare differently at different stages of their ministries. Some start off writing manuscripts, then find out they don't have the time to write everything out or that manuscripts are too restrictive in the pulpit. On the other hand, some others begin with a more informal approach, then find they can't trust their memories or that they need more previously thought-out precision of expression and, thus, gravitate more and more toward manuscripting.

This discussion is incomplete, however, without mention of those preachers who regularly shift from approach to approach, depending on the kind of speaking occasion or the length of the message to be delivered. Since I have, over time, become one of those preachers and teachers who shift quite regularly with the varying situation, this kind of flexibility has a warm spot in my heart.

In addition, different styles of *written ministry* should be considered here. Within the wider "genre" of Christian nonfiction writing, there is a range from the scholarly to the popular or devotional.[4] The bulk of writers are specialists at one end of the spectrum or the other. Some write mostly in one style, with an occasional foray into the other.[5] There are some, though, who fairly naturally move back and forth between the more formal and the more informal styles of writing, as well as between longer and shorter "page-counts" of writing opportunities or assignments. They do not evidence a strong preference for a certain type or length of writing, just a focus on getting the job done with the communication need placed before them.

PAUL'S MINISTRY OF PREACHING AND "THE NEXT BEST THING"

Had the apostle Paul lived in our day, he undoubtedly would have evidenced amazing flexibility in both spoken and written communication. Certainly, Paul was, in his day, the kind of highly flexible communicator who felt more or less equally comfortable with quite different kinds of preaching. For example, there is clearly a dramatic difference between Paul's sermon in the synagogue in Pisidian Antioch (Acts 13:16–41) and his presentation to the philosophers on the Areopagus (Acts 17:22–31).

But the apostle was equally adept at producing significantly different styles and lengths of epistolary writing,[6] depending on the needs of the audience and the life situation. For a classic contrast, many view Romans as a tight logical treatise, while Philemon has the feel of a short personal note. Or, there is the startling "black-and-white" difference between the lengthy list of names and greetings that crowns Romans in chapter 16,[7] versus Ephesians, which, though sharing many of the same theological and practical themes with Romans, lists only one name in its closing section: that of Tychicus, Paul's courier (Eph. 6:21).[8]

But beyond this obvious versatility in style, the apostle also understood very well that his apostolic written interaction with his audiences was the next best thing to being there. If Paul could go to visit a particular church at a specific crucial time and preach related to their needs, he did. But often, he could not go, at least not in as timely a manner as was required by the problems in the churches. Thus, a letter laying out his theological and behavioral responses to the church's situation was the best facsimile spiritual "presence" he could offer in lieu of his actual physical presence. And because the apostle was almost surely verbalizing his letters through dictation to an amanuensis (Rom. 16:22), in a very real sense, they should be considered what could be called *written preaching*. That is the way in which they will be considered in the rest of this chapter.

PAUL'S EPISTLES: THE LONG AND SHORT OF IT

In my first pastorate in the Texas hill country, our church did not have a weekly newsletter. However, I wrote a weekly column for a couple of local newspapers for six years. This meant that, week after week (except when I was out of town on vacation), around three hundred times, I submitted a five-hundred-word column for the readers in Canyon Lake and New Braunfels, Texas. In the process, I got to where I could pretty much crank out a creditable five-hundred-word piece in my sleep. However, as a writer I had become a one-trick pony, too much like a baseball pitcher with only one good pitch.

Paul, though observing all the standard epistolary conventions of his day,[9] was anything but stereotypical in the length of his letters. On the one hand, several are fairly short. Philemon is only a single chapter, while 2 Thessalonians and Titus are only three chapters long. Philippians, Colossians, and 2 Timothy are each only four chapters in length.

At the other end of the length scale, Romans and 1 Corinthians each contain sixteen chapters, while 2 Corinthians is thirteen chapters long. Their length (compared to the rest of Paul's epistles) is the reason these three are often referred to as "the major epistles." Just these three epistles encompass forty-five chapters, while the remaining ten Pauline letters contain a total of forty-two.

As a communicator, it can be safely said that Paul was a practicioner of the "enough, but not too much" philosophy. To the extent that there were issues to be dealt with, he continued as long (or as short) as it took to get the job done. Yet, as you read the apostle's letters, you never have the sense of excess verbiage, much less rhetoric for the sake of rhetoric. Nor do his letters ever feel unnecessarily clipped or underdeveloped. Yes, ultimately this is due to the divine inspiration of the Scriptures (2 Tim. 3:16). Still, the human side of the equation is still very much in play, and that fact is the touch-point for those pursuing inspiring preaching today.

PAUL'S EPISTLES: THE EARLY AND LATE OF IT

While not all evangelicals would agree, there is widespread agreement that the apostle Paul wrote thirteen[10] canonical[11] books over a period of less than two decades. These epistles break down naturally into four groupings, based on clustered dates or other related circumstances. These groups can be charted as follows:

Grouping	Books	Dates
The Early Letters	Galatians;[12] 1, 2 Thessalonians	Late 40s–Early 50s
The Major Letters	Romans; 1, 2 Corinthians	Mid–50s
The Prison Letters	Ephesians; Colossians; Philemon; Philippians	Late 50s[13]–Early 60s
The Pastoral Letters	1 Timothy; Titus; 2 Timothy	Mid–60s[14]

The following selective discussion of Paul's letters as "preaching" will follow the above consecutive chronological arrangement. In this way, we will be able to track Paul's way of doing things from the beginning to the end of his specialized ministry of authoring Scripture. Before proceeding, though, there is one other related issue to introduce.

THE "WILD CARD" FACTOR: THE POSSIBILITY OF MULTIPLE OUTLINES

With several of Paul's letters, it is difficult enough to determine one clear and defensible structure.[15] So the thought of *any* of them having more than one intended outline seems outlandish at first. However, enough evidence has been brought forward over time to at least seriously consider the possibility.

For example, as early as 1970 the highly respected Charles Talbert argued for the presence of double, or even triple, structures in works from the same general era as the New Testament, such as Vergil and Horace.[16] His wise conclusion in regard to such structures was: "It is not necessary to discredit one such pattern if there is good support for more than one."[17]

Nor is this a strange idea in wider New Testament studies. The Book of Acts, for example, clearly reflects two distinct outlines, structures which beautifully complement one another: Acts 1:8 unpacks naturally into a threefold structure: (1) witness in the power of the Holy Spirit in Jerusalem (chs. 1–7); (2) witness in the power of the Holy Spirit in Judea and Samaria (chs. 8–12); and (3) witness in the power of the Holy Spirit to the ends of the earth (chs. 13–28). Equally obvious, though, is the side-by-side comparing of the apostles Peter (chs. 1–12) and Paul (chs. 13–28), in which such aspects as sermons, miracles, trials, and incarcerations are clearly parallelled. In this case, the choice of outlines is not either/or, but clearly both/and.

Even a New Testament book as complex as Revelation evidences the likelihood of multiple outlines. In a very creative recent article, Michelle Lee has pointed toward that very real possibility.[18] Persuaded by her argument, my further study has indicated that the Apocalypse quite possibly has three discernible complementary structures,[19] as will be argued in the later chapter on John's Epistles and Revelation.

Thus, it seems fair to say that there is no decisive reason the Pauline Epistles could not have multiple structures. And, although I will not lay out more than one outlining of each book discussed, it should be assumed that, with the repeated rereading *whole* of books in the congregational setting, which would have been the norm,[20] there is a significant "straight-through" outline for each book, which would have been grasped first by the hearer. The presence of a second structure would have been noticed more progressively, by being sensitive to the clues provided in the text through hearing the letter reread and reread.

PATTERNS THAT GIVE CLUES TO CONCENTRIC ARGUMENTS

After sifting extensive evidence related to the use of rhetorical devices in the Greco-Roman world and in the Septuagint,[21] John Harvey isolates eight that are particularly prominent or important.[22] These range from *inclusion*, a "book-ends" effect, such as Paul's use of "grace" at the beginning and end of each his letters,[23] to various kinds of repetition and parallelism (whether to compare, contrast, or complement [i.e., 2 + 2 = 4]). Particularly common in the apostle's rhetorical repertoire, though, is inverted parallelism (sometimes used interchangeably with "chiasmus"[24]), whether at the micro, middle-sized or macro levels. That point is underlined by Davis, who concludes that, in much of the written communication of the era, the impact of orality was that "the flow of narrative and argument was circular rather than linear."[25]

Though much of the focus of the rest of this chapter will be from the "middle-sized" to the "macro-level," I must admit that my own awareness of the extent of the Pauline use of inverted parallelism began with two passages at the micro level. The first was Philippians 3:10–11, from which I explored the meaning of the reversal of the elements "resurrection" (3:10a, 11b) and "sufferings/death" (3:10b, 11a) in the first book I wrote.[26] Since the midpoint of such a mini-structure is often what is being focused on, the meaning here is likely that the only doorway to resurrection power is through suffering and death.

Shortly thereafter, I realized that Romans 10:9–10 was structured in the same way: Mouth (10:9a), heart (10:9b), heart (10:10a), mouth (10:10b). The featured angle here is that the heart is "the heart of the matter" in regard to salvation. In the culture Paul was addressing in his letters, rhetorical flourishes like these would have been immediately noted and appreciated for the clear emphasis they spotlighted.

Harvey agrees that there is extensive use of chiasmus by the apostle Paul, but he evidences serious doubts that the phenomenon of "extended chiasmus" exists.[27] Ian Thomson similarly understands the widespread employment of chiasm by Paul but, in his study, limits it to a maximum of twenty-three verses, though leaving the door open to the possibility of chiasmus at the macro level.[28] As will be seen, though, there is considerable reason to conclude not only that such macro-chiasm exists, but that it is widely used by Paul as a sermon-length rhetorical technique.

PAUL'S EARLY EPISTLES AS INSPIRED PREACHING

What can we learn about how the apostle began his "written preaching" career with Galatians, his first epistle? Was there a rhetorical pattern established when Paul sent his early letters? What is "heard" from the echoed orality of these books (which is strongly inferred by Paul's wording, "See with what large letters I am writing to you with my own hand," because that meant he was taking the pen from his stenographer to add this written comment)?

The normal straight-through outlining of Galatians (i.e., the initial sense of movement the hearer would comprehend) is simply: (1) Paul's apostolic authority defended (chs. 1–2); (2) Paul's gospel "rooted" (in the Old Testament; chs. 3–4); and (3) Paul's gospel applied (in the power of the Holy Spirit; chs. 5–6). But there is a whole series of clear parallels in Galatians, which chart into the following grand chiastic structuring:

THE STRUCTURE OF GALATIANS

A (1:1–5) Introduction/Preview of key themes

    B (1:6–10) Altering the gospel message; Worthy of being accursed; Pleasing God, not man

        C (1:11–24) Biographical: Revelation of Christ converts Paul, who only later confers with Peter over the gospel, then believers glorify God

D (2:1–10) Truth of the gospel (I): Test case of Titus; False brethren; Stood firm; Gospel to the uncircumcised and circumcised

E (2:11–14) Truth of the gospel (II): Peter's withdrawal and hypocrisy (Issue: food); Impact on the Galatians

F (2:15–21) Works of the Law vs. justification by faith; Crucified with Christ; Maintain grace

G (3:1–9) Spirit through the hearing of faith, just as Abraham believed and was reckoned righteous; Those of faith are "sons of Abraham" and thus blessed

H (3:10–25) Redeemed from the curse of the Law by Christ; Priority of promise over Law; The Law as jail/tutor to bring us to Christ

I (3:26–29) Sons of God through faith; Baptized into Christ; One in Christ; Abraham's seed/Heirs according to promise

I' (4:1–7) Heir was slave until appointed time; In bondage until the fullness of time; Adopted as sons/Heirs of God

H' (4:8–20) Turn back to weak "elements"; Observing calendar; Paul's frailty; Enemy's improper zeal; Paul's renewed labor pains over the Galatians

G' (4:21–5:1) Abraham's sons: Older—in bondage/ Mt. Sinai/present Jerusalem; Younger—Jerusalem above/promise/ persecuted/Spirit/ liberty

F' (5:2–6) Circumcised: No profit in Christ; Must keep the whole Law; Estranged from Christ; Fallen from grace; In Christ, faith working through love

E' (5:7–12) Galatians hindered from obeying the truth; A little leaven (Issue: circumcision); Offense of the cross

D' (5:13–26) Lovingly serve others, not the flesh; Flesh vs. the Spirit (against whose energizing there is no Law)

C' (6:1–6) Pastoral: Spiritual ones restore sinner, being careful; Bear one another's burdens, plus your own load; Share with teachers

B' (6:7–10) Sow to the flesh, reap corruption; Sow to the Spirit, reap eternal life

A' (6:11–18) Conclusion/Review of key themes

With this kind of mirror preaching, the main point is made in the middle of the structure. In this case, the apostle is emphasizing that you can become a son/heir of God through faith in Christ without having to keep the law. This makes sense as a central point, given that the Judaizers had been hammering on keeping the law and being circumcised to be right before God.

There is a similar structure present in 1 Thessalonians. In this case, it was, ironically, my coauthor's inability to make a speaking engagement that prompted me to observe it. In the last few days, I was asked to step in to speak at a Jerry Vines Institute of Biblical Preaching[29] seminar in Longview, Texas, in October 1999, the focus of which was 1 Thessalonians. As I hurriedly prepared to deal with the introductory and structural issues related to 1 Thessalonians, I was struck by the seemingly out-of-place presence of "finally" (Gk. *loipon*) in 4:1, roughly 40 percent before the end of the letter. That clue led me to consider the possibility of a book-long inverted parallel structure (which I charted and handed out at the seminar, with my initial thoughts on how to preach such a macro-structure). The following is what I observed:

THE STRUCTURE OF 1 THESSALONIANS

A (1:1–2) Introductory greeting, thanksgiving and prayer for the Thessalonian church

    B (1:3–10) *Note: faith, love, and hope (1:3);* Living as Christians in the midst of short-term "tribulation," but not end-times wrath

        C (2:1–20) Encouragement to continue faithful in the midst of suffering, looking ahead to Christ's coming

            D (3:1–13) Timothy's hands-on encouragement to handle the tribulation, completing "what is lacking" in their growth, toward the end of holiness (Gk. *hagiosune*) before God "finally" (4:1; *with about 40 percent of the book still to go*)

            D′ (4:1–12) Paul's exhortations to "excel still more" in regard to sanctification (Gk. *hagiasmos*), which is God's will

        C′ (4:13–18) Comfort after the death of believers, looking ahead to Christ's coming

    B′ (5:1–11) *Note: faith, love, and hope (5:8);* Living as children of the light/day, not destined for the wrath of the day of the Lord

A′ (5:12–28) Concluding behavioral directions to the Thessalonian church, including a greeting and emphasis on prayer and thanksgiving

Again, it should be asked whether the spotlighted center point of this structure is adequate to provide insight regarding the overall meaning of the book that Paul was trying to get across in his "written preaching" to the Thessalonians. In this case, it appears to fit the bill very well. Since the believers in Thessalonica were still babes in Christ, Paul having been in the city less than a month when he founded the church (Acts 17:1–10), the encouragement to holiness (ch. 3) and sanctification (4:1–12) is most appropriate.

PAUL'S MAJOR EPISTLES AS INSPIRED PREACHING

There are apparent reasons why, in the mid-50s, the length of Paul's letters more than double from the early epistles.[30] (Stretched-out length is, of course, the primary reason for calling Romans and 1 and 2 Corinthians the Major Epistles.) In the case of Romans, Paul had never been to the capital of the Roman Empire at that time, and thus his epistle served as an extended introduction to the church at Rome (Rom. 1:11–13). As far as the Corinthian letters are concerned, it was, so to speak, far and away the most high-maintenance congregation Paul had founded. In other words, the length of 1 and 2 Corinthians was pretty much in direct proportion to the depth of the problems in, and questions from, the congregation at Corinth.

As far as I can tell, none of the three major letters is structured in a fully inverted parallel manner, probably at least partly because they are so long as to be very difficult for an author to plan and dictate. The outline of Romans seems to unpack 1:16–17: "For I am not ashamed of the gospel, for it is the power of God for salvation to everyone who believes, to the Jew first and also to the Greek. For in it the righteousness of God is revealed from faith to faith; as it is written, 'But the righteous man shall live by faith.'"

This unfolds into an overview outline like this:
    I.   Introduction (1:1–15)
    II.   Theme statement (1:16–17)
    III. The universal sin of mankind (1:18–3:20)
    IV.   Justification by faith (3:21–5:21)
    V.   Sanctification and glorification (chs. 6–8)
    VI.   Israel and the Gentiles in God's plan (Chs. 9–11)
    VII. Living by faith (12:1–15:13)
    VIII. Paul's apostolic ministry and travels (15:14–33)
    IX.   Concluding greetings (ch. 16)

Though Romans seems to reflect a primarily forward movement, there is still evidence of Paul's awareness of the circular in his argumentation. As seen above, he employed chiasm to emphasize a key point in 10:9–10, as well as structuring the section on the Jews and Gentiles in God's wider plan as inverted parallelism:

A (9:1–29) God's election, especially related to Israel
    B (9:30–10:21) Israel's responsibility for their unbelief
A' (ch. 11) God's plan for Israel and the Gentiles

The point here seems to be to underline that, in spite of the fact that God is sovereign in regard to Israel's unbelief, the Jews are still fully responsible before him. Whether we understand (and God's ways are often far beyond our comprehension) or agree with the "fairness" (from our limited human perspective), it is still true.

Nor is 1 Corinthians developed along parallel lines. Very clearly, it is structured around information provided to Paul by "Chloe's people" (1:11) about problems in the church (chs. 1–6) and an extensive list of questions sent to the apostle by the Corinthian church (chs. 7–16). However, again, there is an extremely significant section that is arranged chiastically: the well-known, sometimes controversial section on spiritual gifts (1 Cor. 12–14). It is clearly laid out in the following manner:

A (ch. 12) Spiritual gifts and the Body of Christ
   B (ch. 13) The worthlessness of spiritual gifts without love
A' (ch. 14) Use of spiritual gifts in the worship context

The indisputable practical point here is that, even though a church be incredibly gifted (as the Corinthians definitely were; 1 Cor. 1:7), it was counterproductive unless they were energized by love, not selfishness. That was foundational to edifying the body and operating within appropriate guidelines for worship.

Paul's remaining major epistle, 2 Corinthians, is different. It has proven difficult, even frustrating, to outline. And it is *possible* that 2 Corinthians is an example of a lengthy work that was written at different times (i.e., Paul stopped the epistle and picked it up later, maybe more than once, after a change in the tone with which he is communicating). Whatever the case, 2 Corinthians feels almost like three different letters:[31] (1) Paul's apostolic ministry, against the backdrop of new covenant ministry (chs. 1–7); (2) the collection for the church in Jerusalem, against the backdrop of new covenant giving (chs. 8–9); and (3) Paul defending his apostleship, against the backdrop of the onslaught of the false "super-apostles" (chs. 10–13).

The very first persuasive study laying out an extended chiastic treatment that I ever encountered was by Craig Blomberg, dealing with 2 Corinthians 1:12–7:16.[32] He laid out a rigorous listing of criteria for extended chiasmus, which is still the best I have seen,[33] demonstrating that his proposed structure was anything but "seeing a chiasm under every bush." His structural layout is as follows:

BLOMBERG'S STRUCTURING OF 2 CORINTHIANS 1–7[34]

A (1:12–22) The Corinthians can rightfully boast in Paul
   B (1:23–2:11) Grief and comfort over the painful letter; Hope for forgiving the offender
      C (2:12–13) Looking for Titus in Macedonia

    D (2:14–4:6) A series of contrasts—belief vs. unbelief, centered on
        Christians as the letters of the living God, in glory being
        transformed into his image
        E (4:7–5:10) Surviving and triumphing despite every hardship
           (see esp. 4:8–10)
           F (5:11–21) *Theological climax: The ministry of reconciliation*
        E' (6:1–10) Surviving and triumphing despite every hardship
           (see esp. vv. 8b–10)
    D' (6:11–7:4) A series of contrasts—belief vs. unbelief, centered on
        Christians as the temple of the living God, in light of being trans-
        formed into his holiness
  C' (7:5–7) Finding Titus in Macedonia
 B' (7:8–13a) Grief and comfort over the painful letter; Joy after forgiving the
  offender
A' (7:13b–16) Paul can rightfully boast in the Corinthians

The parallels in this structure are exceedingly clear and, thus, very difficult to deny. Thus, the biggest remaining question here is, "Why would the
apostle center this elegant example of written preaching on his explanation
of the ministry of reconciliation (2 Cor. 5:11–21)?" The most obvious
answer is that the high-maintenance Corinthians needed to be reconciled at
two levels: theologically, with God; and relationally, with Paul. Hence, the
issue of reconciliation is seen as disproportionately important for circumstances in Corinth at this point.

PAUL'S PRISON EPISTLES AS INSPIRED PREACHING

The circumstances behind the Prison Epistles change things in Paul's life
and ministry dramatically in the direction of "preaching through writing."[35]
The reason for that, quite obviously, is because, for a very extended period of
time,[36] he was only able to preach in person to those who visited him, so to
speak, "behind bars" (Acts 28:31).

It is most likely that *three* of the apostle's Prison Epistles were carried by
Tychicus on the same journey: Ephesians (6:21–22), Colossians (4:7–8) and
Philemon (the mention of Onesimus, the focus of Paul's letter to Philemon,
in Col. 4:9, as a traveling companion of Tychicus, makes it clear that
Philemon was delivered along with Colossians). Logically, since all three letters had to have been written very close together time-wise, the "preaching
through writing" that was the apostle's best remaining option for pastoral
oversight of the churches likely was quite similar. To test that thesis, we will
consider the structure of all three in rapid succession:

Often, the probing of the structure of Ephesians goes no further than a
citation of the pivot verse of the letter: "Therefore I the prisoner of the Lord,

implore you to walk in a manner worthy of the calling with which you have been called" (4:1). In this understanding, chapters 1–3 are "the calling with which you have been called," while chapters 4–6 deal with "walking worthy" of that calling. Sometimes, the well-known "armor of God" passage (6:10–20) is broken off as a third main section of the epistle.

However, a grand chiastic structure is discernible:

THE STRUCTURE OF EPHESIANS

(1:1–2) Introduction ("grace"; "peace")
A (1:3–6) God the Father's role in our salvation
  B (1:7–12) Christ's role in our salvation
    C (1:13–14) The Holy Spirit's role in our salvation
      D (1:15–23) Love for the saints; Raised from the dead
        E (2:1–10) No longer walk according to the world
          F (2:11–22) Apostles and prophets; Growing into a holy temple
            G (3:1–7) *toutou charin;* Church; Rulers and authorities in the heavenly places
            G' (3:14–21) *toutou charin;* Every family in heaven and on earth
          F' (4:1–16) Apostles, prophets, etc., a body growing up
        E' (4:17–32) Don't walk like the Gentiles
      D' (5:1–14) Walk in love; Rise from the dead
    C' (5:15–21) The filling of the Spirit
  B' (5:22–6:9) The behavioral outworking of submitting to one another in the fear of Christ/Christ and the church
A' (6:10–20) Armor of God
(6:21–24) Conclusion ("peace"; "grace")

This structural understanding makes sense of the parallel mentions of apostles and prophets in 2:20 and 4:11, as well as the seemingly odd command to rise from the dead in 5:14. The centerpoint seems to be focused on the mystery of the gospel and its cosmic dimension.

What about Colossians? Does it reflect a similar inverted parallel structural strategy, even as Paul is "preaching" against the attacks of a quasiphilosophical view (Col. 2:8) that apparently was a blend of Jewish and Greek elements.[37] The structural layout that follows shows that is not unlikely.

THE STRUCTURE OF COLOSSIANS

A (1:1–2) Introductory greetings to the saints/faithful brethren in Colossae
  B (1:3–12) Thanksgiving/prayer; Evangelism in the world, including Colossae, led by Epaphras (vv. 7–8)
    C (1:13–20) Christ's lordship as Creator and Re-creator, Head of the body

D (1:21–29) Proclaiming Christ; Wisdom
  E (2:1–5) Unifying love, in spite of distance ("in spirit")
    F (2:6–7) Walking in Christ individually/gratefully
      G (2:8–19) Avoiding earthly philosophy and religion through identification with Christ
        H (2:20–23) "If you *died* with Christ"
        H' (3:1–4) "If you've been *raised*"
      G' (3:5–11) Identification with Christ's death and putting on the new self
    F' (3:12–13) Living corporately/graciously
  E' (3:14–15) Unifying love in the church body
D' (3:16–17) Word of Christ; Wisdom
C' (3:18–4:1) Serving the Lord Christ in our primary relationships
B' (4:2–14) Prayer with thanksgiving; Evangelism and evangelists, significantly Epaphras (vv. 12–13)
A' (4:15–18) Concluding greetings to brethren in Colossae, to pass on to those in Laodicea

At the very least, the parallelism seen here is impressive. But does it fit with what we know of the background and emphases of Colossians or even focus it better?

There is no conflict with the normal understanding; and, given the profound Christology of Colossians, the twin passages of applied Christology spotlighted in the middle of the book make complete sense ("If you have died with Christ" [2:20] and "If then you have been raised up with Christ" [3:1]).

Does the little Epistle to Philemon follow suit with the same orality-based pattern of written preaching? I have been wrestling with the question of the structure of Philemon since the mid-1990s, and my carefully considered (and reconsidered) answer is yes.[38] The fruit of my research is seen below:

THE STRUCTURE OF PHILEMON

A (1–3) Paul, a prisoner, to Philemon, a fellow worker, and others: Greetings
  B (4–7) Praying for Philemon, having heard of his love and faith, for effective "partnership," because he has refreshed the saints' hearts
    C (8–9) Paul's spiritual position allows Paul to command Philemon to act, but he chooses to appeal lovingly from the weakness of age/imprisonment
      D (10–11) In prison, Paul has "fathered" a new spiritual child, Onesimus, who is now living up to his name (i.e., "Useful")
      D' (12–13) Paul is returning Onesimus to his master, Philemon, saying Onesimus represents "my very heart," meaning that if Philemon should "refresh" Onesimus as Paul's "heart" (see v. 20), as

Philemon has done with other saints (see v. 7)
C' (14–16) Paul seeks the free-will consent of Philemon to view
Onesimus as more than a slave: as a beloved brother to Paul and
Philemon
B' (17–22) Appealing to "partner" status, Paul asks Philemon to accept
Onesimus as he would Paul, charging Onesimus's debt to Paul, as he
looks forward to visiting with Philemon, in answer to his prayers
A' (23–25) Epaphras, a fellow prisoner, and other fellow workers, greet
Philemon

The parallelism is quite clear. Paul employs it to subtly but significantly enhance his case with Philemon in regard to proper treatment of the now converted slave, Onesimus.

The remaining Prison Epistle is Paul's written preaching to the church at Philippi. I have written more on Philippians, notably various angles related to its structure, than on any other biblical book.[39] The following reflects my best understanding of the structure of this elegant letter:

THE STRUCTURE OF PHILIPPIANS

A (1:1–2) "All the saints in Christ Jesus"
B (1:3–11) "Partnership in the gospel" from the first day in Philippi
C (1:12–26) An opportunity to spread the gospel and live for Christ
amidst distress (Gk. *thlipsis*)
D (1:27–2:4) Conduct worthy of the gospel: Unity in suffering through
humble selflessness
E (2:5–18) Example/action: Christ's example of humility and
suffering before glory, plus behavioral instructions
F (2:19–24) A model gospel partner (I): Timothy; *Note:* (1) The
out-of-place "travelogue" (2:19–30); and (2) the odd use of
"finally" (Gk. *to loipon*, 3:1a), both in the middle of the book
F' (2:25–3:1a) A model gospel partner (II): Epaphroditus
E' (3:1b–21) Example/action: Paul's example of humbling and
suffering before upward call/ transformation, then behavioral
instructions
D' (4:1–9) Conduct worthy of partners in the gospel: Joyful harmony
through prayer and right thinking
C' (4:10–14) An opportunity for the Philippians' generosity and Paul's
contentment amidst distress (Gk. *thlipsis;* used only in the 'C' layer)
B' (4:15–20) Ongoing partnership generosity from the first day since Paul left
Philippi
A' (4:21–23) "Every saint in Christ Jesus"

The problems related to the church at Philippi had to do with the fact that their "partnership in the gospel" (1:5) was unraveling because of pride and self-centeredness. Paul's unusual step of "naming names" in regard to Euodia and Syntyche (4:2) marks these ladies as the "ringleaders" of factions dividing the church. It was a dangerously escalating situation, but one Paul was not "free" to go to Philippi to referee. So the next best things were (1) sending his written preaching and (2) sending the exemplary models of gospel partnership, Epaphroditus and Timothy, in his place (2:19–30). These points are forcefully spotlighted by this inverted parallel structuring.

PAUL'S PASTORAL EPISTLES AS INSPIRED PREACHING

The Pastoral Epistles are a different ballgame from the rest of the Pauline materials. Their style and "feel" are clearly different from the earlier letters, to the point that it has been widely doubted whether Paul wrote them.[40] However, there are good explanations available for the differences, including the use of different amanuenses (e.g., Luke, who is stated as being the only person with Paul in his imprisonment, in 2 Tim. 4:11).

As we conclude our consideration of Paul's letters as preaching written, we will think through the new perspective that Paul would have now had at this point in his ministry. It is not necessary to check this through looking at more structural layouts, though. It is enough simply to consider what had changed and where Paul was in life.

First, and foremost, the apostle was now free to visit the churches . . . and he did, as reflected by the indications of movement in 1 Timothy and Titus. However, if Paul was not just a couple of years older but was indeed also wiser as a result of his extended free stay provided by the Roman legal system, he realized that his presence as a preacher could be multiplied through the permanent record of the written Word.

But during this stage of his ministry, Paul added yet another dimension to his written preaching. He sent epistles to trusted ministry associates (i.e., Timothy and Titus), with counsel on how to conduct their leadership responsibilities and deal with other challenging realities. In the process, he creatively kills two birds with one stone. In addition to the advice he provided to Timothy and Titus, the letters were designed to be read over their shoulders, so to speak, as indicated by the presence of the closing plural "you" in all three epistles (1 Tim. 6:21; Titus 3:15; 2 Tim. 4:22).

So as the swan song of Paul's ministry approached, he demonstrated even more versatility in communication: He could speak with great care and concern to his lieutenants, who could hear his voice through the reading of his letters to them, at the same time that he was "preaching" crucial content that would impact the pastoral leadership of the church of Jesus Christ for the next twenty centuries.

CHAPTER 10

HEBREWS, JAMES, AND JUDE AS INSPIRED PREACHING

A. BOYD LUTER

"Epistle" or "letter" in the New Testament period, however, was an extremely broad category. . . . The wealth of rhetorical devices in Hebrews has suggested to many (probably rightly) that this work was originally a homily or series of homilies that have been turned into the published form of a somewhat anomalous letter.

CARSON, MOO AND MORRIS[1]

[Hebrews is] a homily in written form, with some personal remarks added at the end.

F. F. BRUCE[2]

The letter of James [is] a series of loosely related homilies.

CARSON, MOO AND MORRIS[3]

In light of the very frequent use of chiasmus in the Old Testament, especially in Hebrew poetry, one can easily understand why New Testament authors, familiar as they were with the Scriptures, similarly employed this literary device in their own writings.

JEFFREY WEIMA[4]

Sometime in early 1993 I had a less-than-satisfying interchange with a significant editorial figure about the need for a New Testament resource volume to be produced. At that point, a highly successful volume on the Gospels[5] had been released, and a second on the Pauline Letters,[6] to which I had contributed, was scheduled for imminent release. I was fervently attempting to argue the need for, and the realistic feasibility of, a third volume, dealing with the remaining New Testament books. However, I was rebuffed, because of the unusual breadth of the material and, as much as anything else, the title to be given to such a volume. I still remember vividly his rejoinder on that last point: "What would you call it? The 'Dictionary of the Rest of the New Testament'?" In his mind, such a title seemed to imply "the New Testament leftovers." To him, at least at that moment, the title problem loomed as a huge obstacle . . . and, since he didn't care for the off-the-top-of-my-head title I offered, that was the unceremonious end of our conversation.[7]

The titles of written works can indeed be a major problem. If they are apt and inviting, they usher you in to partake of the contents. If they are forbidding, fuzzy, or just boring, most readers just pass on by without even sampling, in search of something more exciting or attractive or, at least, something they can "get into." Having been personally guilty of succumbing to the embarrassing shallowness of "title turnoff" too often to remember in my "grazing" of bookstores, I freely admit that, when it comes to audience response, titles definitely do matter.

ANYTHING BUT "GENERAL" EPISTLES

As far as the interest factor of at least many contemporary lay readers is concerned, the title "General Epistles" is a most unfortunate designation. "General information" is what you always have to wade through to get to the specific information in which you are vitally interested. In the student's academic experience, "general education" courses are the core curriculum offerings everyone has to take before they get to "the good stuff" in their major field of study. To quote my kids, "Boring!"

But, such a response, though understandable, is short-sighted. After all, the reason for the title "General Epistles" has nothing to do with them being of a general nature or containing just general content. It was because of a very parallel titling problem to that which the editor spoken of above experienced: What do you best call this group of letters?[8] "General Epistles" stuck because their authors, for the most part,[9] "designated the recipients in general terms, rather than with a specific location."[10]

It is fair to say, though, that contemporary readers would welcome a better (though accurate, of course) title for the non-Pauline letters of the New Testament. Is there another live option worth considering? Well, from the earlier centuries of church history, these letters have also been known as the "Catholic Epistles." Let's try that one on for size.

NOT VERY "CATHOLIC" EPISTLES, EITHER

The name *Catholic Epistles* derives from the period in early church history prior to the existence of the Roman Catholic Church. The term *catholic* (note the little 'c' in "catholic") means "universal," so that, in the Apostles' Creed, the wording, "I believe in the holy catholic church," has nothing at all to do with Roman Catholicism. It is simply an affirmation of the universal body of Christ, set apart to holiness. Were an Apostles' Creed being framed for the twenty-first-century church, we would probably say something like "I believe in the church as the body of Christ, set apart in him to holiness."

Thus, the term *Catholic Epistles* was intended only to mean those letters that were addressed to the church at-large. But is that assumption strictly true? What about the overwhelmingly Jewish nature of Hebrews? What about the virtual "Old Testament" feel of James? Why does Peter address his hearers as *diaspora* (1 Pet. 1:1), a distinctively Jewish way of referring to their being scattered outside the land of Palestine? How should we account for the dramatic stacking up of Old Testament citations and allusions in Jude and 2 Peter 2?

Each of these questions is difficult to answer, *if* these epistles were intended for all churches. There is no ready explanation for the Jewish feel of these books, if they were intended for overwhelmingly Gentile congregations or groups of churches.

But there is a disarmingly simple explanation. Each of these questions points to the reality that these letters were not only written *by* Jews, but also were written *for* (at least predominantly) Jewish audiences. We will follow up on the implications of that answer in the next section.

In the meantime, it is probably safe to say that most evangelical Christians are at least slightly uncomfortable using the term *catholic*, whether it is written with a big *C* or a little *c*. It may be embarrassing to admit, but it is true, at least for many. That being the case, it seems wise to put aside Catholic Epistles as a descriptor for these letters.

THREE "JEWISH-CHRISTIAN EPISTLES"

Although the phrase is not equally applicable to all the letters that have been called "General Epistles" or "Catholic Epistles," at least the three we are dealing with in this chapter (i.e., James, Hebrews, and Jude) can be very accurately described as "Jewish-Christian Epistles." They are all targeted to those of Jewish ethnic stock and all are at least professing believers in Jesus Christ.[11]

The question must be asked why there might be a problem with this designation. One commonly held answer is, given the widespread Jewish rejection of Jesus and persecution of Christians, it is unlikely that there would have been the proportion of Jewish believers, much less distinctively, or predominantly, Jewish congregations, to justify such letters as James, Hebrews, and Jude. But is this a completely accurate reflection of the ethnic state of affairs in the church of the New Testament era?

The half-truth of the above explanation is that, yes, most Jews did reject Jesus as the Messiah and, yes, there was tenacious persecution of the church. But that was not the whole story by any means.

After all, the church exploded from its very birth on Jewish turf, on the day of Pentecost (Acts 2). Peter was the apostle to the Jews, and many Jews did respond to his preaching of Jesus as their long-awaited Messiah. Even Paul, the apostle to the Gentiles, invariably began his ministry in a new city or town by presenting the gospel "to the Jew first and also to the Greek" (Rom. 1:16). His point of departure was preaching in the local synagogue and, even if not overwhelming, there was always *some* positive response by Jewish hearers.

This answers the side of the inferred question having to do with whether there is the likelihood that there were enough Jewish Christians scattered around the Roman Empire to make such Jewish-Christian letters plausible. The numbers, though not massive in comparison to the Gentile evangelist "harvest," were indeed enough to support the thesis that James, Hebrews, and Jude were profoundly Jewish-Christian epistles.

The other side of the coin of the question at hand is whether the Jews who were converted retained their full sense of Jewishness afterwards, including their saturation with the Hebrew Bible.[12] The answer to this aspect would also seem to be yes. In Acts 21 the leaders of the church in Jerusalem inform the apostle Paul, "You see, brother, how many thousands there are among the Jews of those who have believed and they are all zealous for the Law" (21:20). Then there is the presence of Romans 9–11, clarifying the places of Jews and Gentiles in the sovereign plan of God, inferring the presence of many Jewish believers in Rome at that time or there would have been no need for the subject to come up.

It is no accident that James, the traditional author of the letter by that name, is believed to have been the senior pastoral figure in the almost exclusively Jewish-Christian church at Jerusalem at the point when it is thought that the Epistle of James was written. In fact, his mention in Acts 15:13–21, at the Jerusalem council (around A.D. 49) and in Acts 21:18, at the end of Paul's third missionary journey (around A.D. 56 or 57), makes it overwhelmingly likely that James was ministering within a heavily Jewish-Christian context at the time of the Epistle of James.

Similarly, the fact that the Epistle to the Hebrews had something to do with a number of individuals from Italy (Heb. 13:24), where many Jewish believers apparently resided (Rom. 9–11), is doubtless significant. The readers of Hebrews were certainly struggling spiritually, but they were struggling within a heavily Jewish, or Jewish-Christian, context. That observation is completely consistent with the thoroughly Jewish feel of the letter.

PREACHING TO "THE REMNANT" AND THE UNBELIEVING REMAINDER

In the Old Testament, as the ministry of the writing prophets took hold, a more and more developed "remnant theology" unfolded. This was the perspective that, even though the bulk of the Jewish people were not faithful to the Lord, there was still present within the wider nation a small group of those who were faithful to the Lord. It is precisely this kind of theological vantage point on "the remnant" from the Old Testament that Paul draws upon in Romans 11:1–5.

It would seem that James, Hebrews, and Jude, to a greater or lesser extent, all reflect a further phase of this type of outlook. For example, James's initial emphasis on the testing of faith through trials (1:2–4) seems designed to separate "the wheat" and "the chaff" spiritually. Likewise, the call of Hebrews to faith and faithfulness "today" (Heb. 3–4), and not be like the hard-hearted wilderness generation, is the response of a "faithful remnant." Certainly Jude's appeal to deal with the subtle, but highly dangerous, inroads of false brethren (vv. 3–4) strongly implies his own assuming and applying of a "remnant theology."

Thus, it can be said that, when the written preaching of the Epistles of James, Hebrews, and Jude arrived at their destinations to be read, there were very realistic aims in mind. Each of the authors knew that not everyone among their hearers would respond positively, just as Paul made that same point abundantly clear about the realities of mixed response to preaching the Word in 2 Timothy 4:2–5. On the one hand, they were "preaching to the choir," so to speak, in those of the Jewish-Christian remnant present who would respond positively to the reading of the written preaching. But they were also speaking to those who would turn their backs on the Lord. Now, these others had every opportunity to repent and become part of the remnant. But they chose not to do so and, instead, walked away from the Lord. It was tragic, but it was also the continuation of the Old Testament theology of the remnant and the playing out of the apostle Paul's explanation of Israel's current hardness of heart spiritually (Rom. 11).

THE FEEL OF WISDOM LITERATURE: JAMES AS "EARLY-ON" INSPIRED PREACHING

The Epistle of James may well be the earliest New Testament book. Although some evangelicals continue to date it in the early 60s, it has become very common to place it in the 40s, even as far back as the early to mid-40s.[13]

As far as the literary genre of the book (beyond the fact that it, loosely, fits within the wider category of letter), there is a strong similarity between James and Old Testament wisdom literature such as Proverbs or Psalms.[14] That feel may also support an early dating of the letter.

Particularly significant for our focus in this book, it is equally true that "James reads like a sermon, or a series of sermonettes."[15] Some would even say that its Jewish feel reflects strong affinities with "synagogue homilies or sermons."[16]

In terms of what has tended to be the standard perception of the structure of James, it has "been likened to a string of pearls,"[17] just one disconnected subject laid on top of the one before. As Wessel observes, "This phenomenon makes an outline in the usual sense impossible."[18] The following outline tracks such a string-of-pearls understanding through the successive listing of subjects in James[19]:

I. Greetings (1:1)
II. Trials (1:2–18)
III. Hear and Do (1:19–27)
IV. Don't Be Partial (2:1–13)
V. Show Mercy (2:14–26)
VI. Control the Tongue (3:1–18)
VII. Avoid Worldliness (4:1–17)
VIII. Be Just (5:1–6)
IX. Endure (5:7–12)
X. Pray (5:13–18)
XI. Lift the Fallen (5:19–20)[20]

Since James seems to defy conventional outlining, it is exactly the kind of book in which an inverted macro-structure may be present. That is, just because it doesn't operate structurally in the way most other books do doesn't mean there is not an elegant structure present. It may well be that they haven't been looking in the right place . . . or in the right "shape."

The following structure demonstrates that the different sermonic parts of James were anything but "loosely related."[21] It reflects the elegant center-facing written-preaching strategy James utilized to minister to his Jewish-Christian audience:[22]

THE STRUCTURE OF JAMES

A (1:1–4) Dispersed ones, view trials as a means to grow to maturity
  B (1:5–8) Receiving wisdom through the prayer of faith
    C (1:9–18) The temporary nature of wealth, and the blessing and crown for persevering
      D (1:19–27) Be a doer of the Word who bridles the tongue and is blessed
        E (2:1–13) It is sinful and lawless for the rich to be partial and merciless, not loving your neighbor
          F (2:14–26) Faith is displayed by faithful works
            G (3:1–12) The danger of verbal abuse
          F' (3:13–18) Wisdom is displayed by wise behavior

E′ (4:1–10) It is sinful to be worldly, not humble, as well as vulnerable to Satan

D′ (4:11–17) Don't speak against your brother, be arrogant against God's will, or fail to do the right thing

C′ (5:1–12) The rotting of wealth and the need for patient endurance in light of the Lord's coming

B′ (5:13–18) Receiving relief and healing through the prayer of faith

A′ (5:19–20) Straying ones view correction as a means to positive rescue and forgiveness

This understanding fits in well with the prevalent feel of wisdom literature in James. Parallelism is a common characteristic of Hebrew wisdom and poetic literature. In addition, at the center of the structure, the focus on "the danger of verbal abuse" (i.e., the tongue) is a classic theme of the Book of Proverbs. Thus, whether this structuring of James is completely correct or not, it is certainly plausible in its main emphases.

It would seem that, within his Jewish-Christian context, James was a very effective preacher. But what Luke records in Acts 15:13–21 is almost surely just a summary of James's message to the Jerusalem council. Therefore, the Epistle of James turns out to be the classic New Testament example of the preaching of James, one of the pillars of the church (Gal. 2:9).

A STYLISH AND PERSUASIVE TREATISE: HEBREWS AS "GET WITH THE NEW COVENANT" INSPIRED PREACHING

There is no use even opening the door on the Pandora's box that is the ongoing debate over the authorship of Hebrews.[23] Since all we know about the author is that he knew the Hebrew Bible very well, he was an elegant and persuasive communicator, and he knew Timothy (13:23), the better part of wisdom is to agree (for once) with Origen in saying, "But who wrote the epistle, in truth God knows."[24]

But this is not necessarily a loss for the purposes of this book. If anything, it will allow us to focus more on the preaching angle and not be preoccupied with the preacher. And make no mistake, Hebrews has all the earmarks of preaching.

Some years ago, I served as interim pastor of a major church that had a Sunday morning, 11:00 to noon radio broadcast. What was particularly significant for my role as preacher, though, was that the broadcast was *live*. In other words, it didn't matter what else was going on in the rest of the service (i.e., how much music, how many announcements, or any other week-to-week variables). At 11:55 every Sunday the broadcast shifted to the "canned" concluding remarks. It was of absolutely no consequence what (or how long) I had prepared to preach. At 11:55, it was *over*. Some weeks I got to preach as much as thirty-five to forty minutes. But fifteen- to twenty-minute sermons were not at all uncommon, especially during the holiday periods when a lot of extra elements were added to the service.

I know well (and I'm sure many other preachers do also) how the author of Hebrews felt when he broke out the previous pattern of his wonderful exposition of what we often call the "Hebrews Hall of Faith"[25] by saying, "For time (Gk. *chronos*) will fail me" (Heb. 11:32). These are not the words of a writer. This is a clear reflection of one of the realities of *spoken* communication.

So even though this book has been historically referred to as the Epistle to the Hebrews, it is best understood as "a homily or a series of homilies that have been turned into the published form of a somewhat anomalous letter."[26] In fact, the only things particularly letter-like about Hebrews are that it's capped off by a fairly standard benedictory statement (13:20–21), "travelogue" (13:23), concluding greetings (13:24), and "grace" (13:25).

In terms of the structure of Hebrews, it has often been viewed as being shaped like a three-point sermon focusing on the superiority of Christ to anything related to the old covenant, with a brief stylized introduction and an extended concluding applicational section:

Introduction (1:1–3)
   I.   Christ is superior to the angels (1:4–2:18)
   II. Christ is superior to Moses and Joshua (3:1–4:13)
   III. Christ's priesthood is superior to Aaron's (4:14–10:18)
Conclusion: A superior response to God (10:19–13:25)

This is an easy outline to follow from a straight-through-the-book approach and does track the linear progression of thought fairly well. However, it misses completely a huge clue to the shape of the book that stands out like a sore thumb in Hebrews 8:1: "The main point."

This is referring to *the* major point of what the author of Hebrews is trying to get across to his hearers: Christ has a superior ministry because it is built on a superior foundation: the new covenant (Heb. 8). Attempting to turn back to Judaism, which is founded on the old covenant, will therefore prove a tragic failure, ultimately no more successful than the wilderness generation turning back from going into the Promised Land (Heb. 3–4). The following mirroring structural layout of Hebrews captures what the author is emphasizing through comparison and contrast, "swirling" the parallels around the new covenant center point.

THE STRUCTURE OF HEBREWS[27]

A (1:1–2:18) Christ is superior to the prophets and angels, who serve believing mankind

   B (3:1–6) Christ is superior to Moses

      C (3:7–4:13) The generation of unbelief in the wilderness

         D (4:14–7:28) The high priesthood of Christ

            E (8:1–13) The superiority of the new covenant, which Christ mediated (*Note:* "Now the main point in what has been said" [8:1]

         D' (9:1–10:18) The priestly sacrifice of Christ

      C' (10:19–12:17) The need for faith and faithfulness

   B' (12:18–29) Christ, mediator of a covenant superior to Moses

A' (13:1–25) Christians must live faithfully, by faith, as if entertaining angels

Before leaving Hebrews, two other practical points should be made related to its quality and procedure as preaching:

First, Hebrews contains *both* stern exhortation to believers and evangelistic warnings to those who often have been called "professors, not possessors." Often, the presence of these distinct (but complementary) kinds of materials has been argued as an either/or question. The ruling assumption was that the original hearers had to be *either* believers *or* unbelievers. For some reason, it did not seem to occur to most commentators that it could be both/and. Since both evangelistic and exhortive passages pepper the book, it seems likely that the author is indeed very purposefully preaching to both the saved and the unsaved, much like many preachers today design their messages to speak to both the children of God and pagans in different, but complementary, ways.

Second, Hebrews has a feel of urgency about it. That could derive simply from a deep heartfelt concern of the author for his hearers, similar to Paul's longing for his Jewish brethren to be converted in Romans 9:1–5. However, there may be more to it. If Morris is correct in dating Hebrews "near or during the Roman War of A.D. 66–70," just prior to the destruction of the temple and Jerusalem by the Romans, then Hebrews is a powerful sermon written against the backdrop of the rapidly darkening twilight of second-temple Judaism. It would serve as a very pointed exhortation for Jewish-Christians who still maintained any ties to the temple and the Jewish sacrificial system to disengage and grasp the full realities of the new covenant in Christ.[28]

THE CHICKEN OR THE EGG?: JUDE AND 2 PETER

Which comes first, the chicken . . . or the egg? So goes the old unanswerable question. You can argue all you want, but there is no final way to decide whether the chicken laid the egg first or the chicken hatched from the egg first.

The question of the relationship between Jude and 2 Peter is much like that. Which was written first? Was it 2 Peter or Jude? The reason for this debate, of course, has to do with the dramatic similarities (yet with some differences) between the material in 2 Peter 2 and the body of the little one-chapter letter of Jude.

The controversy is, at base, somewhat parallel to the so-called Synoptic Problem. (This is, given their similarities and differences, which of the first three Gospels was written first and which one[s] used the other[s] and how?) Without access to any documents predating the writing of the Gospels, though, this is ultimately an unanswerable question, at least in terms of possible written sources. However, when the angle of orality comes into play, the dynamics may clarify somewhat.[29] What I mean by that is, if at least the bulk of the New Testament books were produced as *preaching written down* (i.e., recorded by an amanuensis), the way a preacher's or orator's memory tends to function needs to be considered.

Let's face it: Most speakers, in most communication settings, are far more concerned about the content of what is being presented than the source from which it was derived. In other words, they love the "quotable quote," but often are a little fuzzy on where it came from (which accounts for the proportion of "It has been said" lead-ins to what I call anonymous-through-forgetfulness-or-ignorance quotes).

Jude could have read Peter's letter (if it was written first). However, since Peter unquestionably read Paul's letters (2 Pet. 3:15–16), he could have read Jude's (if it was written first). If it is objected that Jude was not an apostle (and, presumably, "beneath" Peter to cite him), think about this: Paul clearly quoted Luke (though not by name) in 1 Timothy 5:18 (see Luke 10:7), and Luke was not an apostle. But then, either could have heard the other preach and taken it from there, or the ideas could have even come from another preacher or written document.

When the dust settles, though, it probably does not matter much who wrote first or who copied whose written or oral material. It has often been said (only half-jokingly) that, "in preaching, copying is the sincerest form of flattery" (notice that this is an "anonymous quote," since I have no clue who originated this well-known statement).

A LAST-MINUTE *INSPIRED* CHANGE OF PLANS: JUDE AS "CONTENDING FOR THE FAITH" INSPIRED PREACHING

Most preachers strongly dislike (and avoid like the plague) having to make major last-minute changes in regard to their preaching. They have prepared as thoroughly as possible to present a certain message. It is disconcerting, if not terrifying, to come to the realization at the last minute that the message you *need* to preach is not the one you prepared to preach.

One of the most powerful sermons I ever heard emerged out of exactly these circumstances. While Chuck Swindoll was in the latter years of his lengthy pastorate at First Evangelical Free Church in Fullerton, California, a major problem suddenly emerged, having to do with the sinful behavior of a leader in the church. On the audiotape of his message to which I listened, Chuck explained how the Lord had laid it on his heart overnight to preach on the circumstances that had just emerged, in order to make it crystal clear how serious the sin had been. So out of obedience to the Lord's leading, one of the best-known preachers in the United States, speaking to a massive audience (live and through standing tape requests), in the middle of a sermon series, scrapped what he had carefully prepared to speak forcefully, but sensitively, to the painful issue at hand.

Jude did very much the same thing. As we read in verse 3 of his powerful sermon, "Beloved, while I was making every effort to write to you about our common salvation, I felt the necessity to write to you appealing that you contend earnestly for the faith which was once for all delivered to the saints." Planning then single-mindedly proceeding to communicate with his audience on the subject of "our common salvation," Jude was unexpectedly compelled by the Lord to move in a completely different direction. He obeyed.

Jude's sermon written is the result of this last-minute redirection by the Lord. His new focus is to "contend earnestly for the faith" (Jude 3). The stated reason to contend for the faith is because of false brethren who have sneaked into the church (Jude 4). The following mirroring structuring by Weima tracks how these two aspects play out through the letter.[30]

THE STRUCTURE OF JUDE

A (v. 3) The Appeal (General): Believers must contend for the faith
   B (v. 4) The Reason for the Appeal (General): Danger of false teachers
   B' (vv. 5–19) The Reason for the Appeal (Specific): Judgment of false teachers
A' (vv. 20–23) The Appeal (Specific): How believers must contend for the faith

It is interesting how Jude, as a communicator inspired by God, at once proceeds much like a modern "big idea"[31] preacher (Jude 3–4), then reverses field and densely develops the initial ideas in an elegant manner worthy of any ancient orator (Jude 5–19, 20–23). His skill as a flexible impromptu preacher is proved by his skillful use of the stacked-up illustrations from the Old Testament, by his employment of a relevant quotation from the apocryphal book of 1 Enoch (Jude 14–15), like a moder preacher citing an extra-biblical religious source, and by his pointed application, related to "contend earnestly for the faith" (Jude 20–23).[32]

CHAPTER

JOHN'S EPISTLES AND REVELATION AS INSPIRED PREACHING

A. BOYD LUTER

It is difficult to make a logical division of the letter [of 1 John]. The teaching develops in an ever-widening spiral. The themes, woven into the fabric of the whole book, reappear at intervals.[1]

In many ancient texts terms for "read" and "hear" are used synonymously (as in Rev. 1:3), since reading was always audible because it was always done aloud.[2]

Because writing materials were expensive and scarce, so were copies of the books that were part of the biblical canon. As a rule, only one copy per Christian assembly was the best that could be hoped for. Public reading was the only means that rank-and-file Christians had for becoming familiar with the contents of these books.[3]

Hence, it appears a fairly safe assumption that, from the beginning, understanding of the Apocalypse was to proceed from repeated whole readings of the book.[4]

OLDER, WISER . . . AND MORE FLEXIBLE: THE CROWNING ASPECT OF JOHN'S MINISTRY

The ministry of W. A. Criswell[5] at First Baptist Church in Dallas, Texas, lasted all the way from 1944 until his recent death at well over ninety years of age.[6] Because Dr. Criswell's name is almost synonymous with First Baptist,

Dallas, though, it is often overlooked that he already had a very significant pastoral ministry before coming to Dallas.

Called to ministry early, W. A. Criswell preached extensively in his teens, pastoring while in college at Baylor University and while pursuing his masters and doctoral programs[7] at Southern Baptist Theological Seminary, Louisville, Kentucky. From there, he went to two highly successful pastorates in Oklahoma, from which he came to Dallas in his mid-thirties, following the retirement of the legendary George Truett.

Already a veteran of over fifteen years of pastoral ministry and well known in Southern Seminary and Oklahoma Baptist circles, it was still a major challenge to assume the pastorate of the great First Baptist Church of Dallas. But W. A. Criswell more than rose to the occasion. His pulpit wit and wisdom are well documented. But because so much of it was behind the scenes, he is not recognized nearly as much as is deserved for his role as a creative innovator.[8]

Certainly, one of the most monumental aspects of Dr. Criswell's ministry was his exceedingly imposing list of publications. Some were topical in nature, often dealing with issues of current relevance or debate. He also wrote on pastoral ministry. But what W. A. Criswell was rightly most well known for as a "writer" was his published commentaries on books of the Bible.[9] However, it must be quickly stated that all these volumes are essentially nothing more than book studies he preached in the pulpit at First Baptist, Dallas, simply written down for the purpose of publication.[10] And even though Dr. Criswell's earthly life and ministry are now over, his spoken/written ministry of God's Word continues . . . and, if anything, continues to grow.[11]

For the purposes of this book, it is striking that, although W. A. Criswell did not evidence a scholarly awareness of the residual orality aspect of the New Testament era, he did very much *embody* it in his ministry. He "wrote" because it was a means by which others, who would not ordinarily be able to do so, could hear his "voice" as he expounded the Word of God that he loved so dearly with clarity, passion, and power.[12]

Very much the same kinds of extraordinary things, and even more, can be said for the apostle John, whose ministry likewise likely began very early and certainly lasted longer than most, if not all, the other apostles.[13] He apparently met the Lord Jesus at the point where the telling nickname he was given along with his brother, James, *Boanerges,* which means "Sons of Thunder" (Mark 3:17), presumably reflecting "angry (or, at least, tempestuous) young men,"[14] had already stuck. That makes it doubly amazing that John would be remembered through the tone of most of his contributions to the New Testament, traditionally dated near the end of his life,[15] as the "apostle of love."[16]

As is well known, John was called by Jesus from his fishing nets on the Sea of Galilee (Matt. 4:19, 21–22) to begin fishing for men. Given that his name is always mentioned after that of James, he still clearly is remembered as the more famous apostle of the brothers. That is true, even though both were in the "inner circle"[17] of the apostles who were closest to Jesus, with Simon Peter (Matt. 17:1).[18] The constant positioning of John's name after James's almost surely is because John was the younger of the brothers, and he may have been one of the younger, if not *the youngest*, of the apostles.

Whatever his exact age when he began to follow Jesus,[19] John was relatively young for the level of responsibilities that was about to fall on him after the resurrection of Christ. John is with Peter at the temple in Acts 3, apparently also speaking at that time (4:1), though his words are not recorded in Acts. He does, however, along with Peter, answer the Sanhedrin in Acts 4:19–22. Because of this kind of courageous leadership, and much more, John is referred to by Paul as one of the "pillars" of the church (Gal. 2:9) at Jerusalem, a role he could well have played until the time approaching the destruction of Jerusalem in A.D. 70. If so, his ministry in Jerusalem and the surrounding area could have lasted as much as thirty-five or more years.[20]

John invested the "crowning years" of his ministry, tradition tells us,[21] in Ephesus. If he went there more or less directly from Jerusalem, his apostolic and pastoral oversight in Ephesus and the surrounding communities in the Roman province of Asia also could have lasted over thirty years, if he died around A.D. 100, as reliable historical sources from the second century A.D. tell us.[22] In Ephesus, he would have been following the preaching ministries of Paul (see Acts 19–20)[23] and Timothy (1 Tim. 1:3).[24]

Although it is certainly possible that John wrote some, or all, of his contributions to the New Testament before leaving Jerusalem, it is considerably more likely (especially given the location of Patmos [Rev. 1:9] in the Aegean Sea and the addressing of the Apocalypse to the seven churches in Asia, beginning with Ephesus, in Rev. 1:4, 11; chs. 2–3) that he wrote some, if not all, of them while in ministry in Ephesus. If so, the most commonly attributed date range for the Gospel of John,[25] the Johannine Letters, and Revelation is roughly A.D. 85–95. And, although it is not at all impossible[26] that the order of composition was different, it is customary to conclude that the fourth Gospel was written first, followed some time later by 1, 2, 3 John and, finally, by the Apocalypse. Though the apostle John has been dead for over nineteen centuries, his "voice" is still heard loud and clear, and the impact of his ministry is still felt, through the New Testament books that bear his name

JOHN'S VERSATILITY (I): WRITING DIFFERENT GENRES

It is fascinating to note that John is the only writer in the New Testament to produce books that are categorized in not just two, but all three,[27] major literary genres.[28] The fourth Gospel is a beautiful blending of historical/biographical elements (though neither "history" nor "biography").[29] By contrast, 1 John is a slightly longer than average, more formal epistle, while 2 and 3 John, at one chapter each, are shorter, more informal letters.[30] Finally, the Apocalypse is a unique hybrid of apocalyptic (note the Gk. *apoc-alupsis;* Rev. 1:1), prophecy (1:3) and epistle (note, e.g., the common episto-lary elements of author, recipients, and initial greetings in 1:4).

These literary products demonstrate that, especially if John were older when they were written, he was amazingly versatile in his modes of expres-sion. Now, if it is true that, if John were the last of the Gospels to be com-posed, as is often concluded,[31] John could well have "gone to school" on what Matthew, Mark, and Luke had done, in order to put his preaching about Jesus into writing. Also, by the traditional dating of 1, 2 and 3 John, most, if not all, of the other New Testament book in the epistle-letter category would have been completed. Thus, his decision to dictate letters, in lieu of being able to travel and meet his intended audience face-to-face, may well have simply "followed suit" with the upwards of three-fourths of the New Testament books that are in that literary genre.[32]

But what about Revelation? Here we run into a literary genre "out of the clear blue sky," so to speak. And, as we will see in the next section, John's con-siderable "versatility" reflects itself in a completely different way in the "preaching written" of the Apocalypse.

JOHN'S VERSATILITY (II): PLAYING DIFFERENT ROLES

As Andreas Kostenberger helpfully points out, "In keeping with the dif-ferent genres of John's Gospel, Epistles and Revelation, John respectively functions as apostle (Gospel), elder (Epistles) and seer (Revelation)."[33] This is all true, and reflective of John's great functional versatility in addition to his literary flexibility.

However, this is not the whole story, at least as far as John's role in regard to the composing of the Apocalypse is concerned. While John is, in one sense, a "seer" and, thus, "author" of the content of Revelation, his role is every bit as much that of "amanuensis" of the risen and glorified Christ. To sustain that assertion, it is not necessary to go any further than the repeated command the Son of Man issues to John in 1:11, 19 to "write" (Gk. *grapson*) down on a scroll[34] what he has seen and heard.

Thus, we see here a totally unique role in the New Testament, a role which certainly nails down the question of whether John is the most "versatile" of the New Testament authors. He composes (probably through a stenographer for at least some, if not all, of) the Gospel and Epistles himself, under the inspi-ration of the Holy Spirit (2 Tim. 3:16; 2 Pet. 1:21). But in a very real sense, he also "collaborates" with the Lord Jesus in the recording of the visions, mini-letters,[35] and prophecies of the Apocalypse. He has the mind-boggling privilege and responsibility to "write" down what the risen Christ "preaches" to the churches and pass it on to them as "the-next-best-thing-to-being-there" with John on Patmos and actually seeing the glorified Lord themselves.

SO WHAT?

It is indeed an intriguing point that John served as the Son of Man's "secretary" in the writing of the Book of Revelation. But in the wider scope of things, what difference does it really make?

A great deal (to say the least)! The significance of this point for the thesis of this overall study (i.e., that understanding the high residual orality of the New Testament era greatly impacts our understanding of the New Testament and, thus, many of the related interpretative and critical questions) can hardly be overestimated. Here we see an indisputable example in which the dynamics of the author/amanuensis relationship obviously substantially impacts the vocabulary and style (not to mention the genre) of a New Testament book traditionally attributed to a certain human author (i.e., John), but frequently questioned because of focally divergent vocabulary and style.[36]

Admittedly, in this case, the author who moves John into the stenographer role is none other than the risen Christ. Nevertheless, the point remains the same: If there is any possibility that a different amanuensis comes into play (or that an author who normally dictates his books decides to write them down himself), or that the amanuensis is playing a somewhat different role, all bets are off in terms of presumed critical issues. As Ellis correctly concludes:

> The influence of the secretary on the author's vocabulary
> and style varied from a minimal degree in syllable-by-syllable
> dictation to a very great degree as the author gave him greater
> freedom in composing or enlisted him as the co-author. The
> role of the secretary, then, renders questionable any judgments
> about authorship based solely on internal literary criteria.[37]

Thus, whether it be the authorship of the Pastorals (given their very different "feel" from the rest of Paul's letters),[38] or the asserted drastic differences between 1 and 2 Peter,[39] or the long list of "daylight and dark" distinctions between Revelation and the other books attributed to John the apostle, the likelihood of secretary involvement effectively deflates the critical onslaught. While it does not (and cannot) prove the traditional authorship, it makes it almost impossible to show that traditional authorship is not plausible, given the flexibility of the amanuensis role.

1 JOHN AS INSPIRED PREACHING

The epistle we know as 1 John is, on the one hand, characterized by some of the simplest Greek in the New Testament.[40] On the other hand, though, the prologue of the letter (1:1–4) is, in terms of style, much more like the elegant prologue of Hebrews than the beginning of any other New Testament letter. So if we learned nothing else about 1 John as "inspired preaching," it is that it is possible for such an ancient letter to be simple, yet elegant and profound—a tribute to the balanced maturity of its author.

As has often been observed, 1 John and the fourth Gospel seem to be both (1) connected and (2) complementary. The connectedness comes partly because of an almost astounding number of themes in common.[41] Additionally, the opening words of 1 John are obviously an "echo" of the beginning of the Gospel of John, with their common focus on "the Word" (Gk. *logos*).

The complementary angle is seen in comparing the apparent purpose statement of each book. The purpose of the Gospel is stated in these words: "That you may believe that Jesus is the Christ, the Son of God; and that believing you may have life in His name" (John 20:31). It is generally concluded from these words that the Gospel has a primarily evangelistic purpose.[42]

By contrast, the purpose of John's first epistle is laid out this way: "These things I have written to you who believe in the name of the Son of God, in order that you may know that you have eternal life" (1 John 5:13). Generally, it is understood that this wording reflects a purpose of providing assurance of salvation. Thus, 1 John complements the Gospel of John by the assurance it gives to the newly converted hearer of the fourth Gospel.

First John has proven notoriously slippery in regard to attempts to track its structure by conventional outlines. That often indicates the possibility of a concentric structure. I am not aware of what I would consider to be anywhere close to the "perfect outline" of 1 John. But my sometime coauthor, Kathy McReynolds,[43] has, in terms of explaining what Earle Ellis has described as "an ever-widening spiral" of teaching and themes in 1 John,[44] detected the best structural outline that I am aware of to this point:[45]

A (1:1–4) John's testimony: The Word of Life appeared (*the reality of the incarnation*) and has offered fellowship with himself and his Father.
　　B (1:5–2:17) God is light. We must walk with him in the light and love one another as he commanded us (*the expression of the incarnation*).
　　　　C (2:18–27) Beware of antichrists who deny the Father and the Son (*the denial of the incarnation*).

D (2:28–3:24) Children of God must love one another as he
commanded. Jesus Christ is our supreme example of sacrificial love
(*the reality and the expression of the incarnation*).

C′ (4:1–6) Beware of the spirit of antichrist who denies that Jesus Christ
has come in the flesh (*denial of the incarnation*).

B′ (4:7–5:5) God is love. We should walk in love as he commanded us (*the
expression of the incarnation*).

A′ (5:6–21) God's testimony: The Spirit, the water, and the blood (*the reality of
the incarnation*). God has given us eternal life in his Son. We know him who
is true, and we are in him who is true.

The concentric movement here is simple and clear in its parallelism and,
with the "trained ear" of that culture, would have been quite easy to follow as
they listened to the reading of the letter. And since the only uses of
"antichrist" in the entire New Testament (other than 2 John 7) are found in
the C layer here, there seems to be some persuasive exegetical reasons to sit
up and pay attention to this structuring. In addition, it more or less theologically sets off the problematic understanding infecting John's hearers from the
orthodoxy and orthopraxy needed to secure the church from this danger.

As laid out above, the problem among John's readers was an apparently
rapidly emerging false view that denied the truth of the incarnation of Jesus
Christ and, in doing so, was "antichrist" in its perspective.[46] In response, John
emphasized the reality and the "expression" of the incarnation in believers'
own behavior. Not just proper belief, but loving as God first loved us sacrifi-
cially in Christ, is the best answer to the coupling of such false doctrine and
lifestyle.

Now we have a sense as to why 1 John was written, as opposed to the
apostle traveling and preaching directly to the needs of the situation. As with
2 Thessalonians or Colossians, there were pressing theological problems
among the audience for the letter. And because the particular apostle
(whether Paul or John) was not able to go to the point of need, a letter speaking to the problems (and, undoubtedly, read by a ministry associate of the
apostle, who could "follow up") was, indeed, "the next best thing to being
there."

2 JOHN AS INSPIRED PREACHING

The little letter we refer to as 2 John has all the markings of a personal
note, in contrast to the virtually complete absence of a "personal touch" in
1 John. The only links the two exhibit are some common terms, such as the
use of "love" and, notably, the use of "antichrist" in verse 7.

It could be argued from verse 12 that the wording requires the author also
to be the actual "quill-in-hand" writer.[47] And, that may well be true, which

might partially explain the differences between the style of 2 and 3 John versus 1 John. However, in that culture, to "write" did not necessarily mean any more than that there would be a written product, by whatever process was chosen. For example, in Galatians 6:11, Paul felt it necessary to go beyond by saying, "I am writing to you" and clarify with, "I am writing to you *with my own hand.*"[48]

By all indications, 2 John is a pastoral note from John ("the elder"[49]) to either an unnamed Christian woman with believing children or, if the wording is figurative, a congregation. If a congregation, this veiled reference may imply a similar need for discretion such as motivated Peter to refer to his place of writing in 1 Peter 5:13 as "Babylon," though he was almost surely in Rome. If such is the case, it may be that the same period of persecution[50] that landed John on the island of Patmos (Rev. 1:9) had already begun.

A (1–2) Salutation
   B (3) Greetings and a summary of the "truth" about Christ
      C (4) The gladness of finding children walking in truth
         D (5) Remembering the commandment to love one another
         D' (6) Defining love as walking according to his commandments
      C' (7–8) The danger of not acknowledging Christ's incarnation (which is "the deceiver and antichrist")
   B' (9–11) Caution about true "teaching" and greeting those in error about Christ
A' (12–13) Conclusion

Again, the structure is simple and clear. The doctrinal problem afflicting the recipients of the letter appears to be the same as that in 1 John, given the common emphasis on Christ's incarnation, love, and "antichrist."[51] Interestingly, the focus at the center point of the structure (the D layer) is also very close to that in 1 John: love one another. The use of the "commandment" wording is also very similar to 1 John.

From a preaching standpoint, we see here a phenomenon that calls attention to the likely oral (i.e., dictated, though in at least a semi-preaching manner) nature of these letters. While writers do not seem to have as much of a tendency to repeat themselves in much the same wording, speakers often tend to do so—sometimes consciously, sometimes subconsciously, especially when there are pressing circumstances.

Consider, for example, Paul's letters to the Ephesians, Colossians, and Philemon, all of which may have been delivered on the same trip by Tychicus, who was accompanied by Onesimus (Eph. 6:21–22; Col. 4:7–9; Philem. 10–18).[52] The similarities between Colossians and Philemon are almost surely conscious and intended to overlap, given that Philemon is involved in the church at Colossae. However, scholars have noted the intriguing common inclusion of the "household codes" in Ephesians and Colossians, as well as puzzling over the fact that the empowerment for living out the marital, parent-child, and master-slave relationships is to "be filled with the Spirit" in Ephesians, but the indwelling "word of Christ" in Colossians. Whatever the proper exegetical explanation, the similarities *and* differences here make it appear that, in his epistolary "preaching," Paul is subconsciously drawing on what he has recently had on his mind and heart, not to mention expressing as "preaching written."

3 JOHN AS INSPIRED PREACHING

Of all the other New Testament letters, 3 John is most reminiscent of Philemon. It is initially "private" (in this case, from "the elder" to Gaius; v. 1), though designed to be read publicly later. Apparently, like Philemon, its initial private nature has to do with the stickiness of the situation it details: the dictatorial, and evil, conduct of one Diotrophes.

In this case, it may be fairly obvious why John sent a private letter instead of going and preaching: John had written a previous letter to the church[53] (v. 9), the contents of which Diotrophes had flatly rejected. Thus, Diotrophes almost certainly would not have allowed either another letter to the church or an appearance by the apostle. This letter, which "stands in" for a personal conversation between John and Gaius, is indeed the next best thing the apostle could do, given Diotrophes's conduct.

The structure of the little letter of 3 John shows the striking contrast between the proper conduct of church leaders and that of "Diotrophes, the dictator":

A (1–2) Salutation
  B (3–4) Speaking well of Gaius
    C (5–6) Acting faithfully toward other believers
      D (7–8) Support the fellow workers who serve the Name
      D' (9–10) Diotrophes does not support the fellow workers and wants
        to have the biggest "name" himself
    C' (11) Doing good, not evil
  B' (12) Speaking well of Demetrius
A' (13–14) Conclusion

While following the linear flow of the book will bring you to understand most of the situation, as has been laid out above, the beautiful center-facing structure John chose to use underlines one very ironic point: whose "name" is most important in the church. As John spotlights the focal point of his "preaching" structure, true believers serve "for the sake of the Name" (i.e., of God; v. 7), but, at the heart of the matter, Diotrophes was in it to make a name for himself (v. 9). This "sermon written" is proof that the apostle John would not hesitate to "name names" (excuse the pun!), when necessary.

THE APOCALYPSE AS INSPIRED PREACHING

I will never forget, back in 1994, receiving from my former graduate assistant, (now Dr.) Michelle Lee, a copy of a paper she had done in a doctoral seminar on Revelation at the University of Notre Dame under Dr. Josephine Ford.[54] The reason I will never forget is because, when I opened it up and looked at Michelle's structural diagram of the Apocalypse, I was virtually dumbfounded to realize that it laid out this incredibly complex book as a grand chiasm in a completely fresh manner.[55]

Over the following months, I struggled with Michelle's brilliant structural observations, as much as anything trying to come to terms with my own bias against the possibility that a book as complicated as the Apocalypse could be developed as a mirroring structure. As it turned out, Michelle received acceptance for the paper to be published in *Novum Testamentum,* no small accomplishment and a very strong recognition of the viability of her observation of the text and exegetical argumentation.[56]

In the meantime, the strength of the evidence finally won me over, and I began to work with this perspective in classes I was teaching and in professional papers I gave at meetings.[57] I state my great debt to Michelle Lee for a masterful job of sifting all the details of the Book of Revelation and carefully documenting the compelling parallels—which I never would have done—as well as noting the possibility of multiple outlines in the Apocalypse.[58]

Though I am, in the vast majority of the details, still in agreement with Dr. Lee's structuring, I slightly adapted it (see the resulting structural outline below) in the process of preparing and writing a chapter I was asked to contribute on "Interpreting the Book of Revelation."[59] It is my current understanding that there could be as many as three interlocking outlines intended by the author (in this case, the Lord, who is "dictating" to John). I have included two of those below. The third is a standard outline, which focuses predominantly on the sequential progression of the cycles of seven (e.g., seven letters to the churches, seven seals, seven trumpets, seven bowls of wrath, etc.). Such an outline helpfully follows the chronological flow of the end-times events seen in the visions of the Apocalypse.

However, a common (and *divinely intended;* see Rev. 1:3) question that arises when studying Revelation comes into play here: What am I supposed to do (i.e., "heed"), *applicationally,* after I "hear" (aurally) the (oral) reading of the Book of Revelation? The grand chiastic structure seen first "centers" (Rev. 13–14) on the answer to that question: *There are decisions to be made!*

A (ch. 1) Prologue
   B (chs. 2–3) Present Situation: Letters to the Seven Churches
      C (chs. 4–5) Fundamental Paradigm: Worship of God, Worthiness of the
         Lamb
         D (ch. 6) Judgment of God's Enemies (Note rider on white horse)
            E (ch. 7) Faithful Believers (Note "Great Multitude")
               F (chs. 8–10) Judgment of God's Enemies (II; Note First Two
                  "Woes")
                  G (ch. 11) False Power of the Beast: Defeat through the Two
                     Witnesses' Resurrection
                     H (12:1–6) Woman Brings Salvation
                       I (12:7–18) Judgment of God's Enemies (III): The
                         Dragon
                         J (ch. 13) *Decision:* Worship the Beast
                         J' (ch. 14) *Decision:* Worship the Lamb
                     I' (chs. 15–16) Judgment of God's enemies (III):
                       Climactically, Babylon
                    H' (17:1–6) Woman Killing Saints
                G' (17:7–18) False Power of the Beast: Defeat by the King of
                  Kings
              F' (ch. 18) Judgment of God's Enemies (II; Note Repeated "Woe,
                Woe" over Babylon)
            E' (19:1–10) Faithful Believers ("Great Multitude")
         D' (19:11–21) Judgment of God's Enemies (Rider on White Horse)
      C' (20:1–10) Fundamental Paradigm: Damnation of Satan, Worthiness of
         the Saints
   B' (20:11–22:5) Future Situation: The New Heaven and Earth and New
      Jerusalem
A' (22:6–21) Epilogue

Interestingly (and relatedly!), at the "twin peaks" of the centered chapters (Rev. 13, 14), there are twin challenges to faithful endurance (13:10; 14:12), which, in context, tie both back to applicational aspects of the letters to the churches in chapters 2–3: "If anyone has an hear, let him hear" (13:9; and stated in unmistakable orality terminology), and the reference to "the Spirit" (14:13) almost surely echoes the wording at the end of each of the seven mini-letters: "He who has an ear, let him hear what the Spirit says to the churches" (2:7, 11, 17, 29; 3:6, 13, 22).

The bottom line here is to "hear" Christ and the Spirit speaking to the churches (including those today) *now,* not just through the letters, but also through the spotlighted aspects of the visions: Make up your minds! *Who* are you going to *worship?* The beast (Rev. 13) or the Lord God (Rev. 14)?

Ironic, isn't it? In most evangelical churches, there is a preoccupation and ongoing dispute on *how* to worship (i.e., formality and format). In the

Apocalypse, though, the key (and much more foundational) issue is *who* you worship. In many respects, the "how" question gets down to a matter of *personal preference*. In stark contrast, the "who" question boils down to a matter of *eternal destiny*. In other words, in the Apocalypse, Jesus, through John, his secretary/coauthor is "preaching for a verdict," a decision with the gravest eternal consequences.

Before closing this chapter, the other inverted structuring of Revelation deserves a look.[60] It is different from any other structure seen in this book. It can be called a "spread chiasm," an effect I have observed elsewhere in Scripture.[61]

A (1:3) Heed (a), for the time is near (b)
   B (14:13) Death and blessing beyond
      C (16:15) Alertness (echoes Matt. 24:42–44; 25:1–13)
      C' (19:9) Invitation to the marriage supper (echoes Matt. 25:1–13)
   B' (20:6) Resurrection beyond death
A' (22:7) I am coming quickly (b'), so heed (a')
D (22:14) Concluding offer of "blessing" to the newly converted

It is the seven "beatitudes" (i.e., blessing statements) of the Apocalypse that are being considered here. Initially, the reversal of the order of key elements in the first and sixth of the blessings (i.e., heeding and imminency) points to the possibility of some kind of mirroring effect, even if simply as "bookends" (1:3; 22:7) for the body of the book.

But there is much more. The "death" and "resurrection" angles in the second layer (14:13; 20:6) are a prime example of how complementary elements function in chiasms. And, given that the imagery/wording in 16:15 and 19:9 both echo the same sections of the Olivet Discourse, it seems that there is way too much parallelism here to be mere coincidence.

But if it is *intentional* parallelism, what is its purpose? And what about the seventh beatitude (22:14), which has not been mentioned so far?

A viable purpose for this structure would be for the "blessings" to contrast with "the curses," so to speak, of the Apocalypse. Elsewhere in Scripture, the presence of "blessings" often is alongside "curses" (e.g., Lev. 26; Deut. 27–28). In Revelation, it is probably not coincidental that the inner (Layer C) "blessings" (16:15; 19:9) snugly "frames" the portion of the book in which we hear of the "cursing" (expressed repeatedly with the term "Woe!") of Babylon the Great, the consort of the beast (16:17–19:6). Applicational bottom line: You now understand not to worship the beast . . . *but make sure you don't get mixed up in the "curse" waiting for Babylon, either!*

How can you avoid that? That's where the seventh blessing (22:14; the D layer of the structure[62]) comes into play. Utilizing imagery seen earlier in the book, the final beatitude of the Apocalypse makes an evangelistic appeal: To "wash their robes" is to dip them in the blood of the Lamb (see 7:14), which can only take place through saving faith. And the right to "the tree of life" and to enter "the city" is only for believers/"overcomers" (21:7–8; 22:15), who are beyond "the curse" (22:3).

If, indeed, the Book of Revelation is "preaching written," as argued here, considering the "hellfire and brimstone" nature of much of its content, wouldn't you expect an evangelistic call at some point? Well, you are not disappointed. The Lord and John[63] end on exactly that note: In connection with the implied offer of the final beatitude, we hear the "altar call": "The Spirit and the bride say, 'Come.' . . . And let the one who is thirsty come; let the one who wishes take the water of life without cost" (22:17). Powerful preaching! Inspired preaching! *Heavenly* preaching!

PART III

Issues Related to Preaching and the New Testament:

The Forest, the Trees, and Beyond

CHAPTER

12

THE NEW TESTAMENT'S USE OF THE OLD: INSPIRED EXEGESIS AND APPLICATION FOR PREACHING

A. BOYD LUTER

> *No subject is perhaps more important for the understanding of the Christian faith than the use of the Old Testament in the New Testament. The Hebrew and Aramaic Scriptures were, of course, the only Bible that the early thinkers and writers had.*[1]

> *In addition to the over 400 passages consciously using the explicit words of an OT text, there are well over 1,000 places where there is an allusion to an OT text, event or person.*[2]

> *The apostolic message and the traditions about Jesus are primary, and the OT comes into use for the defense and explication of the faith.*[3]

> *The New Testament writers believed the Old Testament to be directly relevant to them, and they used it accordingly. Their statements indicate that the Old Testament in its entirety is meaningful and relevant for the first-century church as well as for us today.*[4]

Preachers have always used external illustrative material for identification and clarification (i.e., an "Aha!" moment), or to provide additional authority, in their messages. In the New Testament, Jesus' mastery of analogies and stories (i.e., parables) based in nature and agriculture stands unparalleled. Paul was no slouch at analogies, either. For example, in writing to a Greek audience in 1 Corinthians, he employs what would have been a readily understood sports illustration in that context (9:24–27).[5]

161

However, just about as often, many preachers will choose to utilize scriptural material to illustrate or clarify their points. And *why not*? Some of the most interesting, and *timeless* (though, as we will see, amazingly *timely*) stories in all of human experience are found in the Bible.

In addition, it "packs a wallop." That is exactly what Billy Graham has in mind when, over and over, he proclaims, "The Bible says!" It has an inspired authority (2 Tim. 3:16; 2 Pet. 1:21) not shared by any other document.

Finally, there is the immensely popular "flexibility of use" factor. Biblical quotes or allusions ("echoes" of wording or imagery) can be employed in so many different and creative ways. From using well-known wording from another passage in an ironic way in a sermon title, to concluding and hammering home an applicational point by reference to another pointed passage on the subject and everywhere in between, the possibilities, though not endless,[6] are virtual "fields white unto harvest." *Oops!* Well, you see what I mean.

As I started thinking about it, in the roughly twelve hundred sermons or messages I have preached over the years, I suspect that I have quoted Scripture from somewhere else in the Bible at least an average of four or five times per message. If that is anywhere close to accurate, that would mean that I have very possibly employed five thousand or more uses of Scripture (in many different ways) to add salt and pepper (and sometimes Tabasco!) to my messages. And I doubt very seriously that my experience is much different from that of many, if not most, preachers.

To focus more closely on how my preaching experience parallels the subject of this chapter, about 750 of my twelve hundred messages have been from the New Testament. I freely admit that there have been some in which I did not turn to the Old Testament at all, usually because there was no reason or circumstance that led me to do so. However, in the vast majority of those messages, I did have occasion to quote or "echo" the Old Testament, often numerous times. Overall, I would conservatively estimate that my total references to the Old Testament in New Testament messages would be at least fifteen hundred times in 750 messages. Again, I believe my experience is pro-bably close to "average" among experienced preachers and teachers of the Bible.

QUOTING SCRIPTURE IN AN "INSPIRED SERMON"

It may well be that the experience of the New Testament authors is closer to that of modern preachers than we might think, at least in regard to this issue of the use of the Hebrew Bible in the New Testament books. As will be seen, there are some New Testament books in which there is no (at least obvious) Old Testament quoting at all.[7] However, most New Testament books, to a greater or lesser degree, do, consciously or subconsciously, breathe out in their "preaching written" the biblical language of the Old Testament that the authors have heard and understood virtually all their lives. More on that later.

Frankly, though, is that not what almost anyone who knows much about the background of the New Testament era would expect? After all, the New Testament writers, with the exception of Luke,[8] were Jewish. The Hebrew Scriptures had always been their "Bible," though now it was, much more often than not, read from the Greek translation, the Septuagint (LXX).[9] And, with the expansion of the gospel to "the ends of the earth" (Acts 1:8 NIV), in obedience to the Great Commission command to preach the Good News to "all the nations" (Matt. 28:19)—almost the entirety of which spoke koine Greek as their first or second language in that day—it was necessary to communicate in "the universal language of their time."[10] This explains the fact that the majority of quotations of the Old Testament in the New Testament are fairly close to the LXX wording.

But it doesn't explain a lot of other things, most of which come across as being much more naturally related to the dynamics of the spoken word than those of the written word. For example, why, alongside standard LXX citations, would there also be phenomena such as: (1) tight translations from the Hebrew Bible; and (2) (what appear to be) "paraphrases" of both the LXX and the Hebrew; and (3) occasional "summaries" of Old Testament events (or their significance).

While there are certainly important reasons directly related to the prevailing hermeneutical approaches of the day,[11] many times the better explanations may well be as much (or more) homiletical in nature. To help clarify here, allow me to employ some analogies to common situations today.

For example, the need for exact "pulpit precision" will, on occasion, press even pastors who prefer not to flaunt their Hebrew or Greek skills in the pulpit to use such to "split hairs" on certain terms, in order to carefully make their point. How is that fundamentally different from Paul arguing from the distinction between "seed" (Gk. *spermati*) and "seeds" (Gk. *spermasin*) in Galatians 3:16?

Or what about those fairly common situations in which the precise wording is not terribly important and a reasonable paraphrase (Living Bible and Phillips have long been the staple here, though some of us just do our own paraphrasing in mid-message) will get the job done just fine? You could quote your regular pulpit translation, but paraphrasing lends a little color and variety to your messages. How do we know that some of the paraphrases in the New Testament are not of a similar nature? If nothing else, in a culture that placed such a premium on memory, what would have been done if a New Testament author was proceeding through the "preaching written" process and his memory got caught "in between" the Hebrew and LXX wording of a verse he was about to quote, with no ready reference available?

If no doctrinal or applicational point was riding on the precise wording, he probably would have paraphrased.

Finally, what do most preachers do when pulpit time is short? They hurriedly begin to summarize (often after saying in so many words, "My time is almost gone"). I've yet to meet a veteran preacher who did not think that is more or less exactly what happened in Hebrews 11:32: "For time will fail me if I tell of Gideon, Barak, Samson . . ." (then he immediately turns to expertly summarize the exploits of the rest of the Hall of Faith). This is a common situation when preaching, and the way the writer of Hebrews handled it is almost as common a reaction to that kind of situation.[12]

WHAT'S ON YOUR LIPS IS WHAT FILLS YOUR MIND AND HEART

Jesus voiced some very strong concerns about "heart of the matter" related to the spoken word: "Do you not understand that everything that goes into the mouth passes into the stomach, and is eliminated? But the things that proceed out of the mouth come from the heart, and those defile the man" (Matt. 15:17–18).

If anything, James' words are even stronger: "But no one can tame the tongue; it is a restless evil and full of deadly poison. With it we bless our Lord and Father; and with it we curse men, who have been made in the likeness of God; from the same mouth come both blessing and cursing. My brethren, these things ought not to be" (James 3:8–10).

What is the answer to this problem of a darkened heart that overflows in dastardly speech? In the context in James, it is "the wisdom from above" (3:15, 17). In Romans 12:2, it is to "be transformed by the renewing of your mind." In Ephesians 5:18, it is to "be filled with the Spirit."

All of these perspectives are very helpful. However, since the issue is *the words that come out of our mouths,* based on the passages above, is not our speech more or less directly related to *the words that fill our hearts?* If so, Colossians 3:16–17 comes center stage: "Let the word of Christ richly dwell within you, with all wisdom teaching [i.e., speaking] and admonishing [i.e., speaking] . . . singing [i.e., speaking] . . . giving thanks [i.e, speaking]."

In effect, that is exactly what we encounter when we study the use of the Old Testament in the New Testament. We keep "hearing" the Old Testament (either in quotation, allusion, or image) when we read the New Testament, almost to the point of saturation in some books, because it was the Old Testament Scriptures that saturated the writers' minds and hearts.[13] If we all tend to talk about what we think about or love deeply, it is not at all difficult to determine what was on the minds and hearts of the New Testament authors. The process of producing the New Testament books, then, was, to a great extent, a "channeled overflow" of the beloved Hebrew Scriptures that they had heard and cherished all their lives.

HOW IS THE OLD TESTAMENT USED IN THE NEW TESTAMENT?

It is now widely recognized that the New Testament authors were operating from several commonly held assumptions as they utilized the Old Testament.[14]

First, they proceeded from the assumption of *corporate solidarity*. This means that the person or act of the individual could stand for the wider community, and, occasionally, vice versa. In regard to Jesus, "He was representative of Israel and in solidarity with her. God's purposes for Israel were now taken up in his ministry."[15]

Second, we consistently encounter the assumption of typology. This is sometimes referred to as *correspondence in history*, meaning "there is a correspondence between what happened to God's people in the past and what happens now or in the future."[16]

Third, the New Testament writers assumed that, in a real sense, the end times had begun and they were living in a time of *eschatological fulfillment*. They viewed the Old Testament passages they handled, especially prophecy and apocalyptic, with that kind of expectation in mind.

Fourth, they operated from the presupposition that the Old Testament Scriptures were *Christological*, and they did so with full "Christological warrant." After all, on the road to Emmaus, Jesus reminded the disciples who heard him: "These are My words which I spoke to you while I was still with you, that all things which are written about Me in the Law of Moses and the Prophets and the Psalms must be fulfilled" (Luke 24:44). It is widely agreed that the wording "Law of Moses," "Prophets" and "Psalms" refers to what we call "the Old Testament canon,"[17] which was complete, as we know it, during the New Testament era. Thus, based on nothing less than the statement of Jesus himself, it is safe to say that their assumption that the Old Testament is heavily Christological is correct.

Two other techniques used by New Testament writers that are worthy of mention here are: (1) "pearl-stringing"; and (2) *testimonia*.[18] Both have to do with what could be called the "clumping" of Old Testament passages in different ways.

Pearl-stringing means that passages that have to do with a certain subject (often theological) are just "strung" in successive fashion in the text to get all the relevant content out on the table, so to speak. In the New Testament, two obvious examples of theological pearl-stringing are Paul's treatment of sin in Romans 3:10–18 and the writer of Hebrews' stacked-up references to Christ and angels (Heb. 1:6–12).

Testimonia were "collections of Old Testament texts that had been grouped thematically for apologetic, liturgical, and catechetical purposes."[19] This largely explains why certain passages are used repeatedly in the New Testament to make similar points (e.g., Gen. 15:6 or Hab. 2:4 for justification by faith). They were well-known, and widely used, "pet passages" of the New Testament churches, beginning from their initial Jewish base in the earlier chapters of Acts.

Interestingly, other than reservations on the parts of some about "corporate solidarity" (in spite of the use of the prevailing "head-body" analogy in the New Testament, to illustrate the close identification between Christ and his church), none of the above assumptions or approaches seem particularly odd, or even significantly different from the ways many evangelical preachers and teachers deal with the Old Testament text and preach today. Thus, in many respects, it seems fair to say that, in regard to the use of the Old Testament in the "preaching" of the New Testament, "the more things change, the more they remain the same."

WHAT'S USED THE MOST, WHERE, AND WHY?

The top five Old Testament books, as far as number of citations in the New Testament is concerned,[20] are Psalms (79 times), Isaiah (66 times), Deuteronomy (50 times), Exodus (44 times), and Genesis (34 times). This is as expected, given the amount of messianic prophecy in Psalms and Isaiah, and the constant need to look back to the historical and legal roots of Israel seen in Genesis, Exodus, and Deuteronomy.

By contrast, fourteen Old Testament books are apparently not quoted at all: Joshua, Judges, Ruth, 2 Kings, 1 Chronicles, 2 Chronicles, Ezra, Nehemiah, Esther, Ecclesiastes, Song of Solomon, Obadiah, Nahum, and Zephaniah.[21] Such selectivity is also to be expected, given the purposes of the New Testament authors and the kinds of background issues their books reflect.

Among the New Testament books, the five that include the most Old Testament quotes are: Romans (64), Matthew (62), Acts (42), Hebrews (37), and Mark (32). Of these, the only mild surprise might be the Gospel of Mark, given its likely Roman audience.[22] However, since Mark was Jewish, and since he was likely recording Peter's sermonic material about Jesus, it is hardly a shock.[23] With the other four books: Romans evidences major issues related to the Jews (especially in Rom. 9–11); Matthew is the most Jewish of the Gospels; Acts reflects the Jewish roots of Christianity and the ongoing offering of the gospel to the Jews, amidst great opposition; and Hebrews consistently goes back to the old covenant Scriptures to back its case for the superiority of Christ and the new covenant.

It is obvious why the bulk, if not all, of the eleven New Testament books that do not cite the Old Testament at all are silent on that front.[24] Their original audiences were almost entirely Gentile and thus had comparatively little background or exposure to the Hebrew Scriptures. Yet, to balance the perspective here, it is important to realize that Revelation, which has no phraseology long enough to qualify as an Old Testament "quotation," may indeed be the New Testament book most saturated with the Old Testament (i.e., in "echoes" and images), as will be examined briefly below.

The remainder of this chapter consists of two "samplers" in regard to the use of the Old Testament in books in which (1) the usage is very frequent and (2) the usage is most striking.[25] These case studies are necessarily brief but are nevertheless powerful. Several of the principles and practices introduced above are seen, and they are seen to work together in the service of "inspired preaching written."

THE HEBREW BIBLE AND MATTHEW'S GOSPEL

Uses of the Old Testament are spread throughout the first book of the New Testament, Matthew's Gospel. But they are particularly interesting, and, in certain ways, controversial in regard to the earliest chapters. Here we see extremely densely clustered usage of the Hebrew Bible: (1) the Old Testament names in Jesus' family tree (Matt. 1:1–17), which is considerably different from Luke's; (2) the virgin birth passage, citing Isaiah 7:14 (Matt. 1:18–25); (3) the prophecy of Jesus' birth in Bethlehem citing Micah 5:2 (Matt. 2:1–12); (4) the use of Hosea 11:1 to speak of Joseph and Mary leaving Egypt after Herod the Great's death (Matt. 2:13–15); (5) the citation of Jeremiah 31:15 in regard to the slaying of the infants by Herod (Matt. 2:16–18); (6) the "Nazarene" reference (Matt. 2:19–23); (7) the Isaiah 40 citation in relation to John the Baptist (Matt. 3); (8) Jesus' quotations from Deuteronomy and Psalms in answering the temptations of the devil (Matt. 4:1–11); and (9) the Isaiah 9 quote having to do with Jesus' making Capernaum his ministry headquarters (Matt. 4:12–16).

Of these uses, most people view the majority as reasonably straightforward. Troubling to some, for various reasons, are the application of the Isaiah 7 passage to the virgin birth, applying the Jeremiah 31 quote to this context and the seemingly out-of-thin-air feel for the "quote" related to Jesus as "Nazarene."

It should be said up front that, although there are several promising possibilities,[26] there is presently no "open and shut" answer to the "Nazarene" issue. There is simply no Old Testament passage which comes close to corresponding to the wording in Matthew 2:23. However, there are better answers for the other two purportedly problematic uses.

A key ongoing issue in the interpretation of the use of the Old Testament in the New is whether the "upper hand" is with the Old Testament passage or the New Testament passage.[27] Often the more decisive factor is the Old Testament passage and its context. However, in both these passages, it seems to be the other way around.

Isaiah 7:14, which, in context, otherwise seems to focus exclusively on Isaiah's day, allows for a virgin birth, due to the fact that the Hebrew *almah* ("young woman of marriageable age") is rendered in the LXX by the Greek *parthenos*, which cannot mean other than "virgin."[28] Thus, Matthew "applies" that meaning to the virgin birth.

The Jeremiah 31 passage is similarly used in an "applicational" manner. One of the most memorable times in Israel's history in which the kind of grief related to such overwhelming loss of life as all the boy babies in and around Bethelehem dying (Matt. 2:16) was in relation to the Exile, as the Jeremiah passage poignantly portrays. Since "Rachel," wife of Jacob and mother of several of the tribes of Israel, was not present at the time of slaughter related to the Exile, either, that served as an interpretive pointer for Matthew.

Although some interpreters would be more comfortable if Matthew's hermeneutics were more like our own in some of these passages, very few will fault him for powerful "applicational preaching." That is especially true, since Matthew's "preaching written" is also divinely "inspired preaching."

ECHOES OF THE HEBREW BIBLE IN THE APOCALYPSE

There are no Old Testament quotations in Revelation, the last book in the New Testament, though even to make that assertion is a close call. In the "collage" effect of Daniel 7:13 and Zechariah 12:10 found in Revelation 1:7, either usage is very nearly long enough to qualify as a "quote." That point, however, does not impact the amount of usage of, and indebtedness to, the Old Testament in the Apocalypse. Estimates of the number of Old Testament allusions and images vary widely, ranging from a low of about 275 to one estimate that goes all the way up to 1,000.[29]

Where do the echoes and "pictures" come from in the Old Testament? "Over half of the Old Testament books are represented," with Psalms, Isaiah, Ezekiel, and Daniel being the most heavily utilized.[30] The allusions cover Old Testament ground "all the way from the earliest chapters of Genesis (echoed extensively in Rev. 21–22) and Exodus (many of the plagues and the 'Song of Moses' [Rev. 15:3–8; cf. Exod. 15:1–18]) to Zechariah (e.g., the four horses [Rev. 6:1–8; cf. Zech. 1:8, etc.] and Malachi (the Elijah prophecy [Rev. 11:6a; cf. Mal. 4:5])."[31]

At the end of the day, the "big picture" effect of the Old Testament saturation of the Apocalypse turns out to be that all the Old Testament typology
("preview" images) and all the Old Testament prophecies with "dangling
ends" find their fulfillment here. In so doing, the world kingdoms of Daniel
(Dan. 2, 7, etc.) all give way to the final, and ultimate, reign—the kingdom
of God. The final fulfillment of the first biblical prophecy, of the ultimate
victory of the "seed of the woman" over the serpent and his "seed" (Gen.
3:15), signaled as "in play" in Revelation 12:1–2, 9, is sealed in Revelation
20:2, 7–10. Even the "curse" related to sin on the human race (Gen. 3) is
"reversed" (Rev. 21:4; 22:3) for all believers for eternity; at least that is the
effect on the hearer of Revelation 21–22, which portrays "Paradise Regained
. . . and Never to Be Lost Again," or "Eden, Only Better."

Suffice it to say that the Apocalypse, because of this "saturation" effect, at
once has the "feel" of the Old Testament at every turn, yet also represents a
dramatic quantum leap forward beyond it. As "inspired preaching," its seemingly never-ending echoes and vivid images of the past that will assuredly
find fulfillment in the future are designed to challenge the hearer to "heed"
its grave and terrifying warnings (Rev. 1:3), especially if the hearer is not a
believer (22:14, 17).[32]

TODAY!: "GETTING THE POINT"
ABOUT THE USE OF THE OLD TESTAMENT IN THE NEW

Often, when the application related to the sermon does not seem to be
urgent (i.e., "right then"), a preacher will say something like, "As you are
reflecting on this truth throughout the coming week, you may wish to consider (and he will proceed to enumerate a laundry list of practical applicational possibilities)." In other words, you don't have to do it now, but don't
forget about the message when you walk out the door today.

Such "suggestions" are, of course, dramatically better than no applicational emphasis at all. However, having heard what we have in this chapter
makes you wonder: Would Matthew have been satisfied if those who heard
the reading of the first Gospel just turned away and said, "I'll think about
Jesus later?" Would not the glorified Son of Man and the apostle John be
absolutely appalled if the response to the climactic call ("Come!") of the
Hebrew Bible-saturated Apocalypse was, "Maybe I'll think about it when I get
around to it"? And, to add one other classic New Testament example: Would
not the writer of Hebrews, in whose pointed applicational exposition of
Psalm 95 (Heb. 3:7–4:13) we find the rapid-fire fivefold repetition of "Today"
(3:7, 13, 15; 4:7 [twice]), not be utterly amazed at this "take your time, no
hurry" approach to response and application?

What we have here is sort of a "hard-edged" flip-side of the old Doublemint slogan, "Double your pleasure, double your fun." In the case of the use of the Old Testament in the New, it can be said, "Double your authority, double your responsibility (to act)." The Hebrew Bible was the "Bible" of the New Testament era, as the New Testament was being written. It is still 72 percent of the Bible today, equally authoritative and spiritually powerful as the New Testament (2 Tim. 3:16; Heb. 4:12). It expects Christians to listen. Even more, it expects believers to act upon what they hear. And most pointedly, it expects action *today*![33]

CHAPTER 13

INSPIRED PREACHING— THEN AND NOW

C. RICHARD WELLS

The condition of man would be lowered if God had not wished to have men supply his word to men.

AUGUSTINE, *DE DOCTRINA CHRISTIANA*

In *The Difference of Man and the Difference It Makes,* philosopher Mortimer Adler wrote that, however humans may differ from the lower animals, the really important thing is to say how the "difference" matters.[1] Our thesis is quite simply that the New Testament consists by and large of preaching, and that the New Testament documents are best described (essentially) either as sermon *transcripts* (written records of actual preaching) or *manuscripts* (intended for delivery as a near-substitute for the living voice of the preacher). As we bring the work to a close, we want to ask, "What difference does our thesis make for preaching the New Testament today?"

We answered that question in part earlier, when we suggested that recognizing the original orality of the Gospels should alter our understanding of them dramatically.[2] But the fundamental orality of the New Testament can and should shape our preaching in ways that are more specifically "homiletical." That in itself deserves an entire volume; but even in such brief compass we can sketch out some possibilities. We will begin by asking how the oral form of the New Testament ought to inform contemporary homiletics. Then, on the assumption that the New Testament faithfully portrays the preaching and teaching of Jesus and the apostles, we will ask what it means to "preach like Jesus." We will close our work with Paul's farewell sermon to preachers.

171

"MYTH BECOME FACT":
THE PARADOXICAL POWER OF PREACHING

The apostle Paul summarized his theology of preaching in a single memorable sentence: "God was well-pleased through the foolishness of the message preached [kērugma] to save those who believe."[3] As culture-without-Christ sees it, preaching is pure nonsense. Yet, according to Paul (and with him, the whole of the early church), this human folly authenticates itself, because God has determined to use it to transform human lives. It is worth noting here that this one verse, in and of itself, almost demands our thesis. If preaching is God's appointed means of salvation, in what else could the New Testament possibly consist, if not in preaching? But Paul's approbrium speaks as well to our immediate *homiletical* concerns. For preaching combines the divine and the human as no other form of communication can do.

C. S. Lewis once described Christianity as "myth become fact."[4] Man's longing for his lost but true home—expressed in the mythologies of long ages in every race—has at last become a reality. God himself has come. And how do we know? Because "on a silent night in Judah's hills, a baby's cry was heard!"[5] The glory of God in a manger of hay—an extraordinary paradox that helps explain the origin of the New Testament, and, in turn, helps us preach the New Testament today.

PREACHING WITH FULL CONVICTION—
THEN AND NOW

To say that the New Testament consists of preaching is to beg the question—why did the early preachers preach in the first place? The answer is simple. They had experienced the power of the kingdom of God in Christ, and they could not stop speaking what they had seen and heard (Acts 4:20).

George Beasley-Murray helps us appreciate this dynamic by inviting us to "listen" to Peter's voice in the Markan account of Jesus in the synagogue at Capernaum:

> There he stood in the synagogue, in the grip of an unclean power! He shrieked in terror before the holiness of the Lord. We were breathless as Jesus faced him. He used no magic. He performed no sorcery. He gave a command, and the demoniac was free. You should have seen his face and heard his shout when he realized what had happened! He was more than healed, he was a new creature! The crowd was filled with astonishment to witness such an act of power. But our Christ has done that to multitudes, and he's doing it still!

Let me tell you about my wife's mother. On that very afternoon, when we reached home, we found her stricken with
fever. My wife was apprehensive. The old lady could not stand
many more of these attacks! But the Lord was with us. He had
demonstrated what he could do for a person in the grip of an
evil power; why should he not do the like for her in her physical weakness? I hurried out of her room to him. "Teacher,"
I said, "she's very ill, but God is with you. You can help her,
can't you?" He went to her bedside and looked at her. What
followed was incredible but for seeing. He simply took my
mother-in-law's hand and sat her up. "God is good to you," he
said. "You're well now." And so she was! All trace of the fever
had gone. "Thank you, Rabbi," she replied. "Yes, I am well.
God is good. And You are very kind." Then she added, "But
I don't see the sense of sitting here. I feel as fit as a fiddle." She
got up, dressed herself, and prepared a meal for the whole
company of us! That's the Jesus I preach to you! He sets a man
or a woman free from the shackles of sin and makes them of
use to God and man![6]

In its preoccupation with critical minutiae, modern scholarship
has tended to blunt the vitality, freshness, and conviction of the earliest
preaching. Without going beyond what is written, without eisegetical psy-
chologizing, without overactive imagineering, the modern preacher must
seek therefore to reenter the "kingdom context" of the New Testament
preachers. Paul reminded the Thessalonians that he preached the gospel to
them "with full conviction" (1 Thess. 1:5). Whatever else he meant by those
words, they certainly indicate that Paul did not merely repeat a history. He
was not an eyewitness of Jesus as were the Twelve—a status he shared with
preachers today—but he nonetheless proclaimed the historical factuality of
the gospel *as a present reality.*

The modern preacher must, of course, bridge the gap between the
"then" and the "now." At one extreme, the preacher may simply preach
Bible history. At the other extreme, the preacher may simply excerpt proof
texts that have some verbal or topical affinity with the supposed felt needs
of a congregation. But if the New Testament itself is really preaching, the
key to biblical proclamation is already *in the text.* The preacher's task is,
using all the best resources of historical and theological analysis, to understand why the first preacher preached as he did, and then, by the power of
the Spirit, to preach the ancient sermon in contemporary language, "with
full conviction."

SACRED LANGUAGE

It is a commonplace that "since [God's] nature is by definition infinite it is impossible for it to be fully revealed through a finite medium to a finite mind."[7] God is, we might say, beyond words; and yet, words "create and reflect their culture, and to read them outside that culture is to invite a basic level of misunderstanding."[8] So here we meet another paradox of preaching—to speak the unspeakable, to express the mind of Christ in the language of the street. In recognizing the New Testament as preaching, we are encouraged that the task is not hopeless. The language of the New Testament, we recall, is *koinē*, the language of everyday. The modern preacher need not doubt that eternal truth *can* be proclaimed understandably and relevantly. The New Testament itself is living proof!

While we must make every allowance for the necessary operation of the Holy Spirit in all effective preaching, we must also recognize that the New Testament is necessarily rhetorical as well. The early preachers used *means* to capture infinite truth in finite language and to communicate that truth for the purpose of salvation. We have seen, especially in our studies of the speeches in Acts, how carefully the first preachers crafted their preaching, depending all the while on the Spirit for results. Augustine opined that without the necessity of communicating the Word by man to men, the "condition of man would be lowered."[9] The very acts of probing the Word, analyzing human nature, reflecting on the application of Scripture, seeking effective forms of expression, and all the rest that goes into good preaching—these foster growth, encourage love, broaden knowledge, and have countless other benefits, quite apart from the effect of the message itself!

The inspired preaching of the New Testament is a kind of "sacred language" whereby God's truth enters human life. As such, it testifies to the necessity of rhetoric, but also (as Augustine said) to the value of rhetoric for the whole body of Christ. And because it is *sacred* language, it provides the modern preacher with a sense of rhetorical direction besides. For that, there is no better place to turn than the Master Preacher himself.

PREACHING LIKE JESUS

In their book *Learning to Preach like Jesus*, Ralph and Gregg Lewis ask, "Can we really preach like Jesus today?"[10] The answer, in a word, is "no." Jesus was (and, of course, is) unique, on any scale of comparison. His spiritual vitality never slumped, because the will of the Father was his very food (John 4:34). He had no need to study rhetoric or psychology, for "He . . . knew what was in man" (John 2:25). His credibility never suffered from a misdeed, because no one could lay an error to his charge (e.g., John 8:46). Furthermore, the *works* of Jesus perfectly conformed to and confirmed his *words*, as when he preached the royal rule (kingdom) of God in Capernaum, and in the same synagogue service, exercised that rule by exorcising a demon (Mark 1:21–28). Even a popular teaching form like the parable is, in the mouth of Jesus, something utterly different, for he himself is the center of each one.[11] And yet, it is not too much to think that *imitatio Christi*, the age-old aspiration to pattern the Christian life after Christ, should not apply to preaching and preachers.

"They Heard Him Gladly": The Preaching Style of Jesus

Commenting on Jesus' teaching during the passion week, Mark says that "the common people heard him gladly."[12] Because the setting here is confrontation with Jewish leaders, William Barclay may be right that the people merely enjoyed Jesus' "denunciation of the scribes." There are certain minds to which invective is always attractive.[13] Even so, the contrast of teaching styles between Jesus and the scribes must have played a part in the crowd's "enjoyment," and in any case, the syntax of the verse suggests that Mark was summarizing the response to Jesus' teaching as a whole.[14] Precisely because Jesus stands alone as a teacher, we may well ask how he "connected" with people, why the crowds "heard him gladly," what gave him the freshness that so captivated those who listened to him.[15] We find at least three answers.

1. **The preaching of Jesus was simple and accomodating.** Pheme Perkins writes:

> Jesus spoke with a prophetic voice to all people.
> Understanding his message did not require special education
> or even a life . . . marked by holiness in a special way.
> Ordinary people heard Jesus' words as the word of God
> addressed to them. Jesus did not use a 'scholarly' or 'technical
> language' such as we find in philosophical writings of the time
> or in legal disputes over the meaning of the Law.[16]

His listeners often failed to understand his teaching, but never because Jesus spoke an unintelligible language. He used everyday figures, experiences, and phenomena to engage his hearers. He found great truths in simple things. He cloaked eternal verities in images like harvests, new wine, physician and sickness, a city on a hill, lamps and platters, leaven, sparrows, serpents and doves, and dozens of others known by all from their mother's knee. In short, he enabled his hearers (in Blake's poetry)—

> To see a world in a grain of sand
> And a heaven in a wild flower,
> Hold infinity in the palm of your hand
> And eternity in an hour.[17]

Simplicity made the teaching of Jesus accessible. Jesus began where his hearers were, with familiar ideas, familiar language, familiar experiences, and led them on from there to a spiritual kingdom. And Jesus never rushed people: "Step by step he led them. 'I have many things to say unto you,' he once told them, 'but you cannot bear them now' (John 16:12). With divine reserve . . . he would keep back part of the revelation . . . until his hearers were able to receive it."[18]

2. The preaching of Jesus was memorable and memorizable. No one who reads the Gospels can fail to see how *parables* dominate the teaching of Jesus.[19] As we have seen, Jesus explained to his disciples that parables *reveal* to those with eyes to see; but to others, they *conceal*. Whether they reveal or conceal, however, the parables cannot be ignored. They are vivid and memorable, indeed unforgettable.

Parables constitute only the most striking feature of the Master Teacher's style. He employed forms and techniques of speech that enabled his hearers to remember what he said. He could use hyperbole—camels through needles or logs in eyes—"as a kind of shock treatment to help people see the truth."[20] He used riddles[21] and paradoxes[22] to focus attention and drive home a point. He used word play[23] and he "knew the truth of the formula *repetitio est mater studiorum*" ["repetition is the mother of learning"].[24] Although we have only Greek translations of Jesus' words, attempts to retrovert them to the original Aramaic (or Hebrew) suggest that the great majority of the Lord's separate sayings have poetic forms or employ poetic techniques such as alliteration, assonance, and rhyme.[25]

Even in Greek translation, it is clear that Jesus "condensed the main points of his theological and ethical teaching in summaries."[26] Birger Gerhardsson and others have dubbed these summaries "*meshalim*," from the Hebrew *mashal*, which can denote any "short, carefully formulated text."[27] Gerhardsson has identified more than fifty "narrative *meshalim*" (roughly equivalent to "parables"), but scores of other "*aphoristic meshalim*," which, according to David Aune, "is the single literary form most frequently attributed to Jesus."[28] Aphorisms belong to the stock wisdom of most ancient societies. They functioned mnemonically, "as vehicles for articulating and preserving traditional values . . . by expressing general and typical truths."[29]

Jesus likewise used *meshalim*, but—and this is important—Jesus did not use them simply to pass on traditional wisdom. Many are radically disorienting—as in "the first shall be last"[30]—and almost none deal with the usual themes, such as friendship, family, personal habits, or politics. Jesus sought rather to make memorable his message about the kingdom of God.

Jesus consciously formulated his preaching and teaching to make it memorizable. Ruth Finegan has shown how, under certain conditions—especially when (a) the leader is regarded as inspired, (b) the material is given in some more or less fixed form, and (c) the remembering group is specially trained—religious groups can ritualize tradition.[31] Thus it is hardly a stretch to imagine that the disciples would have memorized many of Jesus' sayings even during his earthly ministry.

3. **The preaching of Jesus was original and personal.** In words now familiar to us, Matthew records that when Jesus finished the Sermon on the Mount, "the crowds were amazed at His teaching; for He was teaching them as one having authority, and not as their scribes" (Matt. 7:28b–29). Martin Lloyd-Jones sought to recapture that remarkable reaction by distinguishing Jesus from the scribes. First, unlike the scribes and Pharisees who taught by compiling citations of other authorities, "there was a freshness about [Jesus'] teaching . . . [an] originality of thought and of manner." Second, Jesus spoke with "extraordinary assurance." When he teaches, "There is no doubt about it, and no questions; . . . no mere supposition, or possibility only." Finally, "what really astonished these people . . . was what He said, and in particular what He said about Himself." He calls attention to his own person and his own teaching.[32]

As we saw in chapter 4, the "real reason" for putting Jesus to death was this peculiar claim to authority. The Jewish leaders could not endure "Jesus' quiet assumption, unmediated by appeals to Scripture or tradition, that he knew God's mind and was doing God's work."[33]

Effective Preaching

Can we really preach like Jesus today? Perhaps the answer is not absolutely no, but "no . . . and yes." Luke gives us reason to think so, with his accounts of the apostolic preaching and its effects.

Hermann Ridderbos once remarked that the speeches of Acts "have a decidedly 'old-fashioned' character."[34] They certainly follow a well-established pattern: *Exordium* (*proem*) followed by testimony to Jesus of Nazareth, ending with a call to repentance (*epilogos*). Form critics have seized on this stereotyped form as "evidence" that Luke freely invented the speeches, and that they do not in any meaningful way represent the actual preaching of the apostles.[35] A far better explanation, however, is that the first preachers had only one mission—to preach the gospel. They proclaimed the crucified and resurrected Lord Jesus Christ as the fulfillment of the prophetic hope. This message, as Paul explained to the Corinthians, is "of first importance" (1 Cor. 15:1–4). "Old-fashioned" form simply followed function.

Luke gives us other reasons in any case for regarding the Acts speeches as authentic. He sets the speeches in historical context, and he shows that, like all good communicators, the first preachers used rhetorical means to connect with their hearers. The most telling historical evidence for the speeches, however, is that when the preachers preach, things happen. As we might expect

from someone with trained powers of observation, Luke provides us remarkably detailed accounts of homiletical effects, that is, of how the first hearers
responded to the first preachers. Luke reserves his most thorough descriptions
for those instances where the audience is unsympathetic, notably Peter at
Pentecost and (twice) before the Sanhedrin, Stephen before the synagogue and
the Sanhedrin, and Peter before dissenters in Jerusalem. Then there is Paul on
Areopagus, before the mob in Jerusalem, before the Sanhedrin, before Felix,
before Agrippa (with Festus present), and finally, before Jews in Rome.

Luke seems thereby to emphasize that *effective* preaching does not equal
(what we normally think of as) *good communication*. Preaching differs quali-
tatively from every other human speech—whether the oratory of the ancient
rhetors, or the polish of today's communication meisters. Good communication connects with people and moves them along with the speaker. Effective
preaching also connects with people and moves them—but sometimes they
move *against* the speaker! Preaching has a different criterion of success than
mere communication.

"Uneducated and Untrained Men":
Peter (with John) before the Sanhedrin

Nowhere does the paradoxical success of "spiritual rhetoric" stand out
more clearly than in Luke's account of Peter's first defense (with John) before
the Sanhedrin (Acts 4:5–22). Following the speech, the Sanhedrin marveled
"as they observed the confidence of Peter and John, and understood that they
were uneducated and untrained men"; and, Luke adds, they "began to recognize them as having been with Jesus" (4:13). The apostles succeeded, after a
fashion, in that the Sanhedrin "had nothing to say in reply" (Acts 4:14).

To understand the apostles' "success" more fully, it may be helpful to say
a further word about classical rhetoric. From Aristotle on, persuasiveness was
thought to depend on *logos, ethos,* and *pathos*.[36] *Logos* is simply logical argument (which Aristotle thought should be sufficient to persuade, but in the
real world is not). *Ethos* denoted something like "credibility" combined with
"winsomeness." Said Aristotle: "[There is persuasion] through character
whenever the speech is spoken in such a way as to make the speaker worthy
of credence; for we believe fair-minded people to a greater extent and more
quickly [than we do others] on all subjects in general and completely so in
cases where there is not exact knowledge but room for doubt."[37]

Finally, speech persuades when "hearers . . . are led to feel emotion by the
speech [*pathos*]; for we do not give the same judgment when grieved and
rejoicing or when being friendly and hostile."[38] *Pathos* is emotion evoked
from the hearers that inclines them to respond. The link between *logos* and
pathos is *ethos*. Therefore, Aristotle said, "Character [*ethos*] is almost, so to
speak, the controlling factor in persuasion."[39]

Homiletics and Ethos

Translated to homiletics,[40] *ethos* is the link between message and response, as Peter (with John) illustrates in the case before us. Luke calls special attention to the way *ethos* effected "persuasion."

1. Engaging attention. The apostles *got the attention* of the Sanhedrin. Arrested by the Council for their preaching, they now "arrested" the Council by their *ethos*. Luke specifically points out that the apostles shattered a stereotype.[41] In modern communications terms, we might say the Sanhedrin had a negative "anticipatory set." All of us listen with "emotional filters"[42] that render us more or less receptive to what we hear. Researchers have verified what most of us now consider good common sense. People "tend to act in accordance with their dominant attitudes,"[43] or, as we say, people "hear what they want to hear."

Luke portrays the Sanhedrin's stereotype of Peter and John with remarkable fullness. First, Peter and John lacked credentials. The Greek for "uneducated" *[agrammatoi]* literally means "unlettered" or "illiterate," but in actual usage, the term only indicates that Peter and John had no formal rabbinical training. The Council also considered them incompetent. The Greek term for "untrained" *[idiōtai]* suggests a contrast between the "amateur" and the "professional," or the "layman" and the "expert." It is as if two laborers have appeared to argue before the Supreme Court.

No doubt the Council associated the apostles with the common people they scorned. Bruce Metzger reminds us that the so-called "people of the land" (*am ha-ares*) could not be summoned as witnesses in court, nor was their testimony admissible.[44] Some months before, members of this very Council had denounced Jesus partly on the basis of class appeal: "No one of the rulers or Pharisees has believed in Him, has he? But this crowd which does not know the Law is accursed" (John 7:48–49). In the eyes of the Sanhedrin, Peter and John (like Jesus) may have roused the rabble, but they hardly qualified as religious authorities.

The Council thought to make short work of their pretensions. The very arrangement of the room—Peter and John in the center of a semicircle—put the apostles on notice and put the Council in control. They had not come to listen to a message but to dispose of amateurs.

2. Confidence and character. The Sanhedrin "observed"[45] the "confidence" of Peter and John (4:13a). The scene calls to mind an excerpt from the controverted life of Herod the Great. Josephus relates that Alexander and Aristobulus, sons of Herod by Mariamne, had fallen out of his favor, when Herod put Marianne to death for supposed political intrigues and turned his affections to his eldest son, Antipater. Meanwhile, Herod's reputation in Rome was being undermined by accusations of various enemies. Herod responded by scapegoating Alexander and Aristobulus before Caesar Augustus in Rome.

Josephus describes an emotional scene. Caesar permitted the young men to speak, but they "wept, and were in confusion." They "knew in their own consciences they were innocent, but because they were accused by their father, . . . it was hard for them." Yet "they were afraid, that if they said nothing, they should seem to be [guilty]." Still, they had no defense prepared, "by reason of their youth, and the [duress] they were under." At long last, however, emboldened by both *innocence* and *love*, Alexander spoke for himself and Aristobulus, with the result that Augustus and all who heard were "moved by it."[46]

This account illustrates the difference between what we normally think of as "confidence," and what the Sanhedrin detected in Peter and John. Alexander had no "confidence" in the psychological sense. His boldness had nothing to do with temperament, skills, training, or experience. He was frightened, confused, timid, and ambivalent. But Alexander stood on moral high ground. He knew he was innocent, and (despite everything) he loved his father. His *character* (*ethos*) quite literally produced *confidence*. Just so with Peter and John.

Luke often uses this word *confidence* [Gk. *parrēsia*] to characterize the preaching of early Christians.[47] The word nearly always implies a hostile or threatening context, which the preacher meets with openness or candor, and passion for truth. The context here, of course, is Jewish; but we have much to learn by tracing the roots of the term in the politics of ancient Greece. *Parrēsia* is that "freedom of speech" necessary for real democracy—where free people openly speak truth according to the dictates of conscience, all for the greater good of the *polis*. So *parrēsia* is rhetorical ability, of sorts,[48] not image-casting, self-promotion, or mere facility of speech, but the persuasive power of a true citizen. Such is the "confidence," *mutadis mutandis*, of Peter and John. Before the forum of contradictory and hostile opinion, they speak openly, transparently, without affectation. They speak the truth as it is in Jesus for the good of all people. Under arrest, they themselves *arrest*, first the attention, then the conscience, of the Council.

3. Preaching like Jesus. Finally, Luke informs us that the members of the Sanhedrin "were amazed, and began to recognize them as having been with Jesus" (Acts 4:13c). The language here is a bit ambiguous. What does Luke mean? F. F. Bruce represents a good many evangelical scholars when he suggests that Jesus had imparted to his followers something of his own "sure handling of the Scriptures, his unerring ability to go back to first principles for the confirming of his own teaching and the discomfiture of his opponents."[49] Jesus had "rubbed off" on Peter and John, so to speak.

Chrysostom, however, took Luke rather more literally. In his view, the Council recognized that Peter and John "had been with Jesus" precisely because the members had *seen them with Jesus* at his trial! But "at that time . . . they had seen them humble, dejected: and this it was that most surprised them: *the greatness of the change."* The *transformation* of Peter and John, since the trial of Jesus less than two months earlier, is what impressed the Sanhedrin.

It is entirely possible, even likely, that both interpretations are legitimate. Chrysostom himself hinted that Peter learned his "very manner and method" from Jesus.[50] Luke may well have chosen his words specifically to create a double entendre. Peter and John had in fact been with Jesus at his trial. They had in fact been "dejected." (Peter even denied his Lord.) And now Peter and John were in fact "confident." They had in fact changed. And, in fact, there was no explanation for the change but Jesus. The preaching manner and method—in short, the confidence—which they had seen in Jesus a few weeks before, the Council now saw in those who followed Jesus and proclaimed him as Lord.[51]

There is then a fundamental likeness between the preaching of Jesus and the preaching of his followers. Like Jesus, Peter and John preached with *authority.* The *authority* of the apostles was precisely at issue in their defense (Acts 4:7). As we have seen, these uneducated rabble-rousers had no quarter with the Council. Neither had Jesus. His authority was constantly in question,[52] his credentials constantly under scrutiny (cf. Mark 6:1–3; Luke 4:22.). But Jesus taught "as one having authority, and not as [the] scribes" (cf. John 8:45–47; 18:19–23). His preaching was authenticated by character. So was the preaching of Peter and John. And so must ours be. The "Truth, to which we bear witness, is no longer a bare word, but Truth in the form of personal being."[53] Only Christ himself can be called "the Truth," but any Spirit-transformed preacher "can be a witness to the Truth in parallel fashion."[54]

Who Dares to Preach?

Councils and priests questioned the authority of Jesus and the apostles in the first century, and the questions keep coming in the twenty-first. "Who dares to preach?" asks Wallace Fisher. "By whose authority [does] anyone [presume] to preach?"[55] One trained in theology and exegesis, perhaps, or schooled in communications theory? One skilled in pastoral care or literate in liturgy? Perhaps. But as one of the older homileticians said it, these "ministrations" may be nothing more than worthless compounds. The medieval alchemists, said Spencer Kennard, spent their days and nights attempting to make gold by chemical process. They always failed, because they could never isolate the secret ingredient, and without it their most ingenious concoctions lay worthless in mortars and crucibles. But authentic preaching is a kind of successful alchemy, whereby the secret ingredient, "Christ shining in the life," makes gold out of common clay.[56]

Among the many kinds of authority a preacher might claim, transformed character is "of utmost importance."[57] Luke will not let us forget that. Character transformed by Christ is his "explanation of the marvelous pulpit power of . . . men of very modest talents,"[58] notably in Peter but also in Stephen, and in Paul. It was true then; it is true now: "The living force of a self-forgetful, sacrificial soul, pressing, urging itself upon other souls for their impregnation with the truth and their transfiguration from the dark and sordid life of the flesh into the true life for which Christ made and redeemed them, is indeed a spectacle for angels and men."[59]

EPILOGUE:
PREACHING TO PREACHERS ABOUT PREACHING

Like Peter, Paul was called to preach through the "grim abyss" of personal failure—but there the similarities nearly end. While Peter failed through a weak will, Paul failed through a strong will. Peter lapsed; Paul raged. A slave girl exposed Peter; Stephen exposed Paul. Jesus restored Peter; Jesus humbled Paul. As they differed in their pilgrimage to the preaching ministry, they differed also in what they brought to it—personality, education, socioeconomic class, pedigree, and the like.[60] Paul, the rabbi, is a systematic theologian, a scholar trained in disputation, if not formal rhetoric. Peter, the working man, is a lay theologian and a people person. Still, in both Paul and Peter we meet with "spiritual rhetoric." The rhetoric of Peter is Spirit-filled and *intuitive*. The rhetoric of Paul is Spirit-filled and *schooled*.

It should come as no surprise, therefore, that Paul gives us the first known systematic pastoral theology. Long before Chrysostom wrote his *Treatise Concerning the Christian Priesthood* (as a defense of lying to avoid ordination!),[61] or Augustine wrote *De Doctrina Christiana*,[62] or Gregory the Great commenced his episcopacy in Rome with *Liber Regulae Pastoralis*,[63] Paul set out the duties of the pastoral office before the elders of the church in Ephesus (Acts 20:18b–35). Luke records it in a form we should best regard as the synopsis of an extended lecture on preaching and pastoral ministry.

"Apart from the Pastoral Epistles," wrote William Chadwick at the turn of the last century, "[this sermon] contains the only extant advice of St. Paul addressed directly to those holding an office or position of special responsibility in the Church."[64] Despite its brevity, the context of the address renders it uniquely valuable. Paul called for the elders from Miletus as he hurried to Jerusalem at the end of the third journey (20:15–17a). He did not expect to see them again,[65] and the speech is breathless with urgency—as if Paul is doing his best to deal as fully as possible with things that matter most. The result is an impassioned call to the first principles of pastoral theology, "a mirror for self-examination, . . . a standard whereby [a pastor] may test his own aims and conduct."[66]

Chadwick devoted an entire chapter to the Miletus speech in his *Pastoral Teaching of Paul*. The context of the speech, he writes, not only suggests urgency but indicates "that St. Paul knew intimately the Church to whose responsible officers it was addressed." Here, as always, "insight" is the "key to foresight," for "the true pastor is a *watchman*, as well as a prophet; indeed, because he is a watchman he can be a prophet."[67] "Therefore" Paul says to the elders, "be on the alert" (20:31). Chadwick despaired, however, of discovering "any formal arrangement, or even . . . logical sequence of thought" in the speech, preferring to analyze it line by line in light of the major emphases.

Chadwick may have given up too easily. While it is true that several themes weave their way through the speech, it is also true that Paul seems to follow a train of thought, as indicated by the phrase "and now" which appears at three critical points (20:22, 25, 32).[68] On this interpretation, the speech consists of four major sections: (1) a testimony—summarizing Paul's preaching ministry in Ephesus (20:18b–21); (2) a prophecy concerning himself—summarizing Paul's calling to ministry (20:22–24); (3) a prophecy concerning the church—summarizing the responsibilities of the elders (20:26–31); and (4) a prayer for the elders—summarizing the link between ministry and *ethos* (20:32–35).

Paul's Ministry in Ephesus

Recounting his *ministry in Ephesus* (vv. 18b–21), Paul highlights his (a) personal investment, (b) ministry methodology, and (c) ministry objective. First, Paul gave himself without reserve to the work, "serving the Lord with all humility and with tears and with trials" (v. 19). He disavowed the ministerial persona and status-seeking ("humility"), and he grieved over sin and its effects ("tears"). Second, Paul's method consisted primarily in preaching and teaching[69] "anything that was profitable"—as opposed to pet topics, his or theirs[70]—in public and in private conversation. Finally, Paul's ministry objective was always repentance and faith for all, Jews and Greeks (v. 21).

Paul's Personal Prophecy

Paul's *prophecy concerning himself* (vv. 2–4) emphasizes the pastoral calling. Chadwick likened Paul here to Jesus with his face set toward Jerusalem (cf. Luke 9:51). The apostle says he is "bound in spirit" (v. 22), suggesting personal resolve combined with "divine necessity."[71] Paul does not know what awaits him (v. 22), other than "bonds and afflictions" (v. 23). But the "how" is irrelevant to the "what," *namely*, "that I may finish my course and the ministry which I received from the Lord" (v. 24). Thus does Paul "raise up [the elders] minds" to the nobility of the pastoral calling.[72]

The Savage Wolves

Paul's *prophecy concerning the church* (vv. 25–31) illustrates the principle that "insight is the key to foresight."[73] Indeed, the "prophecy" is more like an observation than an oracle, a warning to *expect the expected!* The apostle calls the elders to minister within what Richard John Neuhaus calls "the thus and soness of the church."[74] The "pilgrim people of God on their way to the New Jerusalem," says Neuhaus, "are still pedestrians."[75] So the pastor must guard against "savage wolves" (v. 29) who do not spare the flock, and traitors who use "ministry" as a power grab (v. 30). Ministry is "people business" on a grand scale. A *person* alternately defends *people*, or nurtures *people*, or (when necessary) opposes *people*.

The rhetoric of this section suggests that Paul has come to the heart of his pastoral theology. First, he summarizes his entire ministry in Ephesus in terms of preaching, specifically, "preaching the kingdom" (vv. 25–27; Acts 28:28). Clearly, preaching is not a line item on the job description; it *is* the job description! This explains the apostle's famous impassioned disclaimer—he has proclaimed all of God's Word ("the whole purpose of God," v. 27) to all persons ("innocent of the blood of all men," v. 26). These words about declaring "the whole purpose of God" have "an important application to study as well as to teaching and preaching," says Chadwick, "for the 'counsel of God' has to be *learned* before it can be expressed."[76] Second, Paul issues a final, urgent exhortation to the elders (vv. 28–31). They are to be "on guard" (v. 28) in two directions at once—(a) to themselves, since "doing depends on being,"[77] and (b) to the flock. They are also to be "on guard" in two ways at once—(a) by taking their commission seriously (v. 28b) and (b) by taking the threats seriously (vv. 29–30).

A Prayer for Preachers

In view of the demands that ministry will impose, Paul closes with *a prayer for the elders*, which links ministry with character (*ethos*; vv. 32–35). He commends them to God and to the "word of His grace" as the "*mediatorial instrument*,"[78] which has the power "to build up" and to give a godly "inheritance" (v. 32). Perhaps the mention of "inheritance" prompts Paul to recall another distinctive of his ministry in Ephesus. Just as he is innocent of failing his office (vv. 26–27), he is innocent of using his office for gain (33–35).

Paul ends his message just as he began—by adducing, as Chrysostom says, the testimony of the elders themselves (vv. 34–35). Rhetorically, the strategy allows Paul to use his ministry in Ephesus as a model for the elders. They must "not imagine his works to be mere boasting" since "he calls the hearers themselves as witnesses of the things he says."[79] Richard Baxter found here a call to preachers to "deal as plainly and closely with one another, as the most serious among us do with our flocks."[80] Preachers need to be discipled in their preaching.

For, whatever the world may think, it has pleased God—then and now—to save those who believe by the foolishness of inspired preaching.

Endnotes

Chapter 1, Inspired Preaching in the New Testament: An Introductory Look

1. Sidney Greidanus, "Preaching from the Gospels," *Dictionary of Jesus and the Gospels,* eds. Joel B. Green, Scot McKnight and I. Howard Marshall (Downers Grove: InterVarsity Press, 1992), 625.

2. This Markan phraseology, portraying the beginning of Christ's public ministry, furnished the title for George Buttrick's famous 1931 Lyman Beecher Lectures at Yale, published as G. A. Buttrick, *Jesus Came Preaching: Christian Preaching in the New Age* (New York: Scribner, 1931).

3. Fred Craddock, "Preaching," *Anchor Bible Dictionary,* gen. ed. David Noel Freedman (New York: Doubleday, 1992), 5:452.

4. John B. Polhill, *Acts,* NAC (Nashville: Broadman, 1992), 43.

5. If Peter began preaching fairly soon after "the ninth hour" (i.e., 3:00 p.m.; Acts 3:1) and did not conclude until "it was already evening" (i.e., past 6:00 p.m.; Acts 4:3), his actual message was, to say the least, many, many times longer than the summary presented in 3:12–26, which can be read aloud, at a moderate pace, in just over three minutes.

6. So understands Richard N. Longenecker, "Acts," *Expositor's Bible Commentary,* gen. ed. Frank E. Gaebelein (Grand Rapids: Zondervan, 1981), 9:509. Given the comparative brevity of the average sermon in the early twenty-first century, Eutychus, were he alive today, probably would be congratulated (if not famed!) for amazing "staying power" (Acts 20:7–9).

7. Since the contexts of many of the sermons in the New Testament do not provide the kind of chronological and background information that Acts 3–4 and 20 do, it is obviously practically impossible to have absolute certainty about what is summarized and what is not.

8. Chronologically, e.g., John A. Broadus, *The Preparation and Delivery of Sermons,* 22nd ed. (New York: A. C. Armstrong and Son, 1896), 17–20; D. Martyn Lloyd-Jones, "The Primacy of Preaching," chapter 1 of *Preaching and Preachers* (Grand Rapids: Zondervan, 1971), 9–25; and John R. W. Stott, *Between Two Worlds: The Art of Preaching in the Twentieth Century* (Grand Rapids: Eerdmans, 1982), 15–18.

9. For a more in-depth treatment of the Great Commission by this writer, see, e.g., A. Boyd Luter, "Discipleship and the Church," *BSac* 137 (July-Sept., 1980), 267–73; Luter, "Great Commision," *ABD* II: 1090–91; Luter, "Women Disciples and the Great Commision," *TrinJ* 16NS (1995), 171–85, esp. 173; and Luter and Kathy McReynolds, *Disciplined Living: What the New Testament Teaches about Recovery and Discipleship* (Grand Rapids: Baker, 1996), 31.

10. Because of its form and emphatic position in front of the governing imperative, not a few scholars choose to render the Greek *poreuthentes* here as a virtual command: "Go." Others, however, prefer to translate the participle as "when you go" or "as you go."

11. That is, from Heb. 3:7 to 4:7.

12. See also the discussion of this section in Hebrews in chapter 12, "The New Testament's Use of the Old: Inspired Exegesis and Application for Preaching."

13. David reigned from about 1010 to about 970 B.C. If the conservative dating of the Exodus is accepted (i.e., about 1446 B.C.), with the events in Exod. 17:1–7 not long afterward, the difference would probably be at least 450 years.

14. Hebrews is indeed a remarkable written treatise. But it is also of the highest oral quality. As will be seen in chapter 2, there is no contradiction between those two observations.

15. As will be seen, focally, in the concluding chapter of this book, what is learned from the "inspired preaching" of the first century A.D. in the New Testament can make a decisive difference in "inspiring preaching" in the twenty-first century.

16. The obvious amanuensis in the New Testament is Tertius. Even though it is clear (and basically undisputed) that Paul is the author of Romans, we also encounter the wording "I, Tertius, who write this letter." (Rom. 16:22), referring to Tertius's secretarial duties for Paul.

17. See chapter 11, "John's Epistles and Revelation as Inspired Preaching," for a further discussion of these authorial dynamics and their possible implications for preaching.

18. Though the reader should always be a "Berean" (i.e., to search the Scriptures and validate whatever is asserted; Acts 17:11), a classic discussion of these terms is John R. W. Stott's *The Preacher's Portrait: Some New Testament Word Studies* (Grand Rapids: Eerdmans, 1961). Another helpful succinct discussion is found in Craddock, "Preaching," 452. This writer has briefly dealt with some of these terms in A. B. Luter Jr., "Homiletics," *Evangelical Dictionary of World Missions,* ed. A. Scott Moreau (Grand Rapids: Baker, 2000), 453–55.

19. There is nothing in Acts or any of the Pauline letters in which Timothy is mentioned that seem to indicate he had the gift of evangelism. If anything, the usage in 2 Tim. 4:5 has more applicational force for the bulk of those in preaching ministry, who, like Timothy, do not appear to have the gift of evangelism, but whom the Lord expects to be faithful to do that "work" (4:5) anyway, to his glory and the salvation of some of those who hear the Good News under their ministry of preaching the Word (4:2).

20. Excuse the play on words on the classic set of lectures by D. Martyn Lloyd-Jones, *Preaching & Preachers* (Grand Rapids: Zondervan, 1971).

21. For an excellent discussion of this structuring effect in Matthew, see D. A. Carson, "Matthew," *Expositor's Bible Commentary,* vol. 8, gen. ed. Frank E. Gaebelein (Grand Rapids: Zondervan, 1984).

22. Both the feeding of the 5,000 (Matt. 14:21) and the 4,000 (Matt. 15:38) passages record that beyond the numbered men there were "women and children." It is not unlikely that the presence of the wives and children could easily quadruple the recorded numbers.

23. Mary's words have become famous as the *Magnificat.*

24. See especially chapter 4, "As One Having Authority: The Inspired Preaching of Jesus in the Gospels."

25. There is no way to know the length of time between these two episodes. It seems clear, though, that Matthew is intent on reflecting Peter's inconsistency by placing them virtually back-to-back.

26. That is., when the hearing by the audience would be anything but hospitable and positively responsive.

27. It is this comparison that probably explains why there are no sermons by Barnabas recorded in Acts. Given the extraordinary effectiveness of his preaching ministry in Syrian Antioch (Acts 11:20–26), he undoubtedly was an excellent preacher.

28. For a recent in-depth discussion of Paul's Ephesian ministry by this writer, see A. Boyd Luter, "Deep and Wide: Education Overflowing as Evangelism from Ephesus," *Faith and Mission,* Fall 2001.

29. For further discussion, see chapter 13, "Inspired Preaching—Then and Now."

30. This was a common analogy used to emphasize the effectiveness of straightforward common-sense interpretation of the Bible. While there is definitely much truth in the assertion, it does not adequately grasp the complex literary phenomena of Scripture and the vast differences between contemporary culture and biblical times.

31. Figures of speech, parables, and poetry (perhaps hymns) chief among them.

32. A helpful chapter-length treatment on the major genres in the New Testament is Craig L. Blomberg, "The Diversity of Literary Genres in the New Testament," *Interpreting the New Testament: Essays on Methods and Issues*, eds. David Alan Black and David Dockery (Nashville: Broadman & Holman, 2001), 272–95.

33. Two wise and readable treatments of the characteristics and interpretation of the various major genres of Scripture are Gordon Fee and Douglas Stuart, *How to Read the Bible for All Its Worth*, 2d ed. (Grand Rapids: Zondervan, 1982); and Robert Stein, *A Basic Guide to Interpreting the Bible: Playing by the Rules* (Grand Rapids: Baker, 1994). For help in preaching genre-sensitive sermons, see, e.g., Grant Lovejoy, "Shaping Sermons by the Literary Form of the Text," *Biblical Hermeneutics: A Comprehensive Introduction to Interpreting Scripture*, eds. Bruce Corley, Steve Lemke, and Grant Lovejoy (Nashville: Broadman & Holman, 1996), 318–39; and Mike Graves, *The Sermon as Symphony: Preaching the Literary Forms of the New Testament* (Valley Forge: Judson Press, 1997).

34. For helpful specialized, but succinct, discussions, see Robert H. Stein, "Interpreting the Synoptic Gospels"; Gary M. Burge, "Interpreting the Gospel of John"; and John B. Polhill, "Interpreting the Book of Acts," all in *Interpreting the New Testament*.

35. See Thomas R. Schreiner, "Interpreting the Pauline Epistles"; and J. Daryl Charles, "Interpreting the General Epistles," *Interpreting the New Testament*.

36. John D. Harvey, *Listening to the Text: Oral Patterning in Paul's Letters*, ETS Studies 1 (Grand Rapids: Baker, 1998), xv.

37. See my chapter on "Interpreting the Book of Revelation," *Interpreting the New Testament*. For a specific discussion of apocalyptic, see my "Apocalyptic Literature," *Holman Concise Bible Commentary*, ed. David S. Dockery (Nashville: Holman, 1998), 659–60.

38. Harvey, *Listening to the Text*, xv.

Chapter 2, The New Testament as Inspired Preaching: Appreciating the Orality Factor

1. F. F. Bruce, *Paul: Apostle of the Heart Set Free* (Grand Rapids: Eerdmans, 1977), 16.

2. Casey W. Davis, *Oral Biblical Criticism: The Influence of the Principles of Orality on the Literary Structure of Paul's Epistle to the Philippians*, JSNT Sup 172 (Sheffield: Sheffield Academic Press, 1999), 13.

3. Given the relevant wording in 2 Timothy, and the history of its interpretation throughout the bulk of church history, the only approach that would *not* view 2 Timothy as Paul's final letter is pseudonymity: the view that Paul did not write some, or all, of the so-called "Pastoral Epistles." For a helpful recent conservative discussion, see Terry L. Wilder, "Pseudonymity and the New Testament," *Interpreting the New Testament: Essays on Methods and Issues*, eds. David A. Black and David S. Dockery (Nashville: Broadman & Holman, 2001), 296–335.

4. Jeffrey A. D. Weima, "Literary Criticism," *Interpreting the New Testament*, 151–52, summarizes the main contours of the widely used model of Roman Jakobson.

5. C. W. Davis, *Oral Biblical Criticism*, 13.

6. See, e.g., Richard N. Longenecker, "Ancient Amanuenses and the Pauline Epistles," R. N. Longenecker and Merrill C. Tenney, eds., *New Dimensions in New Testament Study* (Grand Rapids: Zondervan, 1974), 281–97. For a succinct, more recent treatment, see Harry Y. Gamble, "Amanuensis," *Anchor Bible Dictionary*, gen. ed. David Noel Freedman (New York: Doubleday, 1992), 1:172–73.

7. E. Randolph Richards, *The Secretary in the Letters of Paul*, WUNT 2 (Tubingen: J.C.B. Mohr [Paul Siebeck]), 1991.

8. For concise recent discussions of the dating of Galatians by the present writer, see A. Boyd Luter, "Galatians," *Nelson Study Bible*, gen. ed. Earl D. Radmacher (Nashville: Thomas Nelson, 1997), 1966; and A. Boyd Luter, "Galatians," *Holman Concise Bible Commentary*, ed. David S. Dockery (Nashville: Broadman & Holman, 1998), 566.

9. Though a legitimate distinction can be made between the more formal "epistle" and the less formal "letter," the terms will be used in their common interchangeable sense in this study.

10. The most common evangelical dating of 2 Thessalonians is about A.D. 50–51.

11. A thought-provoking recent study related to the function of letter carrier in the New Testament is E. Randolph Richards, "Silvanus was not Peter's Secretary: Theological Bias in Interpreting *dia Silouanou . . . egrapsa* in 1 Peter 5:12," *JETS* 43/3 (September 2000), 417–32.

12. For Paul's recent, and quite brief (apparently less than a month in duration) stay in Thessalonica, in which he founded the church, see Acts 17:1–10a.

13. Conservative dating of 1 Corinthians is generally about A.D. 55–57.

14. Evangelicals usually tend to group Colossians among the so-called "prison letters," and date it between the late 50s and early 60s of the first century A.D.

15. The letter to Philemon is closely related to Colossians and was probably delivered at the same time (see above).

16. Bruce, *Paul*, 16.

17. It is in the great care (similar to that of the legendary Jewish scribes) given to the accuracy of the transcribed text that evangelicals can "rest easy" in regard to the inerrancy of the original "autographs."

18. See Rev. 1:3 for the dynamics of this role, as will be explained briefly below: "He who reads" (note the *singular*) read the entire book aloud to "those who hear" (note the plural).

19. Michael W. Holmes, "Textual Criticism," *Interpreting the New Testament*, 47.

20. It makes sense, given that Paul apparently wrote Romans from Corinth, with Cenchrea being the nearby seaport for Corinth.

21. Although they certainly did not invent this terminology, I credit Paul Achtemeier (*"Omne Verbum Sonat: The New Testament and the Oral Environment of Late Western Antiquity,"* JBL 109/1 [1990], 3–27), and John Harvey (*Listening to the Text: Oral Patterning in Paul's Letters*, ETS Studies 1 [Grand Rapids: Baker, 1998]) with branding it (and its significance) on my consciousness.

22. E.g., A. Boyd Luter Jr., "Philippians," *Evangelical Commentary on the Bible*, ed. Walter A. Elwell (Grand Rapids: Baker, 1989); Luter and Michelle V. Lee, "Philippians as Chiasmus: Key to the Structure, Unity and Theme Questions," *New Testament Studies* (1995), 89–101; Luter, "The Role of Women in the Church at Philippi," *JETS* (1996).

23. See my 1989 argumentation, with which I am still comfortable in the main, in Luter, "Philippians," *ECB*, 1,035–36.

24. There is a discussion ongoing of letters as so-called (substitute) "apostolic *parousia*" (i.e., presence), the, so to speak, "next best thing to being there."

25. A view that I first recall seeing among the writings of F. F. Bruce (e.g., "St. Paul in Macedonia 3. The Philippian Correspondence," *Bulletin of the John Rylands Library*, 63 [1980–81], 260–84).

26. Which I do hold to be a unified document. See my 1995 *New Testament Studies* article (which deals fairly directly with that subject), with Michelle Lee.

27. I have teased out my general reconstruction of the problems at Philippi in the *New Testament Studies* and *JETS* articles (see above), as well as in "Women in Philippi: Partners in the Gospel," chapter 10 in Boyd Luter and Kathy McReynolds, *Women as Christ's Disciples* (Grand Rapids: Baker, 1997), 142–55.

28. Harvey, *Listening to the Text*, 302–303. Brackets added.

Chapter 3, The Gospel and the Gospels: The Inspired Preaching of the Evangelists

1. Laurence Cantwell, "Immortal Longings in *Sermone Humili:* A Study of John 4.5–26," *Scottish Theological Journal,* 3 (1950), 74.

2. Several noncanonical "gospels" are known, though usually only in fragments or citations. Most are entirely alien to the canonical Gospels in spirit, form, and substance. See H. Koester, *Ancient Christian Gospels: Their History and Development* (Philadelphia: Trinity Press International, 1990).

3. Donald Guthrie, *New Testament Introduction* 3d ed. (Downers Grove: InterVarsity Press, 1970), 14.

4. John 21:25; also John 20:30–31.

5. Justin Martyr, *The First Apology,* 66.

6. Morton Smith, "Prolegomena to a Discussion of Aretalogies, Divine Men, the Gospels and Jesus," *Journal of Biblical Literature,* 90 (1971): 174–99.

7. For a helpful survey, cf. Larry W. Hurtato, "Gospel (Genre)," *Dictionary of Jesus and the Gospels,* eds. Joel B. Green, Scot McKnight, and I. Howard Marshall (Downers Grove: InterVarsity Press, 1992), 276–82.

8. Werner A. Kümmel, *Introduction to the New Testament,* rev. ed., trans. Howard Clark Kee (Nashville: Abingdon, 1975), 37.

9. Cantwell, "Longings," 73.

10. William Sanday (ed., *Studies in the Synoptic Problem by Members of the University of Oxford* [Oxford: Clarendon, 1911]) and his student B. H. Streeter (*The Four Gospels: A Study of Origins* [London: Macmillan, 1924]) popularized the source hypothesis, but the theory goes back almost 300 years.

11. Cf. Robert L. Stein, "Interpreting the Synoptic Gospels," David Alan Black; and David S. Dockery, eds., *Interpreting the New Testament: Essays on Issues and Methods* (Nashville: Broadman & Holman, 2001), 338–42. Cf. Marcus Dods, *Introduction to the New Testament* (London: Hodder and Stoughton, 1907), 11–13.

12. B. F. Westcott, *Introduction to the Study of the Gospels,* 3d ed. (London: Macmillan and Co., 1867), 152.

13. Cf. Luke 24:45–47; Acts 1:8; 6:4.

14. Ibid., 15–17 (emphasis added).

15. Eusebius, *The History of the Church,* trans. G. A. Williamson (London: Penguin, 1965), 3.24.

16. See Rudolf Bultmann, *The History of the Synoptic Tradition,* 3d ed., trans. J. Marsh (New York: Harper, 1963 [orig. pub. 1958]).

17. Martin Dibelius, *From Tradition to Gospel* 2d ed., trans. B. L. Woolf (London: James Clark and Co., 1971 [orig. pub. 1933]), 102. For a balanced treatment of evidences for and against a "basic oral Gospel," cf. Guthrie, *New Testament,* 124–29.

18. C. H. Dodd, *The Apostolic Preaching and Its Development* (New York: Harper & Row, 1964), 55.

19. Cantwell, "Longings," 74.

20. William L. Shirer, *Gandhi: A Memoir* (New York: Simon & Schuster, 1979).

21. James Denney, *Studies in Theology* (London: Hodder and Stoughton, 1906), 154.

22. Ralph P. Martin, *Mark: Evangelist and Theologian* (Grand Rapids: Zondervan, 1972), 21.

23. Laurence Cantwell, "Longings," 74.

24. Birger Gerhardsson, *Memory and Manuscript: Oral Tradition and Written Transmission in Rabbinic Judaism and Early Christianity,* trans. Eric J. Sharpe (Grand Rapids: Eerdmans, combined ed., 1998 [orig. pub. 1961]), 197.

25. Ibid., 193.

26. Ibid., 196.

27. George R. Beasley-Murray, *Preaching the Gospel from the Gospels* (Peabody, Mass.: Hendrickson, 1996), 12 (emphasis added).

28. Martin Kähler, *The So-Called Historical Jesus and the Historical, Biblical Christ*, trans. Carl E. Braaten (Philadelphia: Fortress, reprint 1964 [orig. pub. 1897]), 80, n. 11.

29. Westcott, *Gospels*, 197.

30. The Fathers differed, however, on which "face" represented which "Gospel." Cf. note 13 by M. B. Riddle in Augustine, *The Harmony of the Gospels*, 1:6, NPNF 6:80.

31. Irenaeus (*Against Heresies*, 3:11:8) argued that there could be neither more nor fewer than four Gospels "since there are four zones of the world in which men live, and four principal winds, while the Church is scattered through the world." Also Augustine, *De consensus evangelistarum* 1.

32. Cf. Paul W. Barnett, *Jesus and the Rise of Early Christianity: A History of New Testament Times* (Downers Grove: InterVarsity Press, 1999), 388–94; also David A. Black, *Why Four Gospels? The Historical Origins of the Gospels* (Grand Rapids: Kregel, 2001), 60–62.

33. Westcott, *Gospels*, 199.

34. E.g., Luke's use of medical terms. Cf. Adolf von Harnack, *New Testament Studies I: Luke the Physician: The Author of the Third Gospel and the Acts of the Apostles* (London, Williams and Norgate, 1908).

35. Matthew (Levi) appears in all four lists of the Twelve (Eleven in Acts): Matt. 10:2–4; Mark 3:16–19; Luke 6:14–16; Acts 1:13.

36. Papias clearly has the Gospel of Matthew in mind, despite T. W. Manson's ("The Gospel According to St. Matthew," *Studies in the Gospels and Epistles*, ed. M. Black [Philadelphia: Westminster, 1962], 68–104) anachronistic attempt to make *ta logia* the hypothetical "sayings source" (Q). See J. A. Kloppenborg, *The Formation of Theology: Trajectories in Ancient Wisdom Collections* (Philadelphia: Fortress, 1987); also Kümmel, *Introduction*, 43–44.

37. Because Matthew is apparently *not* a Greek translation of Aramaic, many scholars distrust this testimony. Robert Gundry has argued (*Matthew: A Commentary on His Literary and Theological Art* [Grand Rapids: Eerdmans, 1982], 619–20) that Papias was referring to a Hebrew *style*, not Hebrew language. It is also possible that Matthew (or someone else) prepared a Greek edition of the Aramaic Matthew.

38. Eusebius, *History*, 3.39.15–16.

39. *Against Heresies*, 3.1.1; also Eusebius, *History*, 5.8.

40. Eusebius, *History*, 6.25.

41. *Catechetical Lectures*, 14:115.

42. *Lives of Illustrious Men*, 3. Jerome claims to have seen the autograph. Cf. J. N. D. Kelley, *Jerome: His Life, Writings, and Controversies* (Peabody, MA: Hendrickson, 1975), 65.

43. Cited in Eusebius, *History*, 3.24; cf. also Irenaeus, *Against the Heresies*, 3.1.1.

44. Matt. 9:9; Mark 2:14; Luke 5:27–28.

45. Luke 5:29.

46. Matt. 9:12; cf. Mark 2:17; Luke 5:31.

47. Matt. 9:13b; cf. Mark 2:17b; Luke 5:32. Luke adds "to repentance."

48. Matt. 9:13a; Hos. 6:6.

49. Matt. 6:16.

50. Matt. 23:24.

51. Matt. 23:29.

52. Craig L. Blomberg, *Matthew* New American Commentary (Nashville: Broadman, 1992), 157.

53. Hos. 6:6; cf. also Matt. 12:7. See David Hill, "On the Use and Meaning of Hosea 6:6 in Matthew's Gospel," *New Testament Studies* 24 (1977–78), 107–19.

54. Blomberg, *Matthew*, 73.

55. Matt. 6:33; 12:28; 19:24; 21:31; 21:43.

56. Cf. *Shebuoth*, 35b.

57. "Heaven" occurs at least 70 times in Matthew, as compared with Mark (17), Luke (3), and John (18).

58. Matt. 3:2.

59. This phrase alone occurs no less than fourteen times in Matthew.

60. Alfred Edersheim, *The Life and Times of Jesus the Messiah* 3d ed. (Grand Rapids: Eerdmans, reprint 1971 [orig. pub. 1883, 1886]), 1:265.

61. Ibid., 1:266.

62. Eusebius, *History*, 3.39.

63. E.g. Irenaeus, *Against Hereses* 3.1; Clement of Alexandria, *Adumbrationes in epistolas canonicas* (1 Pet. 5:13).

64. Jerome, *Lives*, 8, NPNF 23:364.

65. Some of even the most skeptical critics are reluctant to challenge Markan authorship. But see Willi Marxsen, *Introduction to the New Testament*, trans. G. Busnell (Philadelphia: Fortress, 1968), 142–43.

66. "The Outlines" a commentary.

67. Cited by Eusebius, *History*, 2.15.

68. Ibid., 6.14.

69. Ibid., 5.8.

70. Eusebius, *Proof of the Gospel: Being the* Demonstratio Evangelica *of Eusebius of Caesarea*, trans. W. J. Ferrar (Grand Rapids: Baker, reprint 1981 [orig. pub. 1920]), 3.5.

71. Cf. BAGD; also H. G. Liddell and R. Scott, *A Greek-English Lexicon*, rev. H. S. Jones (Oxford: Clarendon, 1996), 690.

72. Guthrie, *New Testament*, 53. Because we regard Mark as essentially the recorder of Peter's preaching rather than the preacher whose voice we hear, we have little to say about Mark per se. With the consistent witness of the early church, we hold that the second Evangelist was none other than "John who was also called Mark" (Acts 12:12, 25), the son of Mary (Acts 12:12) and cousin of Barnabas (Col. 4:10). Mary's home in Jerusalem was a gathering place for early believers, and the place Peter sought out upon his miraculous release from prison (Acts 12:11–17). John Mark began with Paul and Barnabas (Acts 13:5) as their "helper" (hupēreten)—the exact meaning of which is unclear, though it certainly implies a subordinate ministry, as an aide to the other two (cf. A. T. Robertson, *Making Good in the Ministry: A Sketch of John Mark* (Grand Rapids: Baker, reprint 1976, [orig. pub. 1918], 45–52). Westcott (*Gospels*, 215–17) thinks that Mark was ideally suited to "interpret" Peter not only because he possessed the requisite literary skills Peter lacked, but because his temperament resonated with Peter's—evidence his departure from the first mission journey (Acts 13:13). The close relationship between Peter and Mark is suggested not only by the reference to his home in Acts 12, but by Peter's reference to Mark as "my son" (1 Pet. 5:13).

73. C. H. Dodd, *Apostolic Preaching*, 49.

74. G. F. Maclear, *The Gospel According to St. Mark*, The Cambridge Bible (Cambridge: University Press, 1897), 17–20.

75. Among many examples—Jesus "looked around" or "looked upon" (3:5, 34; 5:32, 10:23, 11:11); he took the children in his arms (9:36); he sat down and called the Twelve (9:35); he sighed (7:34; 8:12). Mark often cites Aramaic words (even though the Gospel was apparently intended for Gentiles), such as *Boanerges* (3:17), *Talitha kum* (5:41), *Corban* (7:11), *Ephphatha* (7:34), and *Abba* (14:36).

76. Again, there are too many examples to cite here. As to *person*, Simon who carried the cross, is "of Cyrene (the father of Alexander and Rufus)" (15:21). As to *number*, only Mark records that Jesus sent the 70 out "in pairs" (Gk. *duo, duo*; 6:7). As to *time*, Mark alone tells us that Jesus was crucified at "the third hour" (15:25). As to *place*, we learn from Mark that the angel sat "at the right" of the tomb (16:5).

77. The NASB marks these instances with an asterisk. A striking example is 15:24, where Mark has *kai staurousin auton* (literally, "and they are crucifying Him [Jesus]").

78. Maclear, *St. Mark*, 20.

79. William L. Lane, *Commentary on the Gospel of Mark*, NICNT (Grand Rapids: Eerdmans, 1974), 26–27.

80. For example, Mark 1:27; 2:7; 2:15–20; 3:22–30; 4:41; 6:51–52; 7:1–5; and others.

81. Lane, *Mark*, 288.

82. Ibid., 601. Mark 16:9–20 is attested by several early texts (as is another "Short Ending"), but not in the best early witnesses.

83. Branscomb, *The Gospel of Mark,* Moffat New Testament Commentaries (London: Hodder and Stoughton, 1937), 310.

84. Larry W. Hurtado, *Mark,* New International Biblical Commentary (Peabody MA: Hendrickson, 1982), 284.

85. Guthrie, *New Testament,* 78.

86. Lane, *Mark,* 592.

87. Mark 16:8.

88. Robert Guelich ("Mark, Gospel of," *Dictionary of Jesus and the Gospels,* 523–24), observes that Mark's Gospel emphasizes the "future" of the Jesus story at several critical points, such as the transfiguration (which the disciples are commanded not to reveal until after the resurrection [9:2–9]).

89. Flavius Josephus, *Antiquity of the Jews: Flavius Josephus against Apion* 1.1.

90. Cf. Luke 1:1. Westcott, *Gospels,* 175.

91. F. N. Farrar, *The Gospel According to Luke,* Cambridge Greek Testament (Cambridge: University Press, 1895), 83.

92. Luke 1:2a.

93. So the AV: "These things which are most surely believed among us." Also Weymouth: "received with full assurance among us." Cf. Rom. 4:21.

94. The "strict meaning" of the term is "to go along with . . . or to accompany" (cf. Mark 16:17: "signs will accompany [*parēkolouthēsei*] those who have believed"). The word occurs four times in the New Testament, never with the meaning, "to investigate," unless here. Cf. 1 Tim. 4:6: "the sound doctrine which you have been following" (*parēkolouthēkas*); also 2 Tim. 3:10: "But you followed (*parēkolouthēsas*) my teaching." Kittel (*TDNT,* s.v. ἀκολουθέω, 1:215–16) cites Josephus (*Against Apion,* I.53, 218) in support of the translation "investigate." But in neither instance does Josephus use the term in this sense. In I.53, he contrasts *personal knowledge* with knowledge gained from others. In 1.218, he bemoans the inability of some writers to "*understand* our writings."

95. Westcott, *Gospels,* 189.

96. See Frederic Godet, *Commentary on the Gospel of John* 3d ed., trans. and ed. Timothy Dwight (New York: Funk and Wagnalls, 1886), 4.

97. Acts 1:1.

98. S.v. λέγω, "B. The Logos in the Greek and Hellenistic World," by H. Kleinknecht, *TDNT* 4:78–79.

99. Cf. NIV, "my former book." See John B. Polhill, *Acts,* NAC (Nashville: Broadman, 1992), 78–79.

100. 1 Thess. 2:13. Cf. also 1 Thess. 1:6, 8; 1 Cor. 2:4 ("my message" = *logos mou*); 1 Pet. 3:1.

101. Darrell L. Bock, "Luke, Gospel of," *Dictionary of Jesus and the Gospels,* 498.

102. In *Against the Heresies,* Irenaeus writes that "Luke was inseparable from Paul, and his fellow-laborer in the Gospel" (3:14.1), and states flatly that "Luke . . . the companion of Paul, recorded in a book the Gospel preached by him" (3.1.1). In his treatise *Against Marcion,* Tertullian calls Luke "an apostolic man; not a master, but a disciple, and so inferior to a master—at least as far subsequent to him as the apostle he followed (and that, no doubt, was Paul) was subsequent to the others" (4.2). Later he avows that Luke's Gospel has "stood its ground from its very first publication" and that most attribute even its "form" to Paul (4.5).

103. Eusebius, *History,* 3.4.

104. Cited by Eusebius, *History,* 6.14.

105. Leon Morris, *The Gospel According to John,* NICNT (Grand Rapids: Eerdmans, 1971), 25.

106. A. T. Robertson, *Epochs in the Life of the Apostle John* (Grand Rapids: Baker, reprint 1978 [n.d.]), 167.

107. Frederic Godet, *Commentary on the Gospel of John*, 3d ed., trans. Timothy Dwight, 2 vols. (New York: Funk and Wagnalls, 1886), 1:94.

108. According to the unanimous testimony of the early church; notably *Irenaeus Against Hereies*, 2.22.5, 3.1.1, 3.3.4. Irenaeus based his own testimony on that of Polycarp, whom he knew, and who in turn knew the apostle John personally. Cf. also Eusebius, *History*, 3.20.23–25, 31, 39.

109. F. F. Bruce, The *Gospel of John* (Grand Rapids: Eerdmans, 1983), 13.

110. Most likely following the destruction of the city in A.D. 70.

111. Godet, *John*, I:216.

112. Cf. Acts 19.

113. Acts 20:29.

114. John 20:31.

115. Cf. also John 21:25.

116. Barnabas Lindars, *The Gospel of John*, New Century Bible (Grand Rapids: Eerdmans, 1972), 46.

117. Eusebius, *History* 3.24. According to the Muratorian Canon (Henry Bettenson, *Documents of the Christian Church*, 2d ed. [London: Oxford, 1963] 28), and Jerome (*Commentary on Matthew*, iv.; *Lives of Illustrious Men*, 9), John agreed to write only after others strongly urged him.

118. B. F. Westcott, *The Gospel According to St. John*, 2 vols. (Grand Rapids: Baker, reprint 1980 [orig. pub. 1908]), lxxxiii–lxxxiv.

119. The Synoptics, by contrast, focus much more attention on Galilee.

120. Friedrich Schleiemacher, *On Religion: Speeches to Its Cultured Despisers*, trans. John Oman, intro. Rudolf Otto (New York: Harper and Row, 1958 [orig. pub. 1799]).

121. John's exhortation "do not marvel" (3:7, Gk. *mē thaumasēs*) implies that Nicodemus was wrestling with "philosophical" doubts. The word group from *thaumazō* has a long history in Greek philosophy where (as in Aristotle, *Metaphysics*, I.2) "wonder" is virtually the beginning of knowledge. In John's Gospel, the word almost always connotes intellectual doubts. Cf. 4:27, 33; 5:20, 28; 7:21; also 1 John 5:13. See TDNT, s.v. θαῦμα, by Georg Bertram, 3:28, 29, 40.

122. John highlights the ambivalence of Nicodemus thematically through the Gospel. See below, chap. 4, pp. 000.

123. John 3:14b–15.

124. For several indications of a change of speaker at 3:16, see Morris, *John*, 228; Westcott, *John*, 119. Cf. RSV.

125. George R. Beasley-Murray, *John*, WBC (Waco: Word, 1987), 46, 51.

Chapter 4, "As One Having Authority": The Inspired Preaching Of Jesus

1. Eusebius, *History*, 3.24.

2. John 20:30; 21:25.

3. John 14:26; cf. 16:13.

4. John 2:19–21.

5. John 2:22b.

6. Frederic Godet, *Commentary on the Gospel of John*, 3d ed., trans. Timothy Dwight (New York: Funk and Wagnalls, 1886), 2:287.

7. George E. Ladd, *A Theology of the New Testament* (Grand Rapids: Eerdmans, 1974), 57.

8. Mark 1:14b–15; also Matt. 4:17; 10:7.

9. More than one hundred with parallels.

10. Neh. 8:1–8. The word *targum* is Aramaic for "translation."

11. Bruce D. Chilton, "*Regnum Dei Deus Est*," *Scottish Journal of Theology* 31 (1978): 267.

12. Ibid., 270.

13. Cf. John 1:20, 41; 4:29; 7:26–31; 12:34; Matt. 21:9; 22:42; Luke 3:15, among many other passages.

14. Ulrich Wilckens, "Jesus' Preaching of the Kingdom of God," C. Marcheselli, ed., *Parola e Spirito* (Brescia: Paideia Editrice, 1982), 1:606.

15. Matt. 5:20.

16. Mark 2:17.

17. Matt. 5:3.

18. Wilckens, "Kingdom," 606.

19. Matt. 11:3–6.

20. Justin, *The First Apology*, 14.5.

21. Cf. A. Duane Litfin, *St. Paul's Theology of Proclamation*, SNTS Monograph Series 79 (Cambridge: Cambridge University Press, 1994), 244–53.

22. Josephus, *Antiquities of the Jews*, 18.3.3.

23. See L. H. Feldman, "A Selective Critical Bibliography of Josephus," L. H. Feldman and G. Hata. *Josephus, the Bible and History* (Leiden: Brill, 1989), 430–34; also Geza Vermes, "The Jesus Notice of Josephus Re-examined," *Journal of Jewish Studies* 38 (1987), 2–10.

24. Rainer Riesner, "Jesus as Teacher and Preacher," Henry Wansbrough, ed., *Jesus and the Oral Gospel Tradition*, JSNT Supplement Series 64 (Sheffield: Sheffield Academic Press, 1991), 185.

25. Matt. 7:28b–29.

26. According to John 1:38, "Rabbi" is a synonym for "Teacher." Cf. also Matt. 23.8.

27. John 1:38, 49; 3:2, 26; 4:31; 6:25.

28. John 20:16.

29. Zeno (335–263 B.C.) founded the Stoics, some of whom, with the Epicureans, heard Paul preach on Mars' Hill. Cf. Acts 17:18.

30. 1 Kings 4:30.

31. Clement of Alexandria. *The Stromata*, I.viii. Clement distinguished three principal categories of "sophistical arts:" (1) Rhetoric, the goal of which is *persuasion;* (2) disputation, the goal of which is *victory;* and (3) sophistry, the goal of which is *admiration!*

32. Riesner, "Jesus as Preacher and Teacher," 191.

33. Josephus, *Against Apion*, 2.17.

34. In Nazareth, for example, Luke tells us, "as was His custom, He entered the synagogue on the Sabbath." Cf. Luke 4:15–16.

35. Cf. Acts 13:5, 14; 14:1; 17:1, 10, 17; 18:4, 19, and others.

36. See on this subject, John Reumann, ed., *Understanding the Sacred Text: Essays in Honor of Morton S. Enslin on the Hebrew Bible and Christian Beginnings* (Valley Forge, Pa.: Judson, 1972).

37. Alfred Edersheim, *The Life and Times of Jesus the Messiah*, 3d ed., 2 vols. (Grand Rapids: Eerdman's reprint 1971; orig. pub. 1883, 1886), 1:446. Cf. also Birger Gerhardsson, *The Origin of the Gospel Traditions* (Philadephia: Fortress, 1979).

38. Cf. Matt. 7:28–29; 13:54 (= Mark 6:2); 22:33; Mark 1:22; 11:18; Luke 4:32; et al.

39. John 7:15. The reference is doubtless to Jesus' lack of formal rabbinical training.

40. John 3:2.

41. The Greek word *nuktos* (3:2), translated "by night," literally means "of night" and indicates the *manner* of Nicodemus's coming, that is, "in a night kind of way."

42. John 7:47b–49.

43. Such as fear that Jesus might incite Rome against them (cf. John 11:50), or that Jewish leaders resented Jesus for his moral castigations, or that Jesus offended Jewish sensibilities by associating with "sinners," or that he seemed to play fast and loose with the law, or others.

44. C. F. D. Moule, "The Gravamen against Jesus,," E. P. Sanders, ed., *Jesus, the Gospels, and the Church: Essays in Honor of William R. Farmer* (Macon: Mercer University Press, 1987), 177.

45. Ibid., 191.

46. As when he characterizes the Mosaic legislation on divorce (Deut. 24:1–4) as an accommodation to sin, not as the intent of holy God (Matt. 19:1–9=Mark 10:1–12).

47. Matt. 12:42 (= Luke 11:31).

48. John 8:56–59.

49. John 8:14b, 18.

50. John 5:18.

51. Moule, "Gravamen," 192.

52. Martin Hengel, *The Charismatic Leader and His Followers,* trans. James C. G. Greig, ed. John Richer (Edinburgh: T. and T. Clark, 1981), 69.

53. 2 Tim. 4:2.

54. A. Büchler ("Learning and Teaching in the Open Air in Palestine," *Jewish Quarterly Review* 4 [1913–14], 485–91) observes that rabbis often taught out-of-doors, but usually with small groups of disciples under the shade of trees.

55. For example, 1:20–33; 8:1–11; 9:1–7.

56. Riesner, "Jesus as Preacher," 192.

57. Luke 13:22–17:10. Cf. Robert H. Stein, *Luke,* NAC (Nashville: Broadman Press, 1992), 378.

58. Pheme Perkins, *Jesus as Teacher* (Cambridge: Cambridge University Press, 1990), 30.

59. Robert Guelich, *The Sermon on the Mount: A Foundation for Understanding* (Dallas: Word, 1982), 33 (emphasis added).

60. Ibid., 35 (emphasis added).

61. On which, in addition to Guelich, see esp. W. D. Davies, *The Setting of the Sermon on the Mount* (Cambridge: Cambridge University Press, 1964). Cf. also Martin Dibelius, *The Sermon on the Mount* (New York: Scribner's, 1940); and J. D. Kingsbury, *Matthew: Structure, Christology, Kingdom* (Philadelphia: Fortress, 1975).

62. Augustine, *The Sermon on the Mount,* 1.1, NPNF 6:3.

63. For a helpful survey, cf. W. S. Kissinger, *The Sermon on the Mount: A History of Interpretation and Bibliography* (Metuchen, N.J.: Scarecrow Press, 1975). A briefer survey is Guelich, *Sermon,* 13–22.

64. A. M. Hunter, *A Pattern for Life: An Exposition of the Sermon on the Mount,* rev. ed. (Philadelphia: Westminster, 1953, 1965), 11. Yet, one "may . . . feel considerable confidence that the sayings . . . collected . . . are substantially authentic" (p. 13).

65. Edersheim, *Life and Times,* 1:525.

66. *History,* 3.39.

67. David Wenham, *The Rediscovery of Jesus' Eschatological Discourse,* Gospel Perspectives 4 (Sheffield: JSOT Press, 1984), 368. Cf. J. A. T. Robinson, *Redating the New Testament* (London: SCM, 1976), 97–106.

68. George A. Kennedy, *New Testament Interpretation through Rhetorical Criticism* (Chapel Hill: University of North Caroline Press, 1984), 144. Cf. B. F. Westcott (*Introduction to the Study of the Gospels* 3d ed. [London: Macmillan, 1867], 331) on the differences and similarities of Matthew's version and Luke's (the so-called Sermon on the Plain [Luke 6:20–49]): "That which was for St. Luke . . . one discourse among many was for St. Matthew the introduction and key to all."

69. Apart from a scholarly prejudice against the original *orality* of the Gospels, the only substantive objection to the authenticity of Matthew's account is the difficulty of *remembering* so much of the sermon so specifically. Kennedy (*New Testament Interpretation,* 68), counters that Jesus may well have preached all or part of the sermon on several occasions. "Given their devotion to Jesus and the striking nature of what he said, "the disciples would have had little difficulty later on "dictating a version . . . for readers who had not personally heard Jesus."

70. Kennedy, *New Testament Interpretation,* 45ff.

71. On the three species of rhetoric, cf. Aristotle, *On Rhetoric,* 1. 7a.

72. Matthew 7:24–27.

73. Matthews does not provide a strictly *chronological* setting for the sermon (cf. Craig L. Blomberg, *Matthew,* NAC [Nashville: Broadman, 1992], 96). Matthew's setting rather

emphasizes two facts about the rhetorical significance of the sermon as a whole. First, Matthew prefaces the sermon with a brief account of Jesus' spreading fame because of his synagogue teaching and miracles (4:23–25). Jesus had created a stir over "the kingdom"; and the "crowds" who gathered on the mount would have come with various preconceptions and expectations about the kingdom. Second, the sermon is both preceded and followed by miracles (4:23–25; 8:1–4), which has the effect of juxtaposing the Lord's *words* and *work*. The works both *call for* the sermon (as an explanation) and *confirm* the sermon.

74. For example, 5:22, 25–26, 29–30.

75. This division is evident from the repetition of *dikaiosunē* in Matt. 6:1, but now put in the context of "acts of righteousness," specifically "alms" (6:2–3), "prayer" (6:5–15), and "fasting" (6:16–18), followed by righteousness in life goals (6:19–34; esp. 6:33), and by righteousness in ordinary life (7:1–20).

76. In rhetoric, this device is called an *enthymeme*. Cf. Aristotle, *On Rhetoric*, 1.–9.

77. Kennedy, *New Testament Interpretation*, 62.

78. Ibid., 63.

79. Adolf Jülicher, *Die Gleichnisreden Jesu*, 2 vols. (Darmstadt: Wissenschaftliche Buchgesellschaft, reprint 1963 [orig. pub. 1899]), 1:168 ff.

80. Craig L. Blomberg, *Interpreting the Parables* (Downers Grove: InterVarsity, 1990), 19–21. According to Blomberg (p. 21), "A majority of the parables make exactly three points."

81. C. H. Dodd, *The Parables of the Kingdom* (New York: Scribner's, 1936), 165.

82. T. F. Torrance, "A Study in New Testament Communication," *Scottish Journal of Theology* 3 (1950), 302.

83. Blomberg, *Matthew*, 211.

84. The sower (13:36–39); the tares (vv. 24–30); the mustard seed (vv. 31–32); leaven (v. 33); the hidden treasure (v. 44); the pearl (vv. 45–46); and the dragnet (vv. 47–50).

85. Cf. Birger Gerhardsson, "The Seven Parables in Matthew XIII," *New Testament Studies* 19 (1972), 16–37. Gerhardsson calls this section "the tract of the seven parables" (p. 16).

86. David Wenham, "The Structure of Matthew XIII," *New Testament Studies* 25 (1979), 516–22.

87. Matt. 13:11–17. The passage in Mark (4:11–12) is straightforward—"those who are outside get everything in parables, in order that [Gk. *hina*] while seeing, they may see and not perceive."

88. D. A. Carson, "The Hōmoios Word-Group as Introduction to Some Matthean Parables," *New Testament Studies* 31 (1985), 277. In the parabolic sermon before us, the formula appears seven times (13:24, 31, 33, 44, 45, 47, 52).

89. The best case teaching always uses actual (as opposed to hypothetical) situations.

90. Carson, *Hōmoios*, 279.

91. We may trace this idea to Calvin. Cf. also Mark 4:33.

92. Torrance, "New Testament Communication," 303–305.

93. Philip L. Culbertson, *A Word Fitly Spoken: Context, Transmission, and Adoption of the Parables of Jesus* (Albany: SUNY, 1995), 111–12.

94. Ibid., 18.

95. Riesner, "Jesus as Preacher and Teacher," 209.

96. John 6:66.

97. For example, John 8:59; 10:31.

98. Cf. Matt. 21:45–46; 22:15.

99. John 14:5, 8; Matt. 13:10 (= Mark 4:10).

100. For example, Luke 4:15–16; Matt. 4:23; Mark 4:21–22.

101. But cf. Paul's sermon in the synagogue at Pisidian Antioch (Acts 13:16b–41).

102. I. H. Marshall (*Commentary on Luke*, NIGTC [Grand Rapids: Eerdmans, 1978], 181) calls it "the oldest known account of a synagogue service."

103. Which would normally encompass the equivalent of about ten verses.

104. Jesus "opened the book," read the text, then "He closed the book."

105. Cf. D. Monshouwer, "The Reading of the Prophet in the Synagogue at Nazareth," *Biblica* 72 (1991).

106. James A. Sanders, "From Isaiah 61 to Luke 4," Craig A. Evans and James A. Sanders, eds., *Luke and Scripture* (Minneapolis: Fortress, 1993), 67–68.

107. For example, F. W. Farrar, *The Gospel According to St. Luke,* Cambridge Greek Bible (Cambridge: Cambridge University Press, 1895), 148–49.

108. William A. Walker, "'Nazareth': A Clue to Synoptic Relationships?" in E. P. Sanders, ed., *Jesus, the Gospels, and the Church: Essays in Honor of William R. Farmer* (Macon: Mercer University Press, 1987), 109–11. Walker takes Matthew and Luke to have access to a common source *other than* "Q" (p. 118).

109. The verb *kataleipō* connotes "abandoning." Cf. Matt. 19:5.

110. Luke 4:23.

111. A. T. Robertson, *A Harmony of the Gospels* (New York: Harper and Row, 1922), 77n. Only Matthew and Mark mention the "works" of Jesus in Nazareth.

112. "Truly I say to you, no prophet is welcome in his home town." Cf. Mark 6:4; Matt. 13:57.

113. Alan P. Winton, *The Proverbs of Jesus: Issues of History and Rhetoric,* JSNT Supplement Series 35 (Sheffield: Sheffield Academic Press, 1990), 133.

114. For example, Jesus tells Nicodemus to "stop wondering" (*mēthoumasēs*) that he must be "born again" (John 3:7).

115. Stein, *Luke,* 158.

116. Paul Hertig, "The Jubilee Mission of Jesus in the Gospel of Luke: Reversals of Fortunes," *Missiology* 26, no. 2 (1998), 169.

117. Cf. Lev. 25:8–55.

Chapter 5, "Begotten Again to a Living Hope": Peter's Epistles as Inspired Incarnational Preaching

1. F. J. Foakes-Jackson, *Peter, Prince of Apostles: A Study in the History and Tradition of Christianity* (New York: George H. Doran, 1927), viii.

2. Ibid.

3. A. T. Robertson, *Epochs in the Life of Simon Peter* (Nashville: Broadman, reprint 1976 [orig. pub.], ix.

4. Eusebius (*History* 3.3.1) mentions at least four works attributed to Peter in addition to 1 and 2 Peter: (1) Acts of Peter; (2) Gospel of Peter; (3) The Preaching of Peter; and (4) Apocalypse of Peter. Of 2 Peter Eusebius says that it "does not belong to the canon," although, "as it has appeared profitable to many, it has been used with the other Scriptures."

5. J. H. Elliott, "The Rehabilitation of an Exegetical Step-Child: 1 Peter in Recent Research," *Journal of Biblical Literature* 95 (1976), 243–54.

6. Though not using the phrase as such, Craig Loscalzo advocates a new "rhetoric of identification" and uses the incarnation as a paradigm. Cf. *Preaching Sermons that Connect: Effective Communication Through Identification* (Downers Grove: Intervarsity Press, 1992), 35–58. See also Clyde E. Fant, *Preaching for Today,* rev. ed. (New York: Harper and Row, 1987), 69–110.

7. Phillips Brooks, *The Joy of Preaching,* intro. Warren W. Wiersbe (Grand Rapids: Kregel, rep. 1989 [orig. pub. 1895], 25.

8. W. M. Taylor, *Peter the Apostle* (New York: Harper, 1876).

9. John 1:29, 35–36. John announced Jesus on successive days; according to Alfred Edersheim, on a Friday and Saturday. Cf. *The Life and Times of Jesus the Messiah,* 3d ed. (Grand Rapids: Eerdmans, reprinted 1971 [originally published 1883, 1886]), 1:344–46.

10. Andrew and "another disciple" (doubtless John himself).

11. "Simon" is a Greek name, though common also among Jews in the first century. Peter evidently preferred "Simon" to his given (Aramaic) name "Simeon." Cf. Acts 15:14; 2 Pet. 1:1.

12. John 1:41.

13. John 1:42.

14. BAGD, s.v. Πέτρος, 660–61.

15. Oscar Cullmann, *Peter: Disciple, Apostle, Martyr*, rev. ed., trans. Floyd V. Filson (London: SCM, 1953, 1962), 21.

16. Ibid., 31.

17. E.g., Mark 8:27–29; also John 6:66–68.

18. E.g., Matt. 18:21; Luke 12:41; John 13:24; 13:36.

19. Matt. 16:16; Mark 8:29.

20. John 20:3.

21. John 20:6–7. Undoubtedly, the "other disciple" is John himself.

22. Matt. 10:2–4; Mark 3:16–19; Luke 6:13–16; Acts 1:13–14.

23. The term *protos* usually, though not necessarily, denotes "priority of rank." At a minimum, use of the term here calls special attention to Peter's place in the list. See BAGD, s.v. πρῶτος, 132–33.

24. Luke 22:8.

25. Matt. 26:40; Mark 14:37.

26. Matt. 17:24.

27. Mark 16:7.

28. Matt. 14:28–33.

29. Robertson, *Epochs*, 58.

30. John 20:3.

31. Matt. 26:35.

32. John 21:7.

33. Matt. 17:4; Mark 9:5.

34. John 18:10.

35. Note Jesus' commendation: "Blessed are you, Simon Barjona, because flesh and blood did not reveal this to you, but My Father who is in heaven" (Matt. 16:17).

36. Matt.16:21–22.

37. See Matt. 15:1–2, 10–15. Cf. also Gal. 2:11–14.

38. Matt. 16:22 (emphasis added).

39. Matt. 16:23.

40. Matt. 26:58. Cf. also Mark 14:54; Luke 22:54; John 18:15. Apparently only John was with him at that time (John 18:15).

41. Matt. 26:41.

42. Robertson, *Epochs*, 135.

43. See Matt. 26:69–75; Mark 14:66–72; Luke 22:55–62; John 18:15–18, 25–27. Foakes-Jackson *Peter*, notes (p. 70): "The very fact the [Peter] had for a moment denied the Lord made an ineffaceable impression."

44. Matt. 26:33.

45. Mark 14:31. Cf. also Luke 22:33; John 13:37.

46. Robertson, *Epochs*, 144.

47. Cf. Anton Boisen, *Religion in Crisis and Culture* (New York: Harper and Bros., 1955).

48. Anton T. Boisen, *The Exploration of the Inner World* (New York: Harper and Bros., 1936), 266–67.

49. Matt. 26:75. Cf. also Mark 14:72; Luke 22:62.

50. Luke 22:24.

51. Cf. Matt. 20:20–28 = Mark 10:35, 45; Luke 9:46–48.

52. Luke 22:31–32.

53. "Surely you too are one of them; for the way you talk gives you away" (Matt. 26:73).

54. Matt. 26:75 (*emnēsthē*); Mark 14:72 (*anemnēsthē*); Luke 22:61 (*hupemnēsthē*).

55. Luke 24:8.

56. John 12:16.

57. TDNT, s.v. μιμνήσκομαι, by Otto Michel, 4:677.

58. Luke 22:61.

59. Luke 22:62.

60. John 20:1–2.

61. John 20:9.

62. Mark 16:7.

63. Luke 24:34.

64. 1 Cor. 15:5.

65. Luke 5:4–10.

66. John 21:7.

67. John 21:15.

68. Alvah Hovey, *Commentary on the Gospel of John* (Valley Forge: Judson, 1885), 415.

69. In Jesus' first two questions, the term for "love" is *agapē*.

70. John 21:17.

71. John 21:18–22.

72. Luke 22:32.

73. John 21:15, 16, 17.

74. Cullmann, *Peter*, 32–33.

75. Foakes-Jackson, *Peter*, 73.

76. Wayne E. Oates, *Religious Dimensions of Personality* (New York: Association Press, 1957), 233.

77. R. Perdelwitz, *Die Mysterienreligion und das Problem des I. Petrusbriefes* (Giessen, 1911).

78. See B. H. Streeter, *The Primitive Church* (New York: Macmillan 1929).

79. F. W. Beare, *The Epistle of Peter* (Oxford: 1958).

80. Paul E. Robertson, "Is 1 Peter a Sermon?" *The Theological Educator* 13 (1982), 40.

81. Peter H. Davids, *The First Epistle of Peter*, NICNT (Grand Rapids: Eerdmans, 1990), 25.

82. C. F. D. Moule, "The Nature and Purpose of 1 Peter," NTS 3 (1956/57), 7.

83. Col. 4:16.

84. Donald Guthrie, *New Testament Introduction* 3d ed. (Downer's Grove: InterVarsity, 1970), 797.

85. J. Spencer Kennard, *Psychic Power in Preaching* (Philadelphia: American Baptist Publishing Society, 1901), 30.

86. 1 Pet. 1:1; 2 Pet. 1:1.

87. For a thorough discussion of all the questions in relation to both 1 and 2 Peter, see Guthrie, *New Testament Introduction*, 771–90; 814–48.

88. Among the parallels: Jude 6/2 Pet. 2:4; Jude 5/2 Pet. 1:12; Jude 4/2 Pet. 2:1; Jude 9–10/2 Pet. 2:11–12; Jude 7/2 Pet: 2.6; Jude 12–13/2 Pet. 2:17; Cf. Guthrie, 919: "Most of 2 Peter ii is paralleled in Jude."

89. Among the several arguments advanced in support of this hypothesis, the most compelling is that since virtually all of Jude is found in 2 Peter, there seems to be "no adequate reason for the publication of the shorter Epistle at all if 2 Peter already exists." See Guthrie, *New Testament Introduction*, 920.

90. Cf. Acts 4:13.

91. Jerome, *Letter to Hedibia*, 120.

92. 1 Pet. 5:12.

93. Robertson, Epochs, 295. Robertson suggested that John's Gospel and Revelation may exhibit the same phenomenon.

94. F. F. Bruce, *The Speeches in Acts* (London: Tyndale, 1943), 27.

95. On Cyril, See *Fathers of the Church: A New Translation*, 77:34. On Theophylact, see *Patriae Araeca*, 126:89.

96. Martin Luther, *Commentary on Peter and Jude* (Grand Rapids: Kregel, reprint 1990 [orig. pub. 1523]), 290ff.

97. 2 Pet. 3:16.

98. Norman Hillyer, *1 and 2 Peter, Jude*, NIBC (Peabody, Mass.: Hendrickson, 1996), 13.

99. Hillyer, *1 and 2 Peter, Jude*, 9. Cf. also E. Earle Ellis (*The Making of the New Testament Documents*, Biblical Interpretation Series 39 [Leiden: Brill, 1999], 122), who argues: "Very probably, 2 Peter and Jude use a common source (or sources), a midrash on the theme of judgment that . . . originated in the Jerusalem church."

100. The phrase is suggested by the late James William McClendon, *Biography as Theology* (Nashville: Abingdon Press, 1974).

101. Likely an allusion to John 20:29.

102. Willi Marxsen calls the letter a "Testament of Peter." Cf. *Introduction to the New Testament*, 3d ed. trans. G. Burwell (Philadelphia: Fortress, 1968), 241.

103. Guthrie, *New Testament Introduction*, 828–29. Many earlier manuscripts have the Aramaic "Symeon," which only compounds the strangeness.

104. Gal. 2:11–14.

105. 1 Pet. 2:4.

106. 2 Pet.1:10–11; cf. also 3:17.

107. Matt. 16:23 (= Mark 8:33).

108. Chrysostom, *The Homilies of St. John Chrysostom on the Gospel of St. Matthew*, iv, NPNF 10:338.

109. Davids, *Peter*, 23.

110. 1 Pet. 2:21a.

111. Cf. Matt. 5:10.

112. Cf. Matt. 5:11.

113. Thomas C. Oden, *Pastoral Theology: Essentials of Ministry* (New York: Harper and Row, 1983), 52–53.

114. Eph. 4:11.

115. Cf. John 10:7–16; Matt. 9:36; Mark 6:34; John 10:26; Matt. 26:31.

116. Oden, *Pastoral Theology*, 52.

117. Paul lists "pastor" (or "pastor-teacher"), the Greek *poimēn*, as one of the Lord's ascension gifts to the church (Eph. 4:11), and he urges the Ephesian elders to "shepherd" (*poimainein*) the "church of God" (Acts 20:28).

118. John 21:15–17. John employs two different Greek verbs—*boskō* in vv. 15, 17; and the more familiar *poimainō* in v. 16. There is no appreciable difference between the words, except that the former might suggest a bit more emphasis than the latter on the *care* of the shepherd. John also uses *agnia* ("lambs") in v. 15, and *probata* ("sheep") in vv. 16–17. Since Jesus spoke in Aramaic, not Greek, it may be that John uses these combinations in an effort to capture the nuances of Jesus' expression, to capture his simultaneous emphasis on both *functional responsibility* and *personal concern*.

119. Gregory (the Great), *The Book of Pastoral Rule*, 1.5.

120. Ibid., Book 1.8.

121. Cf. Paul's "wolves," Acts 20:29.

122. Not surprisingly, the Roman tradition has looked to 2 Peter for support of a "Petrine magisterium." See Raymond E. Brown, Karl P. Donfried, and John Reumann, eds., *Peter in the New Testament* (Minneapolis: Augsburg Publishing House, 1973), 154–56.

123. John 6:67; cf. 6:41–66.

124. John 6:68.

125. F. F. Bruce, *The Gospel of John* (Grand Rapids: Eerdmans, 1983), 165–66.

126. John 6:63.

127. Robert H. Gundry, "'Verba Christi' in 1 Peter: Their Implication Concerning the Authorship of 1 Peter and the Authenticity of the Gospel Tradition," NTS 13 (1966/67),

336–50. Cf. also Gerhard Maier, "Jesustradition im 1. *Petrusbriefe*," *Gospel Perspectives* 5 (Sheffield: JSOT, 1985), 85–128.

128. 1 Pet. 2:25; 5:2, 4; John 10:11–18; 21:15–17.

129. 1 Pet. 1:3; John 3:3–21.

130. 1 Pet. 1:4; Luke 12:33.

131. 1 Pet. 5:7–8; Luke 22:31–32.

132. For example, 1 Pet. 3:1–4; Matt. 5:5.

133. Cf. for example, Mark 12:10 and 1 Pet. 2:4, 6–7, quoting Ps. 118:22.

134. Cf. 2:12, 15, 17, 18–20, 23; 3:1–2, 9–12, 15–16; 4:1. Cf. J. Ramsey Michaels, *I Peter* WBC (Waco: Word, 1988).

135. Mark 1:15.

136. Cf. Matt. 13:41; 16:28; Luke 1:33; 22:29–30; 23:42; John 18:36.

137. Luke 9:31.

138. Hillyer, *1 and 2 Peter, Jude*, 172.

139. Michaels, *I Peter* x1. Peter's use of the Old Testament is comparable to that of Hebrews.

140. Edward Lohse, "Parenesis and Kerygma in 1 Peter," Charles H. Talbert, ed., *Perspectives on First Peter*, NAB Press Special Studies Series, Number 9 (Macon, Ga.: Mercer University Press, 1986), 55.

141. Ibid.

142. 1 Pet. 1:14, 16; see Lev. 19:2.

143. 2 Pet. 3:10–11.

144. Cf. Matt. 24:43–44; Luke 12:39.

Chapter 6, The Inspired Preaching of Acts: The First Theology of Preaching

1. J. Spencer Kennard, *Psychic Power in Preaching* (Philadelphia: American Baptist Publication Society, 1901), 147.

2. Acts 28:23. The conclusion is found in verses 25–28.

3. Acts 28:31.

4. By Gamaliel (5:3–9), Demetrius the silversmith (19:24–27) and the town clerk (19:35–40), both in Ephesus, and by Tertullus the lawyer in Caesarea (24:2–8).

5. The apostles in the temple "about daybreak" (5:21); the preaching of Philip in Samaria, Gaza, and along the coast from Azotus to Caesarea (ch. 8); Peter and John in Samaria and surrounding villages (8:25); Paul in Damascus (9:19b–20) and Jerusalem (19:28–29); preaching to "Jews alone" in Phoenicia, Cyprus, and Antioch (11:19); preaching (by "men of Cyprus and Cyrene") to Greeks in Antioch (11:20); by Barnabas, then Barnabas and Saul, in Antioch "for an entire year" (11:23, 25–26); by Barnabas and Saul (Paul) in Cyprus, in the synagogue at Iconium, and in the cities of "Lycaonia, Lystra and Derbe, and the surrounding region" (14:6–7); by Paul, Silas, and Timothy in Philippi (ch.16), Thessalonica (17:1–3), Berea (17:10–11), and Corinth (ch. 18); by Apollos in Ephesus and Corinth (18:24–28); by Paul in Ephesus (18:19–20; 19:8), and throughout Greece (20:1–2), and in Troas (20:7–12).

6. Cf. I. Howard Marshall, *Acts*, Tyndale New Testament Commentaries (Grand Rapids: Eerdmans, 1980), 17–22.

7. Cf. H. J. Cadbury, *The Making of Luke-Acts* (New York: Macmillan, 1927); William Ramsay, *Was Christ Born in Bethlehem?* (London: Hodder and Stoughton, 1898); W. W. Gasque, *A History of the Criticism of the Acts of the Apostles* (Grand Rapids: Eerdmans, 1975); I. Howard Marshall, *Luke: Historian and Theologian* (Grand Rapids: Zondervan, 1971); *et. al.*

8. Acts 1:1–2a.

9. John R. W. Stott, *The Spirit, the Church, and the World: The Message of Acts* (Downers Grove, IL: IVP, 1990), 32.

10. Charles P. Erdman, *The Acts: An Exposition* (Philadelphia: Westminster Press, 1919).

11. Cf. Acts 1:22–23 with John 15:27.

12. Cf. Acts 2:14.

13. Acts 3:12b–26.

14. Acts 4:4, 8b–12; 5:29b–32.

15. Acts 7:2–53.

16. Stephen was accused of undermining Jewish culture. The false witnesses claimed, "We have heard him say that this Nazarene, Jesus, will destroy this place and *alter the customs* which Moses handed down to us" (Acts 6:14, emphasis added). Cf. 6:14.

17. Acts 8:1, 4; 11:19–21.

18. Acts 8:1a, 3; 9:1–5; 22:3–7; 26:9–15.

19. Acts 8:5.

20. Acts 8:25.

21. Acts 9:19b–22.

22. Acts 9:32–43.

23. Acts 10:1–33. Note the words of Cornelius following the lengthy accounts of the vision that brought Peter to Caesarea: "Now then, we are all here present before God to hear all that you have been commanded by the Lord" (v. 33b).

24. Acts 11:4–17.

25. Acts 15:7–11, 13–21.

26. Acts 9:20, 27–29.

27. Chrysostom, *Acts*, 20, NPNF 11:130.

28. Karl Barth, *Homiletics*, trans. Geoffrey W. Bromiley and Donald E. Daniels (Louisville: W/JKP, 1991), 17.

29. Rom. 1:16.

30. See Roland Allen (*Missionary Methods: St. Paul's or Ours?* [Grand Rapids: Eerdmans, 1962]) for an excellent treatment of Paul's systematic approach to ministry.

31. For example, 14:21–22; 16:4–5; 20:1–2, 6–11; 21:17–19.

32. Cf. 14:21–22, 26; 16:4–5; 18:23; 20:7. On the sermon as a pastoral theology, cf. W. E. Chadwick, *Pastoral Teaching of Paul* (Grand Rapids: Kregel, reprint 1984 [org. pub. 1907]), 19–00.

33. Cf. Rom. 15:20.

34. Acts 1:16–22.

35. Acts 11:2–3, 5–17.

36. Acts 15:7b–11.

37. Cullmann, *Peter*, 34. The Jerusalem council is a notable exception, of course. There, Peter plays a strategic role, but does not preside.

38. Matt. 16:19.

39. Acts 5:1–10.

40. Acts 8:14–17.

41. Acts 8:18–24.

42. John 21:15–17.

43. 1 Pet. 5:1, 2.

44. Acts 15:13b–21.

45. E. H. Plumptre, *The Acts of the Apostles*, in Ellicott, 7:96.

46. Cf. Luke 5:10; also Matt. 4:18–19; Mark 1:16–17. This is Luke's only mention of a "Peter prophecy" (5:8). The Gospels record at least four other prophecies concerning Peter: (1) John 1:42; (2) Matt. 10:2; (3) Mark 3:16 (under the influence of Peter); and (4) Matt. 16:18. Jesus confirmed the "catching men" prophecy with the miraculous catch of fish (Luke 5:4–9), a sign repeated at Peter's recommissioning after the resurrection (John 21:3–11).

47. Cf. Acts 15:7, God chose to extend the gospel to the Gentiles, Peter says, "by my mouth."

48. Cf. Acts 15:14. James finds theological significance in Peter's call to preach to the Gentiles. God was "concerned" to call out for the Gentiles "a people for His name."

49. Chrysostom, *Acts*, 24, NPNF 11:157.

50. Paul habitually began a preaching mission in the synagogue. According to Acts 17:2, it was his "custom."

51. Rom. 1:16.

52. Nine of the twenty total.

53. Acts. 4:8–12; 5:29–32.

54. Acts 11:4–17.

55. Acts 7:2b–53; Cf. 6:12; 7:1.

56. Acts 22:1–21.

57. Acts 23:1b–6.

58. Acts 24:10b–21.

59. Acts 26:2–23.

60. Acts 28:17b–20.

61. Acts 4:18–19.

62. 2 Cor. 10:5.

63. Acts 22:1–21.

64. Acts 21:28.

65. Acts 4:2, 14.

66. Acts 19:8–20.

67. Acts 19:25b–27.

68. Acts 19:35–40.

69. On the species of rhetoric, see Aristotle, *On Rhetoric*, 1.3.

70. Acts 26:2–29.

71. Acts 26:29.

72. Stott, *Spirit, Church, World*, 32.

73. Acts 8:1, 4; 11:19–20.

74. Acts 15:39.

75. Acts 8:4–6; 40.

76. Acts 8:25.

77. J. I. Packer, "Introduction: Why Preach?" in Samuel T. Logan Jr., *The Preacher and Preaching* (Phillipsburg: P&R Publishers, 1986), 19.

78. See J. Reu, *Homiletics* (Minneapolis: Wartburg, 1924), 104.

79. 14:21–22; 15:36, 41; 16:4–5; 18:23; 20:1–2, 6–12.

80. Chadwick, *Pastoral Teaching*, 195–220.

81. Ian Pitt-Watson, *A Primer for Preachers* (Grand Rapids: Baker, 1986), 46.

82. C. H. Dodd, *The Apostolic Preaching and Its Development* (New York: Harper and Row, 1964 [originally published 1936]), 21. The word *kērygma* is Greek, denoting a "proclamation" or "announcement" by "a herald" (*kērux*). In 1 Cor. 1:21, NASB translates *kērugma* as "message preached." The word signifies both the act of preaching and (but especially) the message itself. Cf. BAGD, s.v. κήρυγμα, 432.

83. Dodd, *Apostolic Preaching*, 21–24.

84. Acts 2:16.

85. Acts 13:15–41.

86. Acts 5:29b–31a.

87. Acts 2:33.

88. Acts 10:42.

89. Dodd, *Apostolic Preaching*, 23.

90. Acts 2:38.

91. Acts 3:19.

92. Acts 13:38.

93. Dodd, *Apostolic Preaching*, 24, cf. also Matt. 4:17.

94. Cf. Col. 1:13; Gal. 1:4; Heb. 6:4–5. See esp. George E. Ladd, *A Theology of the New Testament* (Grand Rapids: Eerdmans, 1974), 57–69.

95. Isa. 9:7.

96. Acts 1:3.

97. Acts 28:31.

98. Sidney Greidanus, *The Modern Preaching and the Ancient Text: Interpreting and Preaching Biblical Literature* (Grand Rapids: Eerdmans, 1988), 118.

99. Ladd, *Theology*, 57.

100. 1 Cor. 1:21.

101. The term is characteristic of early preaching and preachers. Cf. Acts 1:8, 22; 2:32, 40; 3:15; 4:33; 5:32; 8:25; 10:39, 41–42; 13:31; 18:5; 20:21, 24; 22:15, 18; 23:11; 26:22; 28:23.

102. Dodd, *Apostolic Preaching*, 7–8. Cf. Acts 10:41.

103. 1 Thess. 2:3–4. Cf. Acts 16:1–17.

104. 2 Cor. 5:11; cf. Acts 17:2–3, 17; 18:4, 19; 19:8; 28:23.

105. Paul's sermon to the Ephesian elders at Miletus (20:18b–35), for example, is one of the longest in Acts; but one can read it easily in two and one-half minutes!

106. Acts 2:40, emphasis added.

107. Acts 20:7.

108. Cf. Martin Dibelius, *Studies in the Acts of the Apostles*, ed. Heinrich Greever, trans. Mary King (New York: Charles Scribner's Sons, 1956). Cf. also H. J. Cadbury, *The Making of Luke-Acts* 2d ed. (London: SPCK, 1958).

109. F. F. Bruce, "The Speeches in Acts—Thirty Years After," Robb Banks, ed., *Reconciliation and Hope: New Testament Essays on Atonement and Eschatology* (London: Paternoster, 1974), 54.

110. On Luke's claim in the Prologue to his Gospel, see above, chapter 3.

111. William M. Ramsey, *Was Christ Born in Bethlehem?* 16.

112. Ibid., 47–48.

113. Marshall, *Acts*, 42. Cf. F. F. Bruce, "Speeches."

114. Cf. Luke 21:12–15; Mark 13:9–11.

115. Aristotle, *On Rhetoric*, trans. George A. Kennedy (New York: Oxford University Press, 1991), 1.2.1., emphasis added.

116. Alfred Barry, The Epistles to the Ephesians, Philippians, and Colossians, in Charles J. Ellicott, ed., *Ellicott's Commentary on the Whole Bible*, 8 vols. (Grand Rapids: Zondervan, reprint 1959), 8:116.

117. Acts 18:4; cf. also 17:2, 17; 18:19; 19:9. Paul also "reasoned" (*dialegōmai*) with Felix, Acts 24:25.

118. This is the background of Paul's avowal to the Corinthians that his "message" and "preaching" were "not in persuasive words of wisdom, but in demonstration of the Spirit and of power" (1 Cor. 2:4). For an excellent analysis of Paul's "rhetoric" here, cf. Duane Litfin, *St. Paul's Theology of Proclamation*, SNTS Monograph Series 79 (Cambridge: Cambridge University Press, 1994).

119. Acts 11:2–3.

120. Acts 11:17–18.

121. 1 Thess. 2:1–13.

122. Acts 6:10.

123. Recall that "rhetoric" is the "ability *in each* [*particular*], *case*, to see the available means of persuasion." Cf. Aristotle, *On Rhetoric*, trans. George A. Kennedy (New York: Oxford University Press, 1991), 1.2.1.

124. For an excellent study of Chrysostom, see J. N. D. Kelly, *Golden Mouth: The Story of John Chrysostom—Ascetic, Preacher, Bishop* (Grand Rapids: Baker, 1995).

Chapter 7, The Inspired Preaching of Peter in Acts

1. NPNF 11:33.

2. (1) In the upper room (1:16–22); (2) at Pentecost (2:14b–36); (3) in Solomon's Portico (3:12b–26); (4) before the council (with John; 4:8b–12); (5) before the council a second time (with the apostles; 5:29b–32); (6) to the household of Cornelius (10:34b–43);

(7) before the disputants in Jerusalem (11:5–17); and (8) before the Jerusalem council (15:7b–11).

3. As well as in the New Testament as a whole. We argue that 1 and 2 Peter most fully represent the *theological* emphases in Peter's preaching. See chapter 5.

4. Cf. Titus 2:10.

5. Cf. Matt. 27:33–35.

6. Luke 22:32.

7. See chapter 5.

8. Acts 1:4.

9. Calvin, *Institutes,* 2.16.14.

10. The Lord's "secret" working was often a source of bafflement. Recall the chiding of his brothers when he declined to go with them to the feast in Jerusalem: "No one does anything in secret when he himself seeks to be known publicly" (John 7:4).

11. In the Upper Room Discourse (John 14–16), the Lord refers no less than five times to his departure (14:2–3, 12–18, 28; 16:5–11, 19–28) and in each case links his departure to some blessing or advantage.

12. Luke alone among the Evangelists develops a theology of the ascension, which serves as the primary link between the third Gospel and Acts. Significantly, Luke sets the stage for Peter's upper room sermon (1:13–14) by noting that all of the disciples, except Judas, were present, along with the (once disbelieving) brothers of Jesus and "the women" (who had followed him throughout his ministry) and "Mary the mother of Jesus" (who had been at the cross). Their very presence testified to the reality of the resurrection, which was now confirmed by the ascension!

13. Acts 1:16a.

14. The Greek text has *Andres, adelphoi* ("men, brothers").

15. See R. P. C. Hanson, *The Acts,* New Clarendon Bible (New York: Oxford, 1971), 46.

16. Chrysostom, *Homilies on the Acts of the Apostles,* 3, NPNF 11:18.

17. Ibid.

18. Cf. R. J. Knowling, "The Acts of the Apostles," Robertson Nicoll, ed. *The Expositor's Greek Testament* (Grand Rapids: Eerdmans, reprint, 1979), 63.

19. Chrysostom, *Acts,* 3, NPNF 11:19.

20. Acts 2:38.

21. See chapter 6.

22. Acts 2:29–36.

23. Ibid., 182.

24. Ibid., 183.

25. To be fair, Kilgallen occasionally shifts his perspective from Luke to Peter. At one point, he restates his analysis this way: "Peter could have simply claimed, at the outset of his speech, that the immediate source of the Pentecost experience was Jesus, but he chose to make the claim only after laying the grounds which would make his claims credible" (p. 187). Later Kilgallen even attributes to Peter a rhetorical strategy. Peter "thought the audience would best react favorably to those revelations which could easily be grounded in the common patrimony of speaker and audience" (p. 196). It is not clear, however, whether Kilgallen has Peter himself in mind, or is only using "Peter" to represent the Lucan reconstruction.

26. There are interesting parallels between Luke's account here and some psychological theories of "consciousness" as applied to religious experience. First, we become *aware.* Then there is a process of *search* ("what is happening?"). Then a *judgment* ("what does this mean?"); then a *decision* ("what should I do?"). The majority at Pentecost were still *searching;* but the mockers had arrived at a (premature and erroneous) *judgment.* Cf. Paul E. Johnson, *Psychology of Religion* (Nashville: Abingdon-Cokesbury, 1945), 34.

27. Chrysostom, *Acts,* 4, NPNF 11:29.

28. Cf. E. Earle Ellis, *The Making of the New Testament Documents,* Biblical Interpretation Series 39 (Leiden: Brill, 1999), 372–73. Also Birger Gerhardsson, *Memory and Manuscript:*

Oral Tradition and Written Transmission in Rabbinical Judaism and Early Christianity, trans. Eric J. Sharpe, Combined ed. (Grand Rapids: Eerdmans, 1998 [orig. pub. 1961]), 221ff. We will encounter this phenomenon again. It is worth asking how we might translate the idea of "communal" preaching today. John McClure (*The Removable Pulpit: Where Leadership and Preaching Meet* [Nashville: Abingdon, 1995]) has attempted something along these lines, but with dubious success. John R. W. Stott (*Between Two Worlds: The Art of Preaching in the Twentieth Century* [Grand Rapids: Eerdmans, 1982], 194–201) offers several helpful suggestions: "I am convinced," he says, "that there ought to be more cooperation between clergy and laity in the process of sermon-making" (p. 200).

29. Cf. Prov. 15:1.

30. Chrysostom, *Acts*, 5, NPNF 11:31–32.

31. Acts 2:17–21.

32. Acts 2:17; Chrysostom, *Acts*, 5, NPNF 11:32.

33. Robert Sloan, "'Signs and Wonders': A Rhetorical Clue to the Pentecost Discourse," *Evangelical Theology* 63:3 (1991), 238 (emphasis added).

34. Acts 2:25–30; Ps. 16:8–11.

35. Cf. Ps. 132:11–12; 2 Sam. 7:12–16; Ps. 89:3–4, 35–37.

36. Cf. Ps. 16:11.

37. Cf. Ps. 110:1. Jesus appealed in the same way to this verse in his teaching against the scribes; Mark 12:35–37.

38. Cf. 2:19. See Sloan, "Signs and Wonders."

39. Chrysostom, *Acts*, 5, NPNF 11:32.

40. Chrysostom, *Acts*, 6, NPNF 11:39.

41. Chrysostom used this precise language. Speaking of Peter's initial mention of Jesus, he says, "Observe how [Peter] forbears to speak of the high matters, and begins with the very low" (6, NPNF 11:37).

42. Chrysostom, *Acts*, 6, NPNF 11:40.

43. Chrysostom, *Acts*, 6, NPNF 11:37.

44. The word *pesher* means "interpretation." *Pesher* was a standard rabbinic homiletical approach whereby a text was applied directly ("this is that") to a present situation, movement, individual, etc. See Walter C. Kaiser Jr., *Toward an Exegetical Theology: Biblical Exegesis for Preaching and Teaching* (Grand Rapids: Baker, 1981), 55–56. J. W. Bowker ("Speeches in Acts: A Study in Proem and Yelammedenu Form" *New Testament Studies* 14 [1967], 96–111) argues that Peter has apparently adapted a well-worn synagogue-inspired homiletical model, whereby an introductory (*proem*) text served as the "bridge" between the *seder* (*Torah*) and *haftarah* (Prophets) readings for a given day. The day of Pentecost was known as *ha atseret* ("the fulfillment"), and the Joel "bridge" text signaled an astonishing "fulfillment" in the present!

45. Chrysostom, *Acts*, 6, NPNF 11:37.

46. Acts 2:22–24.

47. Acts 2:25–31. David foresaw the Messiah ("soft," vv. 25–28). David is dead ("hard," v. 29). David saw the resurrection of the Messiah, who is Jesus! ("hard," v. 3).

48. "God is throughout the central subject who performs these mighty acts with and through Christ." Cf. Sloan, "Signs and Wonders," 230.

49. Gothard V. Lechler, *The Acts of the Apostles*, notes by Charles Gerok, trans. Charles T. Schaeffer, in Philip Lange, ed., *Lange's Commentary on the Holy Scriptures: New Testament* (Grand Rapids: Zondervan; reprint, 1960), 4:51.

50. Chrysostom, *Acts*, 6, NPNF 11:41.

51. Acts 2:43b.

52. Luke identifies it as the "Beautiful Gate" (3:10), probably the Nicanor Gate, the main eastern entrance from the Court of Gentiles. It would have been a place most suitable to beg alms.

53. Webber thinks, for example, that Peter risked "discrediting himself" with "an extremely aggressive strategy" at Solomon's Portico "by accusing [potential supporters] of

murder." Fortunately, Peter catches himself! Says Webber, "He removes his foot from his mouth . . . by admitting to the audience that he judged them too severely" (3:17). The "ploy" (Webber termed it) succeeded, since many believed (Acts 4:4). Randall C. Webber, "Why Were the Heathen So Arrogant?' The Socio-Rhetorical Strategy of Acts 3–4," *Biblical Theology Bulletin* 22 (Spring 1992), 22.

54. Ibid., 24. The proposed "settlement" was the command, at the first defense, not "to speak . . . at all in the name of Jesus"! Cf. Acts 4:18.

55. The phrase is from H. Richard Niebuhr's classic historical study of the struggle. See *Christ and Culture* (New York: Macmillan, 1951).

56. Chrysostom, *Acts*, 8, NPNF 11:52.

57. Chrysostom, *Acts*, 9, NPNF 11:54.

58. Acts 3:12a.

59. Chrysostom, *Acts*, 9, NPNF 11:55.

60. John R. W. Stott, *The Spirit, the Church, and the World: The Message of Acts* (Downers Grove, IL: IVP, 1990), 92.

61. Sloan, "Signs and Wonders," 230, emphasis added.

62. "Men of Israel" (3:12b).

63. Isa. 52:13. "Servant" translates *ton paida*, literally "the Child." But LXX supports this translation, as does the context here and elsewhere in Acts (3:26; 4:27). See Knowling, *The Acts of the Apostles*, in Nicoll, *The Expositor's Greek New Testament* 4:109.

64. Cf. Bruce, *Acts*, 81–82.

65. See above.

66. In this Peter intuits principles of classical rhetoric. Aristotle, for example, believed that as a rule orators spent too much time with introductions, since hearers are *naturally* attentive at the beginning of a speech. He emphasized that the orator might abbreviate the *proem*, or eliminate it altogether, *depending on the receptivity of the hearers.* Cf. Aristotle, *Rhetoric* 3.14.5.

67. "For you first" (3:26) certainly presupposes that the Abrahamic promises (Gen. 12:3) were for "the Jew first," as Paul often declares. But in the rhetorical context of Solomon's Portico, the words are highly personal. The thought is not that "the descendents of Abraham" are heirs of the promise, but that "you, Abraham's children listening to me now," have lived to see the promise fulfilled.

68. Chrysostom, *Acts*, 9, NPNF 11:55.

69. Cf. Luke 21:12–15.

70. Bruce, *Acts*, 92.

71. "Rulers and elders of the people" (4:8b).

72. The sentence is conditional, but there is no explicit apodosis, no "then" corresponding to the "if." It is tantamount to an indirect question: "Are *we* on trial?" Cf. William S. LaSor, *Handbook of New Testament Greek: An Inductive Approach Based on the Greek Text of Acts* (Grand Rapids: Eerdmans, 1973), A112.

73. Cf. R. C. H. Lenski, *The Interpretation of the Acts of the Apostles* (Minneapolis: Augsburg, 1934), 161.

74. Perhaps Tuesday of passion week. Cf. 4:11; Matt. 21:42.

75. "Asyndeton" denotes a text that has no *grammatical* connection to its context. It commands attention because it "stands alone." Aristotle regarded asyndeton as a most effective *epilogos*, because it naturally called for a judgment. *Rhetoric*, 3.19.6.

76. Acts 4:18.

77. Acts 5:28, emphasis added.

78. Acts 4:20. Chrysostom, *Acts*, 13, NPNF 11:83.

79. Chrysostom, Ibid., 11:82.

80. The only reference to the first trial, cf. 4:19.

81. Acts 5:29–32, emphasis added.

82. Knowling, *Acts*, 4:249. To the same effect is Chrysostom: Peter's "unassuming conduct" in Joppa evidences his "humility." Chrysostom, *Acts*, 21, NPNF 11:137.

83. Ronald S. Witherup, "Cornelius Over and Over Again," *Journal for the Study of the New Testament* 49 (1993), 50–54.

84. Witherup, "Cornelius," 48.

85. Cornelius, 10:2–3; Peter, 10:9–10. In each case, the vision is connected with prayer.

86. Cf. B. R. Gaventa, *From Darkness to Light: Aspects of Conversion in the New Testament* (Philadelphia: Fortress, 1986), 112.

87. Cf. Robert L. Saucy, "Theology of Human Nature," J. P. Moreland and David M. Ciocchi, eds., *Christian Perspectives on Being Human* (Grand Rapids: Baker, 1993), 17–52. Saucy reminds us that "heart" is frequently used in Scripture for the center of personality, not least because "emotions . . . ultimately drive behavior" (p. 43).

88. Deut. 10:17.

89. Acts 10:34b, emphasis added.

90. In this connection we note with interest Paul's reference to Peter's apparent lapse into judaizing (Gal. 2:11–13). We cannot date the confrontation with any precision, although it almost certainly occurred prior to the Jerusalem council. We are left to inquire only about the act itself. Hort suggested that Peter did *not* renege on his theological convictions, but rather adopted a "don't rock the boat" attitude to Jewish believers, who still had scruples about eating with Gentiles. However plausible the argument, Paul regarded it as blameworthy. Cf. F. J. A. Hort, *Judaistic Christianity* (Grand Rapids: Baker, reprint 1980 [originally published 1894]), 76–79.

91. Martin Dibelius, *Die Bekenrung des Cornelius, Coniectanea Neotestamentica* XI (1947), 50–65. Among several differences, Dibelius noted especially a supposed discrepancy in reporting the manifestation of the Holy Spirit (cf. 10:44; 11:15).

92. See John J. Kilgallen, "Did Peter Actually Fail to Get a Word in?" *Biblica* 71 (1990), 405–10.

93. Witherup, "Cornelius," 47. Cf. also Witherup, "Functional Redundancy in the Acts of the Apostles: A Case Study," *Journal for the Study of the New Testament* 48 (1992), 67–86.

94. Several scholars have called attention to the roles that "hospitality" and "home" play in Acts. Cf. Gaventa, *Darkness;* J. Koenig, *New Testament Hospitality: Partnership with Strangers as Promise and Mission* (Philadelphia: Fortress 1985); and John H. Elliott, "Household Meals vs. Temple Purity: Replication Patterns in Luke-Acts," *Biblical Theology Bulletin* 21 (Fall 1991), 102–08.

95. Some have attempted to use this verse as a proof text for universalism. The context rules out such an interpretation. The distinction Peter makes is between the Jew and non-Jew, not the saved and unsaved. His point is that God has not withheld the gospel from non-Jews. Peter came to Caesarea, of course, to preach the gospel, so that those who were *welcome* might also be *saved*. Cf. John J. Kilgallen, "Clean, Acceptable, Saved, Acts 10," *The Expository Times* 109 (July 1998), 301–02.

96. Bruce, *Acts*, 219.

97. Chrysostom, *Acts*, 24, NPNF 11:156.

98. Chrysostom, *Acts*, 24, NPNF 11:156–57.

99. Acts 1:4–5.

100. Chrysostom, *Acts*, 32, NPNF 11:201 (emphasis added).

101. Stott, *Spirit*, 248. Chrysostom, *Acts*, 33, NPNF 11:205. Recall that certain men purporting to be "from James" had imported judaizing tendencies to Antioch (Gal. 2:11–12).

102. Chrysostom, *Acts*, 33, NPNF 11:205.

103. Note James's respectful address ("Brethren, listen to me," 15:13b) and his striking reference to Peter *by his Aramaic name*, "Simeon" (15:14a).

104. Cf. 15:2, 4–5.

105. Luke says, incisively, there was "much debate" (15:7).

106. Sloan, "Signs and Wonders," 230.

107. 1 Pet. 1:3.

Chapter 8, "To the Jew First": The Inspired Preaching of Paul in Acts

1. Bruce Chilton, "The Mystery of Paul," *Bible Review* 14 (February 1998), 36.

2. Chrysostom, *The Acts of the Apostles*, 47, NPNF 11:283. The "Hebrew dialect" (22:2) denotes Aramaic, the everyday language of Jews from the time of the Exile.

3. A. T. Robertson, *Epochs in the Life of Paul* (Nashville: Broadman, 1976), 229.

4. James Stalker, *The Life of St. Paul* (Old Tappan, N.J.: Fleming H. Revell Co., 1950), 21.

5. Cf. Acts 22:3; 26:5.

6. Sir William M. Ramsey, *St. Paul the Traveller and the Roman Citizen* (Grand Rapids: Baker, reprint 1962 [orig. pub. 1897]), 30–32.

7. Cf. Robertson, *Paul*, 7.

8. Among them, Epicureans and Stoics (17:18). The latter flourished in Tarsus. See *IDB*, s.v. "Tarsus," by M. J. Mellink.

9. Cf. Acts 17:28a (Epimenides, or possibly, Euripides' *Bacchae*); 1 Cor. 15:33 (Menander's *Thais*); and Titus 1:12 (Epimenides).

10. Paul may allude to the significance of his hellenistic background in Rom. 1:14. "I am under obligation [*opheiletēs eimi*]," he says, "both to Greeks and to barbarians, both to the wise and to the foolish." Most commentators supply the words "to preach" after "obligation" to argue that Paul only meant to express his calling to preach to all. Paul uses the same phraseology elsewhere in Romans (15:27), however, to express a reciprocal obligation: The saints in Greece contributed to the needs of the (Jewish) believers in Jerusalem because they were "indebted to them" [*opheileta eisin autēn*], since the Gentiles had "shared in their [the Jews'] spiritual things." Elsewhere, Paul says that Christians are no longer "under obligation" [*opheiletai esmen*] to the flesh (Rom. 8:12), indicating that the tie had been broken which previously bound the Christian to the desires of the flesh. Origen thought that Paul intended to indicate such an obligation here, that is, a sense of *duty owed to culture as a beneficiary of culture*: "Given that a man receives the gift of tongues [language] not for himself but for the benefit of those to whom he is called to preach, Paul incurs an obligation to all those whose language he has received as a gift from God." Origen, *Commentarii in Epistulan ad Romanos*, ed. T. Heither, 5 vols. (Freiburg im Briesgan: Herder, 1990–95), 1:128. On the nature of "obligation" in the New Testament see *TDNT*, s.v. ὀφείλω, by Friedrich Hauck, 5:559–66.

11. Mishnah, *Sôṭāh*, 9:15.

12. Acts 9:1. Tom Wright (*What Paul Really Said: Was Paul of Tarsus the Real Founder of Christianity?* [Grand Rapids: Eerdmans, 1997], 25–35) argues that Paul in fact followed Shammai, the opponent of Hillel; but this seems unlikely given Paul's evident respect for his mentor.

13. Robertson, *Paul*, 17.

14. Cf. I. Howard Marshall, *The Acts of the Apostles: An Introduction and Commentary*, Tyndale New Testament Commentaries (Grand Rapids: Eerdmans, 1980), 123.

15. Robertson, *Paul*, 19–24.

16. Cf. Phil. 1:10, where Paul seems to allude to the rabbinical practice of distinguishing (for example) "greater" and "lesser."

17. Robertson, *Paul*, 23.

18. Cf. Acts 23:6; also 26:5; Phil. 3:5.

19. Cf. Acts 22:4–5, 19; 26:9–12.

20. Cf. 1 Cor. 15:9; 1 Tim. 1:13.

21. Chrysostom *Acts*, 29, NPNF 11:183.

22. "Beyond measure," he later says (Gal. 1:13); cf. also Acts 26:11.

23. Robertson, *Paul*, 36.

24. Cf. Acts 13:16; 20:34; 21:40; 26:1.

25. Cf. Acts 13:9; 14:9; 23:1.

26. Ramsey, *St. Paul*, 37–39.

27. Stalker, *St. Paul*, 34.

28. According to the Talmud, 480 different synagogues (Cf. Gotthard V. Lechler, *The Acts of the Apostles*, trans. Charles F. Schaeffer, in Lange, New Testament, 4:109), though F. F. Bruce says that figure should "be taken with a grain of salt." F. F. Bruce, *The Book of Acts*, rev. ed. NICNT (Grand Rapids: Eerdmans, 1988), 124n.

29. Many scholars think Luke has in mind only one synagogue, peopled by freed slaves from different parts of North Africa and Asia Minor, though it is possible that two or more synagogues are in view.

30. John Foxe, *Foxe's Book of Martyrs*, ed. Marie G. King (Old Tappan, N.J.: Fleming H. Revell, reprint 1968 [orig. pub. 1559, English ed. 1563]), 11.

31. The ancient farmer typically plowed with a single-handled plow, and with his right hand would employ a 6-to-8-foot rod to control an unruly ox. When the ox "kicked," the goad would inflict pain.

32. John R. W. Stott, *The Spirit, the Church, and the World: The Message of Acts* (Downers Grove: InterVarsity Press, 1990), 171–74.

33. Richard B. Rackham, *The Acts of the Apostles: An Exposition* 4th ed., Westminster Commentaries Series (London: Methuen, 1901, 1909), 88.

34. John B. Polhill, *Acts*, NAC, vol. 26 (Nashville: Broadman, 1992), 186.

35. Henry Alford, Alford's *Greek Testament: An Exegetical and Critical Commentary* 7th ed. (Grand Rapids: Guardian Press. Reprint 1976 [orig. pub. 1844–74]), 2:65.

36. E.g., Matt. 5:20–48; Matt. 12:1–12; Mark 2:1–12, 15–17; 3:1–6; John 5:39–40; among many instances.

37. Polhill, *Acts*, 186.

38. John Calvin, *Commentary upon the Acts of the Apostles*, 2 vols., ed. Henry Beveridge, trans. Christopher Featherstone (Grand Rapids: Eerdmans reprint 1949 [orig. pub. 1585]), 1:247.

39. Cf. Martin Dibelius, *Studies in the Acts of the Apostles* (London: SCM, 1956), 167–69.

40. Calvin, *Acts*, I:249.

41. Stott, *Spirit, Church, World*, 130.

42. "Brethren and fathers."

43. It is tempting to find here correlations with Aristotle's three modes of persuasion—(respectively) *ethos, logos*, and *pathos*.

44. Chrysostom, *Acts*, 15, NPNF 11:95.

45. Cf., e.g., Exod. 34:9; Deut. 9:6; also 32:9; 33:3, 5.

46. A. T. Robertson, *Types of Preachers in the New Testament* (Grand Rapids: Baker reprint 1972), 112.

47. Ibid., 116. By contrast, Peter's preaching to this point has been in company with other disciples.

48. Lechler (*Acts*, 4:110) says the charges implied "active, enduring, irreverent and fanatical hostility."

49. Robertson, *Types*, 114.

50. Cyrene, also known as Pentapolis, was the chief city of North Africa, an important intellectual and medical city, and home to the Cyrenaic School of Greek philosophy. Alexandria boasted a museum, libraries, and a vibrant university life. Philo, a contemporary of Christ and famed hellenist Jewish philosopher, called Alexandria home. The province of Cilicia included Tarsus, the home of Saul and (as we noted) a leading hellenistic city. The large, prosperous, and populous province of Asia included many cities of culture and learning, notably Ephesus.

51. Bruce, *Acts*, 125. Luke uses the term *suzétountes* (*suzēteō*, "to debate"), a rare term in the New Testament, to denote more or less formal argument. Paul uses a noun form of the word in 1 Cor. 1:20 [to show the futility of worldly wisdom]: "Where is the wise man (*sophos*)? Where is the scribe (*grammteus*)? Where is the debater (*suzētētēs*) of this age?" Cf. TDNT, s.v. συζητέω, by Johannes Schreider, 7:747–48.

52. For Paul's reasonings in Athens and Corinth (Acts 18:4) and elsewhere, Luke uses the term *dialegomai*, which, like *suzēteō*, has its roots in Greek philosophy. The word

denotes verbal engagement such as debate or lecture "likely to end in disputations." Cf. BAGD, s.v. διαλέγω.

53. Lechler, *Acts*, 4:109.

54. Cf. chapter 6.

55. Chrysostom, *Acts*, 17, NPNF 11:109.

56. Chrysostom, *Acts*, 18, NPNF 11:113.

57. Chrysostom, *Acts*, 17, NPNF 11:111.

58. Cf. here the words of Jesus: "For whoever wishes to save his life shall lose it; but whoever loses his life for My sake and the *gospel's* will save it" (Mark 8:35, emphasis added).

59. Ibid., 11:110.

60. Rackham, *Acts*, 88.

61. Robertson, *Types*, 120.

62. On which, see chapter 6, pp. 000.

63. Damascus (9:20); Jerusalem (9:28–29); Cyprus (13:5); Antioch Pisidia (13:14–42); Iconium (14:1); Thessalonica (27:2–3); Berea (27:20); Athens (17:27); Corinth (18:4); Ephesus (18:19; 19:8); Rome (28:17).

64. Lawrence Wills, "The Form of the Sermon in Hellenistic Judaism and Early Christianity," *Harvard Theological Review* 77 (1984), 278–80.

65. The other is Jesus' sermon in Nazareth (Luke 4:16–21), on which see chapter 4.

66. Bruce, *Acts*, 261.

67. David A. DeSilva, "Paul's Sermon in Antioch of Pisidia," *Bibliotheca Sacra* 151 (January-March 1994): 32–49.

68. Lechler, *Acts*, 4:248.

69. See Bruce, *Acts*, 252n; Wills, 278. Cf. Heb. 13:22, where the epistle itself is labeled a "word of exhortation."

70. See above.

71. J. W. Bonker, "Speeches in Acts: A Study in Proem and Yelammedenu Form," *New Testament Studies* 14 (1967–68): 101–10. Some older commentators (Bengel, Farrar, Plumptre, for example) hypothesized that the *Parashiach*, or *seder* (Law) reading for the day may have come from Deut. 1, while the *haftarah* (Prophets) reading may have derived from Isa. 1. Cf. also A. Guilding, *The Fourth Gospel and Jewish Worship* (New York: Oxford, 1960), 78; Polhill, *Acts*, 298. In the final analysis, there is no way to identify either reading.

72. John J. Kilgallen, "Acts 13:38–39: Culmination of Paul's Speech in Pisidia," *Biblica* 69 (1988) 482–83.

73. J. Clifton Black, "The Rhetorical Form of the Hellenistic Jewish and Early Christian Sermon: A Response to Lawrence Wills," *Harvard Theological Review* 81 (1988):10.

74. (1) To render the audience well disposed to the orator (and ill-disposed to the opponent; cf. vv. 38, 41); (2) to amplify the leading facts (cf. v. 38, "forgiveness of sins"); (3) to recapitulate the basic argument (cf. vv. 38b–39); and (4) to excite the emotions (cf. vv. 40–41). Black, "Rhetorical Form," 8–10.

75. Black, "Rhetorical Form," 9.

76. Quintilian, *Institutio oratoria*, 4.2.31–52, 123.

77. Cf. A. N. Wilson, *Paul: The Mind of the Apostle* (New York: Norton, 1977), 15–39.

78. Aristotle, *Rhetoric*, 1.2.1.

79. C. K. Barrett, *The First Epistle to the Corinthians*, Harper's New Testament Commentaries (New York: Harper and Row, 1968), 216.

80. Augustine, *On Lying*, NPNF 1st Series, 42, 3:476.

81. Told by Ovid, in *Metamorphoses*, viii, 626ff.

82. Paul was doubtless the chief speaker (14:12). Note that the crowd identified Paul with Hermes, the god of oratory.

83. The absence of a *narratio* could be due to any number of factors. Aristotle regarded it as unnecessary in most cases, except in court (*Rhetoric*, 3.13.3).

84. "Why are you doing these things?" (14:15b).

85. The legend that Zeus and Hermes had visited Lystra could have heightened the effect of Paul's exordium. The Lycaonians had not welcomed the gods, who in turn punished them with a flood. Far from seeking honor—as Zeus and Hermes had—Paul and Barnabas repudiate honor, and seek to deliver the Lystrans from the cycle of futility to which the gods have subjected them.

86. Paul apparently quotes Ps. 146:6, though the idea that God created the "heavens and earth and sea" recurs frequently in the Old Testament, especially in comparisons with idols. Cf. Exod. 20:11; 1 Chron. 16:31–32; Ps. 96:11–12; Jon. 1:9.

87. Colin Barnaby ("Paul and Johanan ben Zokkais," *Expository Times* 108 [1997], 366–68) has argued that the reference to "rain" as the sign of God's goodness has its roots in Paul's rabbinical training. The rabbis taught "that rain from God formed a common ground for both Jews and Gentiles to praise Him" (p. 367).

88. The site of this sermon is traditionally regarded as a rock outcropping northwest of the Acropolis. But the term *Areios pagos* (17:19, 22) likely refers to the Council of Areopagus (which often met elsewhere in the city), not the Hill of Ares.

89. Bruce W. Winter, "On Introducing Gods to Athens: An Alternative Reading of Acts 17:18–20," *Tyndale Bulletin* 47 (May 1996), 71–90.

90. According to Winter, "Jesus" and "Anastasis." The confusion likely stemmed from Paul's teaching on Jesus and the resurrection (*anastasis*). "Introducing Gods," 80.

91. This is indicated by the council's justification for the inquiry: "For you are bringing some strange things to our ears" (17:20). The "strange things" (*xenizonta*) refers to "deities," but reflects caution on the part of the council. Cf. Winter, "Introducing Gods," 82.

92. Winter translates 17:20b [*boulometha oun gnōna; tina thelei tauta einai*], "We therefore wish to make a judgment . . . on what is being claimed (or decreed) these things are" (p. 83). Relatedly, according to Winter, we should probably translate 17:19b, "we possess the legal right to judge what this new teaching is that is being spoken by you" (p. 82).

93. Aristotle, *Rhetoric*, 1.3.4.

94. Dean Zweck ("The *Exordium* of the Areopagus Speech, Acts 17.22,23," *New Testament Studies* 35 [Jan. 1989], 99–100) cites the *Olympic Discourse* (c. A.D. 97) of Dio Chrysostom as an almost exact parallel—being a deliberative oration on "the topic of religion," in particular "concerning the first conception of God" (p. 99), and containing the standard (a) *exordium*, (b) *propositio*, (c) *probatio*, and (d) *peroratio* (*epilogos*).

95. Literally, "seizure of good will," a technical term in Roman oratory.

96. Mark D. Given, "Not Either/Or but Both/And in Paul's Areopagus Speech," *Biblical Interpretation* 3 (October 1995), 356–72. Paul's *propositio* might also be said to turn the tables on the council. He uses the neuter "what" and "this" for the "(unknown) god" worshiped by the Athenians. Recall that the council had referred to Paul's teaching about Jesus as a "thing" (17:19b–20).

97. Martin Dibelius, *Studies in the Acts of the Apostles* 82.

98. Edward Fudge ("Paul's Apostolic Self-Consciousness at Athens," *Journal of the Evangelical Theological Society* 14 [Summer 1971], 193–98) points out that while Paul does not quote from Scripture, the sermon is filled with allusions.

99. Zweck, *Arepagus*, 100.

100. See Polhill, *Acts*, 372–76.

101. Croy, "Hellenistic Philosophies," 37–39.

102. Stott, *Spirit, Church, World*, 27.

103. Cf. 21:28. These "Jews from Asia" had doubtless encountered Paul in Ephesus, but imagined they could have greater success against him in Jerusalem. See Bruce, *Acts*, 408–10.

104. Notably, the opinions of E. Hachchen, *The Book of Acts* (New York: Oxford 1971), 657; and G. A. Kennedy, *New Testament Interpretation through Rhetorical Criticism* (Chapel Hill: University of North Carolina Press, 1984), 135.

105. Bruce Winter, "The Importance of the *Captatio Benevolentiae* in the Speeches of Tertullus and Paul in Acts 24:1–21," *Journal of Theological Studies* 42 (October 1991),

518–19. Tertullus charged that Paul "stirs up dissension among all the Jews throughout the world" (24:5a).

106. The three purposes of the forensic *captatio*, according to Cicero (*De inventione*, 15:20), Quintilian (*Institutio* Oratoria, iv, 1.5), and other classical rhetors.

107. C. S. Lewis, *Surprised by Joy: The Shape of My Early Life* (New York: Harcourt Brace Jovanovich, 1955), 227.

Chapter 9, Paul's Epistles as Inspired Preaching

1. John D. Harvey, *Listening to the Text: Oral Patterning in Paul's Letters*, ETS Studies 1 (Grand Rapids: Baker, 1998), xv.

2. Casey W. Davis, *Oral Biblical Criticism: The Influence of the Principles of Orality on the Literary Structure of Paul's Epistle to the Philippians*, JSNT Sup 172 (Sheffield: Sheffield Academic Press, 1999), 13.

3. Paul J. Achtemeier, "*Omne Verbum Sonat*: The New Testament and the Oral Environment of Late Western Antiquity," JBL (1990), 26.

4. There are also varying degrees of middle-range writing, somewhere in between the scholarly and popular poles. Undoubtedly, it is easier to write from a strictly scholarly or popular perspective, and not a few appear to think that the two polar styles are like oil and water (i.e., they don't mix). However, if it is possible—and it is—to communicate the fruit of in-depth scholarship (that is not normally accessible to those who desire [or require] more readable materials) in more understandable or interesting wording, is it not "the best of both worlds"?

5. Usually scholars trying their hands at more popular writing (usually to broaden the audience), since established popular writers rarely move across to the scholarly realm (for fear of losing most of their audience).

6. Though the terms *epistle* and *letter* are generally used virtually interchangeably by nonspecialists today (and often will be in this chapter), in the New Testament world an *epistle* was more formal and longer, while a *letter* was less formal and shorter. Since the compositions that make up the "Pauline literature," with the exception of Philemon, are generally much longer than the average letter of that era (according to Paul Achtemeier, the average length of Cicero's letters was 295 words, Seneca's 955 words the Apostle Paul's about 2,500 words ["Oral Environment," 22]), the tendency has been to apply the term "epistle" to them. In terms of their (lack of) stylistic formality, though, at least several of them probably deserve at least as much to be viewed as letters.

7. For an extended discussion of this chapter by the present writer, see "The Women in the Church at Rome" in Boyd Luter and Kathy McReynolds, *Women as Christ's Disciples* (Grand Rapids: Baker, 1997).

8. He was also the one who carried Paul's correspondence to the Colossians and Philemon (Col. 4:7–9).

9. For a helpful and succinct recent discussion, see Thomas R. Schreiner, "Interpreting the Pauline Epistles," *Interpreting the New Testament: Issues and Essays*, eds. David Alan Black and David S. Dockery (Nashville: Broadman & Holman, 2001). This chapter is an abridgement and updating of Schreiner, *Interpreting the Pauline Epistles* (Grand Rapids: Baker, 1991).

10. Although few evangelical scholars today join him, David Alan Black has recently emerged as a champion of the view that Paul also wrote Hebrews.

11. There are textual indications that Paul wrote at least several other letters not included in the New Testament (1 Cor. 5:9, 11; 2 Cor. 2:3–4, 9; and, possibly, Col. 4:16).

12. Though some American evangelicals have opted for a post-Jerusalem council (mid-50s) dating of Galatians over the past 10–15 years, the majority position is still about A.D. 49.

13. Most evangelicals date the Prison Epistles in the range of A.D. 60–62, but some, who understand them to have been written from Caesarea, date them in the late 50s. The

rarely held (because of its total lack of plausibility) view that some (or all) of the Prison Epistles were written from Ephesus would require a dating in the mid-50s.

14. Though freely admitting that the early church historian, Eusebius, dated 2 Timothy, Paul's final epistle, in A.D. 67, Carson, Moo and Morris date it about A.D. 64–65 (*An Introduction to the New Testament* [Grand Rapids: Zondervan, 1992], 231, 378).

15. Notably slippery are Philippians and (at least part of) 2 Corinthians, with the Thessalonian letters and all three Pastorals not far behind.

16. C. H. Talbert, "Artistry and Theology: An Analysis of the Architecture of John 1, 19–5, 47," *CBQ* 31 (1970), 362–63.

17. Ibid., 363.

18. Michelle V. Lee, "A Call to Martyrdom: Function as Method and Message in Revelation," *NovT* XL, 2 (1998), 175.

19. Boyd Luter, "Interpreting the Book of Revelation," *Interpreting the New Testament*, 467–71.

20. As I argue in my chapter on "Interpreting the Book of Revelation," 467.

21. The Greek translation of the Hebrew Bible, often abbreviated as LXX (for its traditionally held 70 translators from Hebrew into the Greek of the era).

22. Harvey, *Listening*, 98–104.

23. A. Boyd Luter Jr., "Grace," *Dictionary of Paul and His Letters*, eds. Gerald F. Hawthorne and Ralph P. Martin (Downers Grove: InterVarsity Press, 1993). Note that, while Paul often uses "mercy" and "peace" in addition to "grace" at the beginning of his letters, and occasionally at the end, the only item that is invariably at both the beginning and end of every letter is "grace."

24. The term *chiasmus* derives from the Greek letter chi, which looks like an X. It is the appearance of crossing in the middle (as does the letter X) that describes the reverse-in-the-middle, or mirroring, effect of this rhetorical technique.

25. Davis, *Orality*, 13.

26. Boyd Luter, *Looking Back, Moving On* (Colorado Springs: NavPress, 1993).

27. Harvey, *Listening*, 98–100.

28. Ian H. Thomson, *Chiasmus in the Pauline Letters*, JSNT Supplements Series 111 (Sheffield: Sheffield Academic Press), 231.

29. The Vines Institute is a ministry of The Criswell College to the churches, named in honor of the well-known pastor of First Baptist Church, Jacksonville, Florida, a great expository preacher and a great friend of the college.

30. The longest of the early epistles is Galatians, with six chapters, while the shortest of the major epistles, 2 Corinthians, contains thirteen chapters.

31. This is not a problem for inspiration and inerrancy, since they have to do with truthfulness and trustworthiness, not whether a document was recorded completely at one sitting.

32. Blomberg, "The Structure of 2 Corinthians 1–7," *Criswell Theological Review* 4 (1989), 3–20.

33. Irrespective of the similar reductionistic critiques of Stan Porter and Jeff Reed, in *New Testament Studies*, and Harvey, *Listening*, 108–09.

34. Blomberg, "2 Corinthians 1–7," 8–9.

35. The significance of these background factors and further refining and development of the following "written preaching" structures will be forthcoming in my Mentor Commentaries volume on *The Prison Epistles*, currently in process for Christian Focus Publications, on which research I am being ably assisted by Roy Metts, a specialist in the Prison Epistles.

36. A majority of evangelical scholars would place the origin of the Prison Epistles in Paul's two years of house imprisonment, while waiting for his appeal through the Roman legal system, as seen at the end of the Book of Acts (28:30).

37. Carson, Moo and Morris, 336.

38. I previously published a less-specific inverted parallel structuring of Philemon in Boyd Luter and Kathy McReynolds, *Disciplined Living: What the New Testament Teaches about Recovery and Discipleship* (Grand Rapids: Baker, 1996), 120. The adjustments are the result of further study and reflection on the rhetorical and orality factors involved.

39. See A. Boyd Luter Jr., "Philippians," *Evangelical Commentary on the Bible*, ed. Walter A. Elwell (Grand Rapids: Baker, 1989), 1037; Luter and Michelle V. Lee, "Philippians as Chiasmus: Key to the Structure, Unity and Theme Questions," *NTS* 41 (1995), 89–101; Luter, "The Role of Women in the Church at Philippi," *JETS* 39/3 (1996), 411–20; and Luter, "Women in Philippi: Partners in the Gospel," in Luter and Kathy McReynolds, *Women as Christ's Disciples* (Grand Rapids: Baker, 1997), 142–55.

40. D. A. Carson, Douglas J. Moo and Leon Morris, *An Introduction to the New Testament* (Grand Rapids: Zondervan, 1992), 359–71.

Chapter 10, Hebrews, James, and Jude as Inspired Preaching

1. D. A. Carson, Douglas J. Moo and Leon Morris, *An Introduction to the New Testament* (Grand Rapids: Zondervan, 1992), 391.

2. F. F. Bruce, *The Epistle to the Hebrews*, NICNT, Rev. Ed. (Grand Rapids: Eerdmans, 1990), 389.

3. Carson, Moo and Morris, *An Introduction to the New Testament*, 409.

4. Jeffrey A. D. Weima, "Literary Criticism," *Interpreting the New Testament: Essays on Methods and Issues*, eds. David Alan Black and David S. Dockery (Nashville: Broadman & Holman, 2001), 162.

5. Scot McKnight, Joel B. Green and I. Howard Marshall, eds., *Dictionary of Jesus and the Gospels* (Downers Grove: InterVarsity Press, 1992).

6. Gerald F. Hawthorne and Ralph P. Martin, eds., *Dictionary of Paul and His Letters* (Downers Grove: InterVarsity Press, 1993).

7. Apparently, a better and similar idea from somewhere else "caught fire" shortly thereafter, since what was finally titled as the *Dictionary of the Later New Testament and Its Developments* (Ralph P. Martin, Peter F. Davids and Daniel G. Reid, eds. [Downers Grove: InterVarsity Press, 1997]), to which I also had the privilege of contributing, was soon contracted, for which I was most grateful.

8. Frankly, there is not even anything close to a full consensus as to which letters are in play under the umbrella title "General Epistles." At different points in church history, and varying from author to author, the title "General Epistles" has been applied to: (1) most broadly, all the letters from Hebrews to Jude (occasionally even including Revelation, which does have an epistolary framework [see Rev. 1:4; chs. 2–3]); (2) middle ground, all those same letters, with Hebrews excluded; or (3) most narrowly, James, 1 and 2 Peter and Jude, excluding the Letters of John (which, under this approach would be grouped with Revelation, due to their Johannine authorship.

9. It should be noted that 2 and 3 John are exceptions to this rule, being addressed to individuals.

10. Thomas D. Lea, "The General Letters," *Holman Concise Bible Commentary*, ed. David S. Dockery (Nashville: Holman, 1998), 617.

11. As will be seen in the discussions below, the audiences for any, or all three, of the letters may be most accurately described as "mixed multitudes" from a spiritual standpoint.

12. Given the Babylonian Exile and the Diaspora of Jews around the Roman Empire in the New Testament era, this point is not affected if the reading was done in Aramaic or koine Greek, not Hebrew.

13. Carson, Moo and Morris, *Introduction to the New Testament*, 414.

14. Lea, "James," *Holman Concise Bible Commentary*, 629.

15. Doug Moo, "James," *Evangelical Commentary on the Bible*, ed. Walter A. Elwell (Grand Rapids: Baker, 1989), 1151.

16. Lea, "James," 617.

17. Walter W. Wessel, "James" *Wycliffe Bible Commentary*, eds. Charles Pfeiffer and Everett Harrison (Chicago: Moody, 1962), 1430.

18. Ibid.

19. Lea, "James," 617.

20. Interestingly, Wessel's "string of pearls" outlining of James contained eighteen (disconnected) points ("James," 1430).

21. Carson, Moo and Morris, *Introduction to the New Testament*, 409.

22. Boyd Luter, "Tandem Explorations of Trust Issues," Luter and Kathy McReynolds, *Disciplined Living: What the New Testament Teaches about Recovery and Discipleship* (Grand Rapids: Baker, 1996), 149–50.

23. For those who are vitally interested, though the spring 2000 issue of Southeastern Baptist Theological Seminary's journal, *Faith and Mission*, was given over almost entirely to that topic.

24. See the helpful and succinct related discussion in Carson, Moo and Morris, *Introduction to the New Testament*, 394–97.

25. It is frequently called "Hall of Fame," but in Hebrews 11 their "fame" rested completely on their faith (Heb. 11:1, 6).

26. Carson, Moo and Morris, *Introduction to the New Testament*, 391.

27. Luter and McReynolds, 151–52. I have continued to pay attention to the structure of Hebrews over time, and this outline is somewhat more detailed than my 1996 structuring.

28. Leon Morris, "Hebrews," *Expositor's Bible Commentary*, vol. 12, gen. ed. Frank E. Gaebelein (Grand Rapids: Zondervan, 1981), 8.

29. See chapter 4 on "As One Having Authority: The Inspired Preaching of Jesus."

30. Weima, "Literary Criticism," 162.

31. See Haddon W. Robinson, *Biblical Preaching: The Preparation and Delivery of Expository Messages* (Grand Rapids: Baker, 1980).

32. Weima, 162–63.

Chapter 11, John's Epistles and Revelation as Inspired Preaching

1. E. Earle Ellis, *The World of St. John: The Gospel and the Epistles* (Lanham, Md.: University Press of America, 1995 ed.), 85.

2. David Aune, *Revelation 1–5*, Word Biblical Commentary 52A (Dallas: Word, 1997), 21.

3. Robert L. Thomas, *Revelation 1–7*, An Exegetical Commentary (Chicago: Moody, 1992), 60.

4. Boyd Luter, "Interpreting the Book of Revelation," *Interpreting the New Testament: Essays on Methods and Issues*, eds. David A. Black and David S. Dockery (Nashville: Broadman & Holman, 2001), 467.

5. Whom this book memorializes. Some of the information in the following paragraphs can be found in W. A. Criswell, *Standing on the Promises: The Autobiography of W. A. Criswell* (Dallas: Word, 1990).

6. Even as pastor emeritus (and chancellor at The Criswell College), Dr. Criswell played active roles as an advisor until the very last days of his earthly life.

7. Surprisingly, even many otherwise knowledgeable people are not aware that W. A. Criswell earned the doctor of philosophy degree in New Testament from Southern Seminary, having studied under, among others, the venerable A. T. Robertson.

8. This was one of the most intriguing aspects of the memorial service for Dr. Criswell at First Baptist Church. A lengthy litany of his innovations (much too long to enumerate here), many of which have become staples of evangelical pastoral ministry, especially in larger churches, was laid out and it was merely selected highlights of his more than half a century of ministry in Dallas.

9. For only one classic example that relates directly to the subject matter of this chapter, not a few have proclaimed Criswell's volumes on Revelation to be among the very best commentary material on the Apocalypse ever published.

10. Admittedly, there was a certain amount of editing necessary to adapt Dr. Criswell's animated preaching style to enough of a culturally expected "written style" to placate the publishers. However, for those who heard him preach in person, or on tape, the "voice" of W. A. Criswell still reverberates through the written page as you read his written commentaries.

11. The W. A. Criswell Legacy Project, which is underwritten by the Criswell Foundation, is nearing completion of the transcribing of all his sermons, with many also already available in the original audio, through the Criswell Legacy Web site.

12. The relaunch issue of the *Criswell Theological Review* (after an extended hiatus) in the fall of 2002 honors W. A. Criswell, and particularly his expository preaching ministry, with a wide range of related essays.

13. For a complementary discussion of John's ministry of preaching written embodied in the fourth Gospel, and background considerations related to it, see chapter 3: "The Gospel and the Gospels: The Inspired Preaching of the Evangelists."

14. Another, though less likely, possibility at their relatively early stage of spiritual growth is that "Sons of Thunder" spoke of James's and John's "zealous commitment to Christ" (Paul D. Gardner, "John, the Apostle," *The Complete Who's Who of the Bible*, ed. P. D. Gardner [London: HarperCollins/Marshall Pickering, 1995], 351.

15. Roughly A.D. 85–95 (though the case for a late 60s dating of all the Johannine writings is currently at a "high-water mark," as much as anything because of reasoning related to the presumed central significance of the destruction of Jerusalem in A.D. 70, which is [directly or indirectly] dependent on the argumentation of J. A. T. Robinson, *Redating the New Testament* [London: SCM, 1976]).

16. Though the phenomenally well-known wording of John 3:16 is certainly a major factor in this characterization, it should be pointed out that, proportionately, the mentions of "love" in 1 John are at least as extensive.

17. Andreas J. Kostenberger, *Encountering John*, Encountering Biblical Studies (Grand Rapids: Baker, 1999), 24.

18. It is certainly partly due to the fact that, tragically, James died very early, among the first martyrs of the church, likely in the earlier 40s, as recorded in Acts 12:1–2.

19. Which, unfortunately, cannot even be surmised any closer than an "educated guess."

20. That is, from c. A.D. 30 to some time in the latter years prior to the progressive siege of Jerusalem by the Romans, which escalated through the period from A.D. 66 to 70.

21. "John the Apostle, Life and Writings of," *Baker Encyclopedia of the Bible*, gen. ed. Walter A. Elwell (Grand Rapids: Baker, 1988), 2:1192.

22. I have discussed this angle elsewhere in A. Boyd Luter, "Revelation" notes, Nelson Study Bible, gen. ed. Earl D. Radmacher (Nashville: Thomas Nelson, 1997); and "Interpreting the Book of Revelation," 462.

23. Probably from about A.D. 53–56. For an in-depth analysis of the method and impact of Paul's ministry in Ephesus by this writer, see A. Boyd Luter, "Deep and Wide: Education Overflowing as Evangelism from Ephesus," *Faith and Mission*, Fall 2001.

24. Probably from about A.D. 63 or 64 to 67.

25. See the specific discussion related to its background in chapter 3.

26. Perhaps not even improbable, especially with John's letters. I am asked frequently by students whether 2 or 3 John could have been written before 1 John, and the answer I give them is yes, though there is no way of knowing. Thematically, 1 John seems to have been something of a "sequel" to the fourth Gospel and, thus, there seems to be a sequential relationship between the two. Also, Revelation exudes a sense of "finality" and, thematically, extends ideas in both the Gospel and letters, implying that it is the "last word" by the apostle John. However, even these measured thoughts are more speculative than rooted in any solid evidence for the order of appearance of the five books of the Johannine corpus.

27. The only other New Testament author who could possibly have written in as many as two different genres is Luke, on the outside chance that he could have written Hebrews, a very uncommon view. However, that view has been vigorously, but carefully, championed by our colleague, David Allen. See, most recently, his defense of Lukan authorship of Hebrews among the symposium articles published in the Spring 2001 issue of *Faith and Mission*.

28. See the brief introductory discussion of the three wider New Testament literary genres at the end of chapter 1.

29. See the related discussion of this point in chapter 3.

30. As stated more than once, the distinctions between the terms *epistle* and *letter* can be somewhat artificial, though, in general, an epistle is somewhat longer and more formal or stylized, while a letter is somewhat shorter and more informal or personal.

31. See the discussion leading to this conclusion in chapter 3.

32. Of the twenty-seven books in the New Testament, twenty-one (almost 78 percent) fall comfortably in the wider category of epistle-letter.

33. Kostenberger, *Encountering John*, 205.

34. Although the Greek *biblion* in Rev. 1:11 could possibly refer to a "book" (codex) here, it is more likely (culturally and imagery-wise, in this kind of apocalyptic literature) to be envisioning a "scroll." See the excellent related discussion in Alan F. Johnson, "Revelation," *Expositor's Bible Commentary*, gen. ed. Frank E. Gaebelein (Grand Rapids: Zondervan, 1981), 12:465–66.

35. For lack of a better term for the seven brief "letters" to the churches in Rev. 2–3.

36. This is certainly not to say that there are no other questions which come into play in questioning the authorship of Revelation. It is to say, though, that the other questions, without the vocabulary and style issues, would hardly be enough to mount a very strong attack.

37. E. Earle Ellis, *The Making of the New Testament Documents* (Leiden: E. J. Brill, 1999), 326–27.

38. See the brief discussion in chapter 8.

39. See the treatment of this issue in chapter 5.

40. This is, of course, why it almost always among the first places in the New Testament where students of koine Greek are taken to begin to learn to sight-read.

41. Kostenberger, *Encountering John*, 204, lists twenty-six such clear thematic parallels.

42. What may not be so evident is that the use of the present tense ("believe") may indicate an aspect of purpose that goes beyond initial evangelism. Though John 1–12 does indeed seem to be specifically evangelistic in tone, John 13–17, the so-called Upper Room Discourse, seems to be much more focused on edification for those who are already believers. So perhaps it is most accurate to conclude that the fourth Gospel is primarily evangelistic and secondarily for edification.

43. Dr. McReynolds and I have cowritten a response article (for the *Christian Research Journal* in 1993) and three books (*Truthful Living* [Grand Rapids: Baker, 1994]; *Disciplined Living* [Baker, 1996] and *Woman as Christ's Disciples* [Baker, 1997], and are currently working on a devotional volume on *The Pilgrim Psalms*, for Christian Focus Publications. In addition, *Women as Christ's Disciples* is being re-published by Christian Focus in 2003.

44. *The World of St. John*, 85.

45. "The Gnostic Error and Recovery: 1–3 John," *Disciplined Living*, 173–74.

46. Perhaps a form of embryonic or proto-Gnosticism.

47. And it should be noted that the wording is also practically identical in 3 John 13.

48. Emphasis added.

49. It cannot be known for sure if "elder" here has primary reference to John as a local church official (see 1 Tim. 5:17; Titus 1:5) or an older (i.e., elderly) man, or both. Given the pastoral nature of the letter, the first angle would certainly seem to be in play, though the element of the wisdom that comes with age may be also.

50. If the traditional dating of the Johannine writings is accepted, the persecution of Christians would be under the reign of the emperor Domitian. If the early (60s) date is taken instead, the imperial persecution would originate from the hand of Caesar Nero.

51. It is not at all impossible that this letter was essentially sent at about the same time as 1 John to a different audience, but to people who were wrestling with the onslaught of the same false teaching.

52. See the discussion of this point in chapter 8.

53. The purpose of this letter is completely unknown, even more so than the apparent "lost letters" to the Corinthian church by Paul (1 Cor. 5:9, 11; 2 Cor. 2:3, 9).

54. Author of the controversial *Revelation* commentary in the Anchor Bible series [Garden City, N.Y.: Doubleday, 1965].

55. That is, I was aware of other (and far less than convincing) attempts to structure the entire book of Revelation in an inverted parallel manner and, at that point, I simply did not think it was possible to do plausibly.

56. It appeared as Michelle V. Lee, "A Call to Martyrdom: Function as Method and Message in Revelation," *Novum Testamentum* 40 (1998).

57. Over the past few years, I have invested three papers at Evangelical Theological Society meetings (two national, one regional) on structural aspects of the Apocalypse.

58. Lee, "A Call to Martyrdom," 173, 193–94.

59. *Interpreting the New Testament*, 470.

60. Ibid., 471.

61. See, for example, my analysis of the chiastic nature of the statements of the Abrahamic covenant (which likewise have a focal "blessing" aspect) spread throughout much of Genesis, in A. Boyd Luter, "Israel and the Nations in God's Redemptive Plan," *Israel: The Land and the People*, gen. ed. H. Wayne House (Grand Rapids: Kregel, 1998), 292–93.

62. Interestingly, my published analysis of the structure of the Book of Ruth is exactly the same as what has been seen here (A, B, and C layers, with a "dangling" D at the end, at least until you look closer at the key role D plays. For the rationale leading to that conclusion, see my "Ruth" commentary in Luter and Barry C. Davis, *God behind the Seen: Expositions of the Books of Ruth and Esther* (Expositor's Guide to the Historical Books; Grand Rapids: Baker, 1995). This commentary will be reissued in 2003 by Christian Focus Publications as the *Ruth-Esther* volume in their Focus on the Bible series.

63. With, obviously, significant off-and-on "help" from a number of angels mediating to John the content of the book to be recorded.

Chapter 12, The New Testament's Use of the Old: Inspired Exegesis and Application for Preaching

1. Klyne Snodgrass, "The Use of the Old Testament in the New," *Interpreting the New Testament: Essays on Methods and Issues*, eds. David A. Black and David S. Dockery (Nashville: Broadman & Holman, 2001), 209.

2. "Quotations of the Old Testament in the New Testament," *Baker Encyclopedia of the Bible*, gen. ed. Walter A. Elwell (Grand Rapids: Baker, 1988), 2:1808.

3. Barnabas Lindars, "OT Quotations in the NT," *Harper's Bible Dictionary*, gen. ed. Paul J. Achtemeier (San Francisco: Harper and Row, 1985), 727.

4. Thomas D. Lea, "New Testament Use of the Old Testment," *Holman Concise Bible Commentary*, ed. David S. Dockery (Nashville: Holman, 1998), 619.

5. This does not necessarily mean that Paul was a "sports fan," so to speak. It does mean, though, that, in his childhood years in the Jewish Diaspora, in Gentile territory in Tarsus of Cilicia (Acts 22:3), as well as in his travels on his missionary journeys in primarily heavily Greco-Roman territory, he had come to understand the events of "the games" (1 Cor. 9:25; i.e., whether the ancient Olympic games or, since this is written to the church in Corinth, the local Isthmian games), in order to work this analogy here.

6. Sadly, certain preachers will stretch this into bizarre "every which way but loose" uses that cause more cautious expositors to cringe, and sometimes to (over)react.

7. The "Index of Quotations: New Testament Order," at the back of the United Bible Society's *The Greek New Testament*, Fourth Revised Edition, eds. B. Aland, K. Aland, J. Karavidopoulos, C. M. Martini and B. M. Metzger (Stuttgart: Deutsche Bibelgesellschaft, 1994), 888–90, includes no citations in Philippians; Colossians; 1 or 2 Thessalonians; Titus; Philemon; 1, 2 or 3 John; Jude; or Revelation. That is, just over 40 percent of the New Testament books (11 of 27) do not contain an Old Testament quote of any identifiable length.

8. In Colossians 4, Luke is mentioned in verse 14, well after Paul concludes his list of Jewish coworkers with the wording, "These are the only fellow workers for the kingdom of God who are from the circumcision" (i.e., Jewish; verse 11). Though it is (barely) possible to attempt to argue that Luke could have been a hellenistic Jew, and, in that way, not "from the circumcision," that is a highly unlikely reading of Col. 4 (Darrell L. Bock, "Luke, Gospel of," *Dictionary of Jesus and the Gospels*, eds. Joel B. Green, Scot McKnight and I. Howard Marshall (Downers Grove: IVP, 1992), 496.

9. The name "Septuagint" and the Roman numerals LXX (i.e., 70) are derived from the Latin *septuaginta*, which means 70. The story that 70, or 72, elders translated the Pentateuch from Hebrew into Greek is fictitous, "yet the label persists by virtue of the tradition" (Melvin K. H. Peters, "Septuagint," *Anchor Bible Dictionary*, gen. ed. David Noel Freedman [New York: Doubleday, 1992], 5:1093).

10. Larry Lee Walker, "Biblical Languages," *Baker Encyclopedia of the Bible*, gen. ed. Walter A. Elwell (Grand Rapids: Baker, 1988), 1:338.

11. For helpful explanations of these Jewish approaches (especially Pesher and Midrash), see (among sources already cited in this chapter) the discussions of Lea (the most succinct and readable), Lindars and Snodgrass (full, but fairly readable). In addition, at the scholarly end of the spectrum, the work of Hans Hubner (in translation) is worth the wrestling ("New Testament, OT Quotations in the," *Anchor Bible Dictionary*, 4:1,096–1,104.)

12. See the discussion in chapter 10 of the homiletical character and feel of Hebrews.

13. As best I could quickly determine, I have somewhere between 750 and 1,000 verses of Scripture committed to memory. And, with even this relatively small amount "on my mind," so to speak, verse after verse (or at least, phrase or image) just (seemingly) automatically pops up in conversation, teaching, preaching, and writing on a constant basis. I can hardly imagine the frequency with which that would happen to those who lived in a culture in which the memorization factor was paramount, such as the New Testament era, especially to those from Jewish backgrounds.

14. See the helpful related discussions by Snodgrass, 214–18, 219–20.

15. Snodgrass, 215.

16. Ibid.

17. Sometimes, the entire Old Testament was summarized as "the Law" (Heb. *torah*). Sometimes, the Old Testament was referred to as "the Law and the Prophets" (Heb. *nebi'im*). However, sometimes, as in Luke 24:44, the threefold breakdown was used. It was generally referred to as "The Law and the Prophets and the Writings" (Heb. *kethubim*). Apparently, Jesus chose to use "the Psalms" for the category of the Writings for one of two (or both) reasons: (1) Psalms is the first book in the order of the books in the Writings; or (2) many of the Psalms is absolutely saturated with messianic prophecy and, hence, is as obviously "Christological" as any book in the entire Hebrew Bible.

18. See, especially, Snodgrass, 219–20.

19. Ibid., 220.

20. According to the "Index of Quotations: Old Testament Order," *UBS4Rev.*, 887–88.

21. It should be pointed out, though, that a number of these books are alluded to (echoed) in the New Testament.

22. See the discussion of the original audience of the second Gospel in chapter 3.

23. See the discussion of the dynamics of the production of the Gospel of Mark in chapter 3.

24. See the listing in footnote 7 above.

25. Of the books chosen, there are only eleven Old Testament quotations in Galatians and none in Revelation. However, the usage in Galatians is very significant in regard to "the truth of the gospel" (Gal. 2:5, 14), which I understand to be the central theme of the letter (see A. Boyd Luter, "Galatians," *HCBC*, 566–68). And with Revelation, from the "Son of Man" imagery in Rev. 1, reflecting Dan. 7, to the "tree of life" and related images at the end of the book in Rev. 21–22, reflecting the Garden of Eden in the early chapters of Genesis, the Old Testament is, so to speak, woven into the very fabric of the book.

26. For a very helpful and careful discussion of the current options, see D. A. Carson, "Matthew," *Expositor's Bible Commentary*, gen. ed. Frank E. Gaebelein (Grand Rapids: Zondervan, 1984), 8:96–97.

27. See my discussion in Boyd Luter, "Interpreting the Book of Revelation," *Interpreting the New Testament*, eds. David A. Black and David S. Dockery (Nashville: Broadman & Holman, 2001), 464.

28. *BAGD*, s.v. "*parthenos*," 627.

29. Gregory K. Beale, *The Book of Revelation*, New International Greek Testament Commentary (Grand Rapids: Eerdmans, 1999), 77.

30. Luter, "Interpreting the Book of Revelation," 463.

31. Ibid.

32. See the discussion of the "altar call" applicational conclusion of Revelation in chapter 11.

33. Lea, 619.

Chapter 13, Inspired Preaching—Then and Now

1. Mortimer J. Adler, The Difference of Man and the Difference It Makes (New York: World, 1971).

2. Cf. chapter 3, pp. 31–33.

3. 1 Cor. 1:21b.

4. C. S. Lewis, "Myth Become Fact," *God in the Dock: Essays on Theology and Ethics*, ed. Walter Hooper (Grand Rapids: Eerdmans, 1970), 66–67.

5. Michael W. Smith, "The Hope of Israel," *Christmastime* (Reunion, 1998).

6. George R. Beasley-Murray, *Preaching the Gospel from the Gospels* (Peabody, Mass.: Hendrickson, 1996), 16–17.

7. George A. Kennedy, New Testament Interpretation through Rhetorical Criticism (Chapel Hill: University of North Carolina Press, 1984), 158.

8. Ibid., 159.

9. Augustine, *De Doctrina Christiana*, Prologue.

10. Ralph L. Lewis, with Gregg Lewis, *Learning to Preach Like Jesus* (Westchester, Ill.: Crossway, 1989), 123.

11. Cf. Eduard Schweizer, *Jesus, the Parable of God: What Do We Really Know about Jesus?* Princeton Theological Monograph Series 37 (Allison Park,Pa.: Pickwick, 1994), 32–34.

12. Mark 12:37 (KJV). Similarly, Mark informs us that Herod enjoyed listening to John the Baptist (6:20).

13. William Barclay, *The Gospel of Mark*, rev. ed., Daily Bible Study (Philadelphia: Westminster, 1954, 1975), 299.

14. Cf. William L. Lane, *The Gospel According to Mark*, NICNT (Grand Rapids: Eerdmans, 1974), 439.

15. On the style of Jesus' preaching and teaching, see especially, William Barclay, *The Mind of Jesus* (London: SCM Press, 1936), 96ff.; J. P. Kealy, *Jesus the Teacher* (Danville, N.J.: Dimension Books, 1978; Pheme Perkins, *Jesus as Teacher*; and Rainer Riesner, "Jesus as Preacher and Teacher," 192–193, 201–208. Cf. also C. H. Dodd, *The Founder of Christianity*

(New York: Macmillan, 1970), 53–79; James S. Stewart, *The Life and Teaching of Jesus* (Nashville: Abingdon, 1978), 77–86.

16. Perkins, *Jesus as Teacher*, 38.

17. William Blake, "Auguries of Innocence," I:1ff.

18. Stewart, *Life and Teaching*, 80.

19. There are approximately fifty to sixty parables in the Gospels (depending who does the counting, and how), constituting about one-third of Jesus' teaching. The great majority appear in the Synoptics, though John also records parables (for example, the "Good Shepherd [10:1–18] and the "True Vine" [15:1–8]), and contains numerous parabolic elements. An outstanding survey is Craig L. Blomberg, *Interpreting the Parables* (Downers Grove: InterVarsity Press, 1990).

20. Kealy, *Jesus the Teacher*, 41.

21. For example, Mark 11:29–30 (= Matt. 21:21–25a).

22. For example, Mark 12:35–37a (= Matt. 22:43–45).

23. For example, on the name of Peter, Matt. 16:18.

24. Riesner, "Jesus as Preacher and Teacher," 201. A notable example of repetition is the saying about seeking and losing life, which occurs in no less than four different contexts (cf. Mark 8:35 = Matt. 16:25; Luke 9:24; Matt. 10:39; Luke 17:33; John 12:25).

25. Riesner, "Jesus as Preacher and Teacher," 202. Cf. also H. P. Rüger, "Das Problem der Sprache Jesu," *Zeitschrift für die neutestamentliche Wissenschaft*, 59 (1968), 111–22.

26. Riesner, "Jesus as Preacher and Teacher," 204.

27. Birger Gerhardsson, "Illuminating the Kingdom: Narrative Meshalim in the Synoptic Gospels," [Henry Wansbrough, ed., *Jesus and the Oral Gospel Tradition*, JSNT Supplement Series 64 (Sheffield: Sheffield Academic Press, 1991)], 267.

28. David E. Aune, "Oral Tradition and the Aphorisms of Jesus," in Wansbrough, ed., *Oral Gospel Tradition*, 211.

29. Aune, "Oral Tradition," 214.

30. Mark 10:31.

31. Ruth Finegan, *Oral Poetry: Its Nature, Significance and Social Context* (Cambridge: Cambridge University Press, 1977), 73.

32. D. Martyn Lloyd-Jones, *Studies in the Sermon on the Mount*, 2 vols. (Grand Rapids: Eerdmans, 1959–60), 2:330. Cf. the conclusion by A. Carr (ed., *The Gospel According to St. Matthew*, Cambridge Greek Testament [Cambridge: Cambridge University Press, 1887], 143): "The thought of the listeners was: 'While He was teaching we felt all along that He was a lawgiver, not merely an interpreter of the law.'"

33. C. F. D. Moule, "The Gravaman against Jesus," E. P. Sanders, ed., *Jesus, the Gospels, and the Church: Essays in Honor of William R. Farmer* (Macon: Mercer University Press, 1987), 191.

34. Hermann N. Ridderbos, *The Speeches of Peter in the Acts of the Apostles* (London: Tyndale, 1962), 10.

35. Martin Dibelius, *Studies in the Acts of the Apostles* (London: SCM, 1951).

36. Aristotle, *Rhetoric*, 1.2; 2–7.

37. Ibid., 1.2.4.

38. Ibid., 1.2.5.

39. Ibid., 1.2.4.

40. Significantly, modern homiletics, dating from the early 1800s, was originally known as "sacred rhetoric." As noted, Aristotle (*Rhetoric*, 1.2.1) defined rhetoric as the "ability, in each case, to see the available means of persuasion."

41. Walter Lippmann (*Public Opinion* [New York: Macmillan, 1922]) is usually credited with coining the term "stereotype," the "picture in the head" by which we tend to classify people and evaluate what they say and do.

42. Ralph G. Nichols and Leonard A. Stevens, *Are You Listening?* (New York: McGraw-Hill, 1957).

43. Jon Eisenson, J. Jeffery Auer, and John V. Irwin, *The Psychology of Communication* (Englewood Cliffs, N.J.: Prentice-Hall, 1963), 282.

44. Bruce M. Metzger, *The New Testament, Its Background, Growth, and Content* (Nashville: Abingdon, 1965), 45.

45. The participle καταλαβόμενοι indicates that they "perceived" or "noticed" or "discovered." Cf. BAGD, s.v. καταλαμβανω.

46. Josephus, *Antiquities of the Jews*, trans. William Whiston (Grand Rapids: Kregel, reprint 1963 [orig. published 1867], xvi, 4, 3–4.

47. For example, 4:29, 31; 9:27–28; 14:3; 18:25–26; 19:8.

48. TDNT, s.v. παρρησία, παρρησιάζομαι, by Heinrich Schleier, 5:882.

49. F. F. Bruce, *The Book of the Acts*, rev. ed. (Grand Rapids: Eerdmans, 1988), 95. Cf. A. T. Robertson (*Epochs in the Life of Simon Peter* [Nashville: Broadman, reprint 1976]), 198, who suggests that perhaps the Sanhedrin "recognized a likeness in Peter's boldness of speech and that of Jesus who spoke as never a man spoke."

50. Chrysostom, *Acts*, 10, NPNF 11:67, emphasis added.

51. Ibid., "Peter and John did all in the character of His disciples," that is, "in the character of those who had followed Jesus."

52. Cf. Mark 8:12, 27–28; 11:27–28; Luke 6:1–2; 13:13–14; 20:1–2.

53. T. F. Torrance, "A Study in New Testament Communication," *Scottish Journal of Theology*, 3 (1950), 310.

54. Ibid.

55. Wallace E. Fisher, *Who Dares to Preach? The Challenge of Biblical Preaching* (Minneapolis: Augsburg, 1979), 18.

56. J. Spencer Kennard, *Psychic Power in Preaching* (Philadelphia: American Baptist Publication Society, 1901), 43–44. Cf. 2 Cor. 4:7.

57. James W. Cox, *Preaching* (San Francisco: Harper and Row, 1985), 21–22.

58. Ibid., 22.

59. Kennard, 44.

60. So much so that some critics imagine a divide between them, as the cultured and the uncultured. Such critics often cite Paul's confrontation with Peter in Antioch (Gal. 2:11) as evidence of deep-seated antagonism, although Peter's affirmation of Paul (2 Pet. 3:15–16) presents strong counterevidence. Of course, many modern scholars deny Pauline authority of 2 Peter, and so discount the evidence.

61. Chrysostom, *Treatise Concerning the Christian Priesthood*, trans. W. R. W. Stephens, NPNF 1st Series 9:31–83. Chrysostom was about twenty-eight years old at the time (c. A.D. 371), although he wrote the *Treatise* some twenty years later.

62. C. A.D. 396–426. Augustine, *De Doctrina Christiana*, trans. J. T. Shaw, NPNF 1st Series 2:515–597.

63. C. A.D. 590. Gregory (the Great), *Liber Regulae Pastoralis*, trans. James Barmley, NPNF 2d Series 128:1–72.

64. Chadwick, *Pastoral Teaching of Paul*, Foreword Warren W. Wiersbe (Grand Rapids: Kregel, reprint 1984 [orig. pub. 1907]), 197.

65. "I know that all of you . . . will see my face no more" (Acts 20:25; also v. 38).

66. Chadwick, *Pastoral Teaching*, 196.

67. Chadwick pointed out that the term "watchman" appears in the Angelican Ordination Service, as it does to this day. Cf. *The Book of Common Prayer* (New York: Oxford, 1928), 539.

68. Cf. Bruce, *Acts*, 389–395, who divides the speech at these points, though he does not call attention to the repetition of "and now." Oddly, Chadwick takes note of the *kai nun* phrase, but does not pursue its significance. Chadwick, *Pastoral Teaching*, 204n, 217.

69. Cf. v. 20, "declaring [*anageilai*] . . . and teaching [*didaxai*]."

70. Cf., "the whole purpose of God" (v. 27). "Mark here the character of a teacher," says Chrysostom, "ungrudging fullness, unshrinking promptness." Chrysostom, *Acts*, 44, NPNF 11:268.

71. Chadwick, *Pastoral Teaching,* 205. Most commentators take the word *spirit* in verse 22 to mean the "human spirit," indicating Paul's self-determination, albeit effected by the Holy Spirit. Some older commentators (Chrysostom, Theophylact, Beza, Calvin, for example) understood Paul to say he was "bound by the Holy Spirit." The difference seems to be a matter of emphasis.

72. Chrysostom, *Acts,* 44, NPNF 11:270.

73. Chadwick, *Pastoral Theology,* 214.

74. Richard J. Neuhaus, *Freedom for Ministry,* rev. ed. (Grand Rapids: Eerdmans, 1979, 1992), 1–18.

75. Ibid., 7.

76. Chadwick, *Pastoral Teaching,* 209.

77. Ibid., 212.

78. Ibid., 219.

79. Chrysostom, 44, NPNF 11:267.

80. Richard Baxter, *The Reformed Pastor,* ed. by William Brown (Carlisle, Pa.: The Banner of Truth Trust, reprint 1999 [orig. pub. 1656]), 51.